THE
AMERICAN
ECONOMY
WE NEED

THE
AMERICAN
ECONOMY
WE NEED

—and won't get from the
Republicans or the Democrats

JOHN B. ANDERSON

New York
ATHENEUM
1984

FOR KEKE

whose concern for the future of not only our children but the children of the world has helped inspire this effort to suggest how that better future might be achieved.

Library of Congress Cataloging in Publication Data

Anderson, John Bayard, ——
    The American economy we need.

    Includes index.
    1. United States—Economic policy—1981–
I. Title.
HC106.8.A53   1984   338.973   83-48832
ISBN 0-689-11464-8

Composition by Maryland Linotype Composition Company,
Baltimore, Maryland
Manufactured by Fairfield Graphics, Fairfield, Pennsylvania
Designed by Kathleen Carey
First Edition

ACKNOWLEDGMENTS

I WISH to acknowledge the assistance of many people who have helped me in the project of writing this book.

First, I wish to acknowledge the assistance of Dr. Clifford W. Brown, Jr., who has been my constant and faithful collaborator over the lengthy period that this book has been in preparation. His insights and analysis are reflected throughout. I am particularly indebted to him for the conclusions which are presented on the strategic challenge by Japan and the methods employed in its penetration and capture of United States markets.

I would also like to acknowledge the assistance of Robert Walker and Dr. H. Berkley Peabody, who thoroughly read most of this manuscript and provided me with many new ideas, insightful comments, and helpful suggestions.

I would further like to acknowledge the assistance of Donald Bliss and Robert Adams, who made major contributions to Chap-

v

ters XIII and XVII respectively and both of whom read the entire manuscript and shared their comments with me.

Donald Reeb, Richard Hunt, Daniel Yergin, Bradley Lewis, Sheldon Sturges, Peter Zimmerman, Grace Pierce, and Edward Renshaw read either the entire manuscript or parts of it and provided helpful insights.

In thinking through our economic problems and in preparing the manuscript, I benefited immeasurably from conversations with a great number of people from both the academic world and those involved in business and the professions. Any list is bound to be only partial; however, it does include Otto Echstein, Henry Aaron, William Abernathy, Bruce Scott, Robert Pindyck, Francis Bator, T. C. Schelling, Bruce Mazlish, Frank Lindsay, Robert Gardner, Gaylord Freeman, Rimmer De Vries, Seymour Pappert, Thomas Aimlee, Andrew Grove, Thomas Parker, and Wassily Leontief.

Needless to say, the views expressed in the book are my own, and none of those named share any responsibility for the material that is presented. However, I do want to acknowledge publicly their courtesy in granting me interviews and stating their own opinions, which greatly enriched my own background and understanding.

In the preparation of the manuscript, I wish to acknowledge the help of Judith Leibowitz, Richard Lindsey, and Brian Sheridan, who provided editorial and research assistance.

I also wish to thank Daniel Boorstin for extending to me the courtesy of an office in the Library of Congress and the facilities of that library during the time I worked on the manuscript. These were of immeasurable help.

I also wish to make a special acknowledgment to Barbara Andrews, who on her own time made innumerable contributions to this project.

Last, but hardly least, I wish to acknowledge the support of my wife, Keke, and my family, who offered encouragement for a project which consumed far more of my time and effort than I ever imagined it would when it began.

CONTENTS

PREFACE

AFTER the election of 1980 many friends and associates urged me to write a book about my experiences in that exciting venture. As the campaign receded into history, however, it seemed to me that the events of 1979 and 1980 had been adequately chronicled. I therefore determined to address the future and not the past.

Two issues will dominate our public agenda during the 1980s: prosperity and security. Can we conquer inflation and unemployment? Can we produce a peaceful world?

These issues are not separate. As people of my generation clearly remember, global economic catastrophe can give way to global war. Moreover, we see today in many parts of the world conditions of economic stagnation that are producing political upheavals which are generating civil and international conflicts. Also, security itself, in a quite literal way, can depend upon prosperity: Our ability to produce arms depends upon the state of the economy. Those who are trying to bankrupt the American economy with a wasteful military build-up seem to have forgotten this.

Crucial to our security, therefore, is solving the problems of our economy. Equally important a lively economy is central to ensuring that all our citizens have the opportunity to live decent, humane, and fulfilling lives. There is more to life than prosperity, but without prosperity, life for many is simply wretched.

I therefore decided to write a book about the economy. It has not been an easy task. First, I am not an economist. Second, the discipline of economics seems more hopelessly divided at present than at any time since the Depression. This circumstance is not helpful for those who are seeking answers. Third, serious economists today seem to state problems more convincingly than they present solutions. Others, alternatively, are quick with solutions, but their theories are mostly rhetorical gimmicks to justify policies that will benefit some special interest. At times I have wondered if economics to many people is not simply a means of convincing some group in society (rich, poor, or in between) that it is cosmically just that it be thoroughly taken.

I have devoted a lot of time to this book. I have spent an enjoyable and instructive year reading most of the current trade books on the economy, many articles in the popular press and serious journals, provocative pieces in such publications as *Technology Review* and the *Harvard Business Review*, studies by the Congressional Research Service, and even scholarly pieces in academic journals (when I could find my way around the equations to reach the conclusions). In addition, I have spent many pleasurable and informative hours talking to economists and leading economic practitioners. I also bring to this project the convictions of a lifetime in politics and the experience of many years on the Rules Committee in the U.S. House of Representatives, where we had to review every piece of substantive legislation that reached the floor.

In this book I address the following question: whether it is possible during the 1980s to break the cycle of stagflation and still maintain a high standard of living in America. Stated differently: Is it possible to have an economy with low rates of inflation, low levels of unemployment, and high levels of compensation for the people who work in that economy? I believe that the answer is yes, but the task is tough, and no single solution will work by itself. Only a comprehensive and coordinated set of policies can bring us out of economic stagnation.

I am fully convinced that the economic doctrines of both Left and Right lack this comprehensiveness. Reaganomics is a blatant failure. Ronald Reagan's supply-side policies have left us with an extraordinary legacy of unemployment and a debt that would embarrass even the most ardent spendthrift of yesteryear. The recovery following the recession of 1981–83 was simply produced by monetary expansion bound to rekindle inflation in 1984 as the stagflation cycle resumes.

The old demand-side aggregate policies don't work either. They fail to encourage the growth of productivity and global competitiveness. They fail to solve the problems of unemployment without inflation. They fail to encourage the creation of real wealth needed to raise our standard of living on a broad basis.

We clearly need to move in new directions. But first we must understand our problems. In the absence of clear signals from economists, this is difficult. A good strategy for the practical economic observer faced with doctrinal confusion seems to be to start with very basic concepts, such as supply and demand, investments, and support systems, and then to build on them in a practical and nonideological way. This I have tried to do. I hope that my recommendations, therefore, strike the reader as being grounded in common sense. At times I have found it necessary to restate the obvious—if only because the obvious is being ignored by the policy makers of today. I present no quick-fix solutions, no waves of a magic wand that will bring us utopia. Intelligently directed hard work for a decade is more to the point. But we really can solve our economic problems. Of that I am convinced. America need not accept stagflation, nor need it accept a status of inferiority to any other economy.

I structure the book around the basic proposition that there is both a supply-side and a demand-side dimension to our economic difficulties. (This means that solutions must be found that operate on both the micro- and macroeconomic level.) In fact, if our quandary can be summarized, it is that we have seen nearly two decades of erratic and irresponsible federal demand-side policies operating on a deteriorating supply base.

The supply base has been deteriorating for many reasons, some of which are related to the demand-side policies themselves and some of which are not. The failure of demand-side policies, in turn, has been a result both of government ineptitude and of government's understandable but misguided desire to compensate for the effects of supply-side deterioration with short-term quick fixes. The outcome has been a vicious feedback which has produced stagflation.

Both the supply side and the demand side, therefore, need serious policy attention. They must be addressed independently, but simultaneously, in ways that do not feed back negatively upon each other. This is why we need a comprehensive approach to economic strategy if we are to break the stagflation cycle.

The political party system as it exists today cannot provide such a solution because one major party effectively represents supply-side interests while the other represents demand-side interests. These special interests are sufficiently powerful in both parties to prevent either one from enacting the comprehensive program America needs to achieve a long-term economic recovery.

Many measures are needed; many changes must take place. In the proposing of these changes, however, it is necessary to do more than spin off a series of proposals. For an economic policy to work, its components must fit together and form a coherent plan.

The book looks at what the economy is and what is wrong with it. It creates a framework for analyzing and discussing the economy constructively, and it outlines a workable and realistic plan for action. It says what we as a nation must do if we are to remain prosperous and secure.

I begin by setting forth the problems we face: those associated with Reaganomics; the longer-term problems of economic stagnation and poor investment policies; the challenge of the new technology and of the Japanese economy. I then proceed to solutions —first those of the supply side with a special emphasis on investment, then those of the demand side, with a special emphasis on employment. Finally, I address the economically related problems of security and end by putting my proposals into a larger cultural and political framework.

My economic recommendations are far-reaching, but they are not radical. Many of them are grounded in ideas as old as the country itself. Some are Jeffersonian in their celebration of personal initiative and economic freedom. Yet some are also Hamiltonian in their belief that government should support the economic progress and well-being of the American people.

There is one proposal that some may regard as revolutionary: We need a new political party in America. A party with a new awareness of our problems, committed to the national interest and willing to ask Americans to sacrifice to achieve long-term objectives. We can no longer look to the tired old parties of the past for solutions to the problems of the future. We need a new American economy and a new American politics to shape it.

John B. Anderson

I

Challenge and Response

1

THE GREAT
RECESSION

T H E recession that began in the summer of 1981 was different
from any other since the Great Depression. It was longer. It was
deeper. It was far more global and far more disruptive. Unemployment reached the highest level in forty years. So did
bankruptcies and foreclosures on homes and farms. One-third of
the nation's industrial capacity fell idle. Corporate profits
plunged, and with them, business investment. Shantytowns began
to appear in the backyards of many American cities for the first
time since the 1930s. As the recession lingered, all kinds of people
across the country faced the devastating prospect that never again
would they find employment in the jobs they had held for a
lifetime.

The old remedies worked slowly or not at all. The largest
budget deficit ever recorded failed to halt the rise of unemployment. New and generous business incentives preceded a sharp
decline in investment. Double-digit unemployment, long thought
to be a sure cure for inflation, slowed, but did not completely halt,

the advance of consumer prices. Interest rates, which dropped significantly at the onset of most postwar recessions, remained very high far into this one and failed to stimulate a quick recovery. Stabilizers and anticyclical measures seemed to lose their effectiveness. Nothing worked according to script.*

Professional sages and practitioners began to waver. Liberal Democrats advocated tax increases and spending cuts to cure unemployment. Many conservative Republicans declared their allegiance to huge budget deficits and a ballooning national debt. Supply-siders, who had stood shoulder to shoulder with the monetarists at the start of the Reagan administration in 1981, broke ranks and joined the demand-side Keynesians in castigating the tight money policies of the Federal Reserve System. Five hundred business leaders, most of whom had endorsed Reaganomics in 1981, launched an advertising campaign in 1983 criticizing the policies of an administration which claimed to be more probusiness than any since Calvin Coolidge. Despite calls to "stay the course," the government as a whole eventually pushed all the buttons, alternating between tax cuts and tax increases, between monetary restraint and monetary expansion, between massive domestic spending cuts and massive military spending increases.

Most alarming was the embarrassment of the nation's financial system. Many of our largest banks found themselves awkwardly exposed to an escalating number of bad loans. Some of the most famous names—Chase Manhattan, Citicorp, and Continental Illinois—became the subject of press speculation about the soundness of their practices and even their solvency. The spectacular failures of Penn Square Bank and Drysdale Securities Corporation served only to overshadow the forced liquidation by merger of countless savings and loan institutions. The New Deal banking reforms of the 1930s were put to the test as never before. Unsung heroes in the Treasury and Federal Reserve intervened to merge and rescue banks, save investors in failing security ventures, and avert domestic and international panic. Without their timely action and agencies such as the Federal Deposit Insurance Corporation, the nation's financial system might easily have collapsed before the

* Reference notes begin on page 329.

4

end of 1982. This recession was different indeed, and the whole country sensed that something was terribly wrong.

The economy is just not supposed to behave this way. In the past, full economic recoveries followed recessions as predictably as day followed night. Recessions were viewed as the normal purgatives of the business cycle. They were mild, short-lived, and manageable. They were tied to swings in business inventories; they quickly corrected themselves as inventories fell and orders increased. But this pattern began to break down in the 1974–75 recession, which was deeper and longer than its predecessors. It broke down completely from 1981 to 1983, as we fell into what I call the Great Recession.

As one looks back on the campaign of 1980, it is tempting to lay the blame squarely on Ronald Reagan, who, of course, blames Jimmy Carter and almost everyone else who preceded him. But two decades of stop-and-go monetary and fiscal policies, two major oil price shocks, a generation of speculative credit expansion, the aging of our capital plant, the rise of effective foreign competition, and the almost universal willingness in both private and public sectors to mortgage a nuclear bomb-threatened future for the sake of short-term gains all have combined to impose a dreadful penalty on our economic system.

Nevertheless, that curious amalgam of policies called Reaganomics was an unmitigated disaster and the immediate cause of the Great Recession, its uniqueness, and its severity.

When Ronald Reagan came to office, he inherited an expanding economy and a falling inflation rate. His "Program for Economic Recovery," therefore, met an economy that was already recovering, at least in the short run. The plan, according to its authors, consisted of four parts: "(1) a substantial reduction in federal expenditures; (2) a significant reduction in federal tax rates; (3) prudent relief of federal regulatory burdens; (4) a monetary policy on the part of the Federal Reserve System which is consistent with those policies." Translated into action, this plan meant a large personal tax cut, some business tax cuts, a large cut in social services spending, a large increase in military spending, and a policy of tight money.

A lot of nonsense has been put forth about what all this really did to the economy, but the facts are not hard to establish. Despite Arthur Laffer's famous curve, the tax cuts resulted in an enormous loss of federal revenues. The defense build-up resulted in a large jump in spending. Social programs were cut, but the savings were nowhere near the size of the tax cuts and defense hikes.

The Reagan program, therefore, had a catastrophic effect not only on people but also on the budget and the national debt. There is no magic to this. As I said in the Iowa debate, when you start with a deficit, cut your income, and increase your spending, the result is a larger deficit. In fiscal 1982 the deficit jumped to a record $111 billion, while the national debt climbed to well over $1 trillion. In 1983 the deficit jumped to $200 billion and threatened to stay there unless the administration abandoned what Senator Howard Baker called its "riverboat gamble." According to traditional Keynesian analysis, the huge deficits should have quickly produced a sharp and vigorous recovery. But the Great Recession was different because fiscal expansion was matched with monetary restraint.

For most of the postwar period, increases in government borrowing to finance tax cuts or new government spending were generally "accommodated" by the monetary authorities. The Federal Reserve would step in to prevent federal borrowing from pushing up interest rates and crowding out private borrowing. It would do so by "monetizing" the deficit—that is, by creating more money through the expansion of bank reserves and lending capability. To the extent that tax cuts or new spending were monetized, changes in fiscal policy injected new money into the economy and generated fresh economic activity, though at the risk of inflation.

In October 1979, however, the Federal Reserve changed its policies and stopped monetizing the federal deficit. Interest rates were permitted to rise when federal borrowing put pressure on the credit market. And rise they did. Money is a commodity; when supply is limited and demand rises, the price of money goes up. Interest rates can rise for many reasons, but large budget deficits are now one of them.

The full impact of the Reagan tax cuts fell upon the already beleaguered savings market. Federal borrowing, as a percentage of the nation's credit, rose sharply from an already high 34 percent in 1981 to a record high of nearly 60 percent in 1982. This meant that three-fifths of all new savings generated in America that year went to finance the federal deficit.

The result was predictable. When the Treasury Department borrows, it moves to the front of the credit line. It can pay whatever the market demands. Private borrowers, on the other hand, stand at the end of the line. The small businessperson in Des Moines, the home builder in Tuscaloosa, the farmer in Kansas, and the would-be car buyers everywhere are crowded out. Contrary to Reaganomic expectations, the crowding out swamped the stimulus of lower tax rates.

Pressures on the money market kept interest rates high. This discouraged investment and consumption alike. Businesses reduced inventories and postponed purchases of new plant and equipment. People could no longer easily finance houses and cars. Interest payments on credit-card balances forced people to retrench.

Demand fell sharply. Business cut back production and laid off employees. Tax revenues fell, unemployment expenditures rose, the deficit got worse, and the pressure on the credit market mounted. Interest rates therefore stayed high. This created another problem: The value of the dollar rose on international exchanges as people abroad rushed to take advantage of the high American interest rates. Because of the dollar's climb, our products became more expensive overseas, and foreign products became less expensive in America. Exports fell. Some imports rose. The result was a large trade deficit and fewer jobs for Americans. By the end of 1982 unemployment had broken 10 percent for the first time since the Second World War. More than $250 billion of the gross national product (GNP) was lost that year alone as a result of the recession.

Meanwhile, with tight credit many businesses could not find adequate financing, and they failed. Others, including some very big ones, went close to the wall. As interest charges soared, financial managers discouraged new investment. "Cut back your debt load," they understandably warned, "or next time you will go under." The loss of business investment caused by the Great Recession rose to $80 billion in 1982 and exceeded $150 billion in 1983. The impact of the tax cuts, made to stimulate investment, was thereby neutered by the deficits. When interest rates finally began to fall just before the 1982 election, many companies and many individuals had given up. They were not going to borrow until they saw how the economy recovered. The supply-side experiment in America had swiftly become a supply-slide experience.

The recession spread overseas. Europe, already in economic turmoil, was seriously affected by the high American interest rates, which forced interest rates up everywhere else. Investment there stalled, and unemployment soared. Many exporting countries in the developing world saw their markets collapse. Suddenly they could no longer easily make payments on their large international debts incurred during the 1970s. The economic downturn thereby rapidly developed into the greatest international financial crisis in half a century.

By the beginning of 1983 the disaster was apparent even to administration economists. The glib optimism of earlier times gave way to a determined, if not calculated, pessimism, despite strong signs of a recovery. The administration sounded the trumpet of retreat on many of its important pledges. Gone was Reagan's campaign promise to cut the federal government's share of the GNP, as the administration released new projections showing that it would be the same in 1986 as it had been in 1981. Gone was Reagan's campaign promise to create "millions and millions" of new jobs, as the administration reluctantly yielded to congressional pressures just to find employment for some of the millions and millions of Americans who had lost their jobs in the Great Recession. Gone was Reagan's campaign promise to balance the budget by 1984 or at any other time during the decade. Even the goal of cutting taxes was put in ultimate jeopardy when Reagan asked for large contingent tax increases for fiscal 1986, the first full fiscal year to follow the election of 1984.

The administration may have been willing to abandon its promises, but it was unwilling to budge in its commitment to wage a relentless campaign to slash domestic spending for health, education, research, and income-support programs. It no longer did so with the conviction or even the pretense that it was just a matter of cutting waste, fraud, and abuse. The "truly needy" were asked to sacrifice alongside the "welfare cheats" and the "ne'er-do-wells," and the administration knew it.

With the financial system teetering on the brink, with the overseas debt problem worsening, and with the captains of industry clamoring for relief, the government finally began to expand the money supply. Under great White House pressure, the Federal Reserve Board (the Fed) eased its restrictive policies and quietly abandoned, at least for a while, the doctrines it had followed since 1979.

An upturn then started, but it was stimulated primarily by monetary expansion. By the summer of 1983 this expansion had become quite rapid. Interest rates began to rise again, spurred by continuing federal deficit pressures on the credit markets and by understandable expectations of renewed inflation in 1984. Since substantial price increases regularly follow substantial expansions in the money supply by about a year to eighteen months, the Reagan administration, when all was said and done, had simply embraced a cure for recession that was bound to cause inflation. This resumption of stop-and-go economic policies was its biggest confession of failure.

Did the Reaganites at any time really think their policies were going to work? Did anyone believe in the Laffer curve? Or was David Stockman right when he confessed that it was all a sham, a fancy Alice in Wonderland or looking-glass illusion to justify a set of policies designed for other purposes? Whatever its motives may have been, the administration's economic failure certainly has been matched by astounding political success in Washington. The extent of this success is easily measured by the degree to which nearly every politician continues to embrace the basic structure of Reaganomics.

Reagan has succeeded in making his program stick because there are two things that Congress is *very* reluctant to do. One is to raise taxes; the other is to cut defense spending. The first takes money out of people's pockets; the second subjects you to an election charge that you are somehow soft on communism or lacking in patriotism. It is therefore not surprising that a majority of my former colleagues in Congress, both Democrats and Republicans, still support Reagan's massive 25 percent cut in personal income taxes and still endorse his large defense build-up. Some are willing to raise other taxes here and there, but hardly anyone seems willing to raise taxes, even over a reasonable period, to levels high enough to bring the deficit to where it was before the Reagan revolution. Some are willing to shave the defense build-up, but hardly anybody is willing to shave it enough to bring the budget under control. Until this thinking is changed or other approaches are devised, Reaganomics will remain in place, with all that this means for the economy and the people of the United States.

The Democrats are not comfortable with this situation, but early on they decided to play politics. "Give Reagan everything he asks for, let the economy go bust, and we'll win the next election" seemed to be the strategy of Speaker of the House Thomas ("Tip") O'Neill. This was as irresponsible as Reaganomics, and the voters knew it in 1982. After that election the Democrats found themselves locked into a taxing and spending pattern which they found politically difficult to escape and economically devastating to maintain. They had been outmaneuvered.

The game is still being played in Reagan's court. It is his game. It is played by his rules. All he has to do is remain adamant about his tax cut and defense build-up, the essence of which he can probably retain, and he wins. In fact, he can just make a speech or two, then sit back, play amiable and determined, let the Senate leadership wriggle around trying to enact a budget with token tax increases and token military spending cuts, enjoy the show between naps and visits to the ranch, and keep on winning. He has created a strategic position where it is politically much more difficult for his opposition to dislodge him than it is for him to maintain himself.

I am sure it has not escaped White House attention that the key to maintaining this strategic position is the deficit, with its spectacular annual projections of $200 billion in the decade ahead. As long as the deficit persists, it will be possible to continue dismantling New Deal and Great Society programs (or to prevent their restoration) under the guise of spending restraints. Reagan knows that Congress would prefer to neglect social spending rather than to raise taxes or take on the defense lobby and its political network. He also knows that if the deficit disappears, civilian spending will increase. It is therefore not surprising that the administration shows little enthusiasm for reducing the deficit.

Using the deficit in this way is cynical right-wing politics at work, grounded in ideology and disguised by an "aw, shucks" script. It is both a debilitating and deceptive attempt to refight the economic battles of the 1930s and dismantle the legacies of that era while continuing to employ such Rooseveltian phrases as "a rendezvous with destiny."

The Great Depression was indeed a remarkable trauma. It lasted about twelve years, and its political impact on America was profound, realigning the electorate almost as much as did that other great trauma, the American Civil War. In addition to creating the welfare state, it established the legal underpinnings of the modern labor movement. The right wing has refused to give up the fight over either of these innovations. Fifty years later it is still trying to win the war over the New Deal and destroy the economic and political power base of the Democratic party in the process. But there can be no winners, only losers, in such a game. The Reaganites did not positively want a recession, but they were willing to accept a severe one rather than abandon their ideological objectives.

Reagan may have temporarily achieved those objectives, but in winning, he has also lost. His policy of helping the well-to-do while hurting the poor has divided the country. He has shattered the hopes of millions. His legacy to America will be one of suspicion, bitterness, and mistrust.

But what of economic policy? Have we at least learned something about the economy from this experience? Are the conservatives who supported Reagan wrong? Are the liberals correct? Where do we stand?

The true believers in what is called supply-side economics had a lot riding on Reagan's great adventure, and their predictions were proved terribly wrong. No longer can they assert that economic expansion always follows a major tax cut. No longer can they affirm with a Kierkegaardian leap of faith that supply creates its own demand. No longer can they say that tax-based business incentives will quickly and automatically lead to investment. No longer can they claim that lower taxes stimulate private savings by themselves. No longer can they argue that John Maynard Keynes was wrong when he asserted that the economy can stall at levels less than full employment.

Still, the term *supply* should not become just a discredited slogan, a fraud, as Stockman claimed, to justify the trickle-down tax breaks for Reagan's wealthy political supporters. Supply and demand are a large part of what this economy is about, and there is certainly a supply crisis in America. When consumer demand increases, "supply" no longer responds as it did when American manufacturers clamored for the customer's dollar with a wide variety of quality products at reasonable prices. Many parts of the economy have become sluggish, inflexible, unresponsive to change, inefficient by world standards, and vulnerable to external attack. Our decline in productivity is part of this problem. So is our widespread loss of global competitiveness.

Supply is an umbrella concept that covers many factors. These have been clearly identified for more than a century and a half. Classically defined, they are entrepreneurship, capital, knowledge, land (or resources), and labor. Today management should be separated from entrepreneurship and added to the list. In traditional economics, each of these factors was given a return, and its name has remained a part of our commercial vocabulary. Profits go to entrepreneurs, interest to capital, royalties to knowledge, rents to land or resources, wages to labor, and salaries to management. Modern economists have made the argument more sophisticated, but the basic elements remain unchanged. In our contemporary economy all components are necessary to make the system work.

Supply-side economists in the Reagan administration paid attention only to entrepreneurship and capital while assuming that somehow these would take care of the rest. With their blind ideological fixation on slashing taxes and repealing the New Deal, they neglected the other factors of supply and our need for them. Support for science, technology, research and development was seriously curtailed. Energy resources were left to the oil companies, while programs for conservation and alternative fuels were chopped. Aid to education was axed. Unemployed labor was sent to look in the want ads. The management-related problems of sluggish and stagnant industries were simply ignored. If this was a policy of supply, it certainly was incomplete, and deliberately so.

Furthermore, the Reagan supply-side policies were not even well designed to accomplish their ostensible objectives in the area of capital formation and entrepreneurial activity. The personal tax cut was intended primarily to stimulate consumption, not investment. The business tax cuts were neutralized in the short run by the recession and will be blunted in the long run by the impact of the deficit on credit and prices. Investors, faced with the economic uncertainties of the Great Recession, used their windfalls for paper speculation, not for real investment.

Moreover, the deficit made it difficult for Congress to increase its support for the neglected factors of supply and made it hard for the private sector to obtain the capital needed to upgrade the quality of its own investments. Long-term prospects for a genuine economic recovery, therefore, fell. So much for Reagan's version of supply-side economics. We don't even hear about it anymore.

The supply-siders were not the only partisans of Reaganomics. The administration had its full complement of monetarists as well. Analytically they fared better. The Great Recession demonstrated that tight money will slow inflation even in the face of an expansionist fiscal policy. It also demonstrated that fiscal stimulants need monetary expansion to be effective. In a sense, therefore, the Great Recession was a major victory for the monetarists. There was, however, little cause for them to celebrate. They now must recognize that monetary policy cannot be used as a cure-all for our economic woes. Tight money may have brought inflation down, but at such a cost to the economy that no one again should be willing to pay that kind of price. Monetarists also have yet to show that they can either define or control the money supply. They have no cure for unemployment, nor do most claim to. They can cure inflation by policies which lead to unemployment, but so can almost everybody else.

At the outset fiscally conservative Republicans felt at home in the Reagan administration. But these advocates of balanced budgets have been orphaned by runaway deficits, and their voices in the administration have been muted by the prevailing ethos, well expressed by Treasury Secretary Donald T. Regan, that deficits no longer count.

For fifty years the alternative to these Republican economic doctrines has been "liberal" demand-side Keynesian economics, still fully embraced by a majority of the Democratic party.

The Keynesians are absolutely correct in their basic assumption: There are times when the economy will not provide full employment and adequate growth without government intervention. They are also right in saying that government by law, tradition, and decency has the obligation to fight unemployment when it occurs. I share fully their instinct that government must act, and act effectively, to solve economic problems.

The Keynesians, however, fared ill in the Great Recession when a record budget deficit and even a record "high-employment" budget deficit failed for a long time to moderate the recession or start a recovery. The missing variable of monetary expansion took on awesome significance as the recession deepened and the deficit did little but hold up the price of money.

Furthermore, demand stimulus in recent recessions has not called forth supply without the economy's succumbing to the temptation of rising prices. For nearly twenty years the reciprocal relationship between inflation and unemployment has been deteriorating despite often frantic attempts to bring both under control at the same time. This condition of stagflation has resisted both fiscal and monetary remedies, used singly or together for more than a decade. Put simply, the system leaks.

Traditional demand stimulus must be rethought. Throwing money into a leaky system and borrowing excessively to do so are

like being a fiscal junkie. With ever-larger deficits needed to produce the same amount of effective stimulation, the system is
rapidly breaking down.

Fifteen years ago, during my early days in Congress, we were
smug in our confidence that the economy was manageable, that
growth could be stimulated while inflation and unemployment
could be controlled. At that time I remember experts both here
and overseas talking confidently about their ability to fine-tune
the economy while young Turks were shaping proposals to eliminate the residual, if persistent, problems of structural unemployment and to remove those pockets of poverty that seemed
unaffected by the general prosperity sweeping the nation and the
world. The mid-sixties were truly heady times for economists and
politicians alike.

What happened? I believe that the economic difficulties of the
last decade and a half have been the result of a series of ill-chosen
fiscal and monetary policies operating on a deteriorating productive base. This base, as we now know, was already showing signs of
weakness in the 1960s. The reasons for its deterioration in many
cases lie beyond the reach of monetary and fiscal policies. Nevertheless, these policies have contributed to the deterioration by
creating an uncertain and inflationary economic environment
which has tended to discourage investment. The weakened supply
base, in turn, has rendered even sound fiscal and monetary policies
less effective in stimulating growth and in fighting economic
downturns. These twin problems have fed back upon each other
and have accelerated our economic difficulties.

Furthermore, the system has been repeatedly shocked during
the last fifteen years. Lyndon Johnson's decision to create a Great
Society at home while fighting a war in Vietnam, the "guns and
butter policy," as it became known, put excessive and conflicting
demands on the economy, channeled scarce resources into non-
productive uses, and unleashed inflationary pressures that have yet
to be fully contained. Richard Nixon shook the international
economic system in August 1971, when he torpedoed the Bretton
Woods arrangements, and ushered in an era of "floating" exchange

rates. The result was created international instability, reduced monetary and fiscal discipline, and world inflation. Jimmy Carter pursued a series of stop-and-go economic policies that generated confusion, pushed up interest rates, and created more inflation. Nineteen eighty saw three different economic game plans presented in one year.

No president, meanwhile, successfully devised policies to meet the external shocks to the system caused by the two OPEC oil price rises, which consequently imposed their awful penalties upon the economy. In 1980, for example, more than $65 billion was drained from our economy just to pay for our imported oil.

The Reagan shocks were the most devastating of all.

The result of these recurrent upheavals has been not only personal hardship for many Americans but also a decade and a half of uncertainty, inflation, and loss of real wealth. Stable fiscal and monetary policies, while absolutely necessary, will not, however, cure our present woes by themselves. Coherent government action designed to solve the supply-side problems of the productive sector is also needed.

Such decisive action, however, will not be forthcoming from either major party in the near future. The Democrats, dominated by the traditional interests of organized labor, are still committed to traditional policies of demand stimulus, even though these no longer work well. Their version of "Industrial Policy," which is designed to be a strategy for solving the supply-based problems of the American economy, will preserve existing inefficiencies, not enliven the economy. Nor can the majority of the Democratic party, as a matter of practical politics, embrace those measures needed to encourage entrepreneurship, capital, and the rapid dissemination of new technologies, all of which are necessary for a long-term recovery.

The Republican party, with its presidential nominating process dominated by the right wing, convincingly supports an equally truncated set of supply-side policies. Its constituencies will prevent it from giving adequate support to nonmilitary spending for science, technology, energy research, education, and job training, all of which are needed to rebuild our economic base. Furthermore, despite the tax cuts, Republicans are still reluctant to enact needed demand stimulus in times of economic downturns. Their ideological fixations prevent them from recognizing that government must play an active role in rebuilding the economy.

Both parties are succumbing to protectionist tendencies. Both seem unable to bring the deficit under control. The political debate between them is the extent to which the New Deal will be liquidated and the extent to which we should use unemployment and inflation as cures for each other. No wonder many Americans feel that neither party can solve the economic problems of today or tomorrow.

The disputes between the majority of Republicans and the majority of Democrats may affect our future, but they do not address our future. They shed no light on our condition of economic stagnation. They offer no new insights about inflation and unemployment. They fail to recognize the impending technological revolution that is filled with vast opportunities and dangers. They fail to provide an understanding of the real nature of the Japanese challenge. They fail to create a framework for analyzing and solving our underlying economic problems.

The wrong things are being debated. The real issues are being ignored. These include how to develop and implement a coherent strategy to rebuild and restructure the supply base of the entire American economy, how to create new instruments and policies of demand stimulus that can operate in a noninflationary way, and how to rebuild the global economy so that all people, Americans included, can have a future based on hope, not on despair.

The American economy can be rebuilt. I agree with the old New England adage, usually applied to some piece of ancient machinery, that "If it ran once, it can be made to run again." Stagflation can be cured. We can have a society enjoying a high standard of living. But it will not be easy. The commitment to drift is great. The political temptation for the old parties to manipulate responsibilities while avoiding solutions is also great.

To succeed, we must first understand just what our problems are. We must recognize that the world of the 1980s is different from the world of the 1920s, when conservative economics had its last days of glory. We must also recognize that it is different from the world of the 1930s, when Keynesian economics was developed to explain the causes of the Great Depression. We live in new circumstances: stagnant companies in many sectors at home and lively competition abroad, a large and permanent government sector, an enormously costly defense establishment, a high and persistent government debt, a scarcity of energy, a growing number of multinational corporations, a changing service economy, a degree of intercourse with other countries that exceeds all previous experience, and a high level of public expectation about the ability of government to solve economic difficulties.

To overcome stagflation, we need new thoughts, new approaches, and a new framework for analysis. Let's put the past behind us. We need a new economics, and we need a new politics. The old coalitions of the two existing major parties will need to be challenged by a new party if these goals are to be achieved.

2

STAGNATION AND
STAGFLATION

THERE is indeed a supply crisis in America. The conservatives are right about that. Ask anybody whose new car has just
been recalled. Many important sectors of the American economy
no longer respond quickly and flexibly to changes in the patterns
of demand.

This is not a problem of quantity. Auto salespeople looking for
tire kickers have all the shiny new cars they need. American shop-
pers are not lined up in a vain attempt to find appliances and
apparel. The shelves are full.

Unfortunately too often they are filled by American products
with rising prices and falling quality alongside imported products
with rising quality and falling prices. People are buying these new
products from Japan, Taiwan, Hong Kong, and Singapore because
they are often a better bargain. Let's not fool ourselves; we are
being beaten at what used to be an American game.

The statistics show it. In 1980 Japanese auto production exceeded that of the United States. In 1982 our trade deficit burgeoned to more than $18 billion with Japan alone. Our total imbalance was over $35 billion. By 1983 it had passed $60 billion. We are in trouble.

Has the American economic miracle perished once and for all? Have we lost the vibrance and resilience that made us the wonder of the world? Carter, after two years of frustration, blamed our difficulties upon some deep-seated malaise. In almost metaphysical terms he labeled it a crisis of the spirit. Reagan talks about fifty years of economic mismanagement. Both miss the point.

There is no malaise in the sense that Carter implied. Our problems, while great, can be understood and, if understood, can be cured. Americans are willing to sacrifice if the need is clear. We have not reached a condition where we can stand neither our vices nor their remedies.

Ronald Reagan is also wrong to talk about fifty years of economic sin. In his fixation on the alleged atrocities of the New Deal he has forgotten that the American economy between the mid-1940s and the late 1960s performed spectacularly. We were the engine of growth for the entire world. We created an economic miracle unique in our own history and matched by few other countries at any point in theirs. If the New Deal ushered in an era of economic crisis, this fact was certainly well disguised for a generation.

The structural difficulties of the American economy which we associate with the phrase *supply crisis* seem to center on three related problems. First, many American industries have become stagnant in the sense that they have lost their dynamism and their ability to adapt to changing circumstances. This loss of liveliness seems to characterize a large number of companies in industries which have relatively static markets and which, for a variety of reasons, find it very difficult to lower their prices.

Second, our economic system during the last two decades has tended to discourage quality long-term investments. Both public and private sectors share responsibility for this development. Since the quality of our investments is related over time to our rate of growth, the result has been economic slowdown.

Third, we have undergone a dramatic credit expansion which has exceeded the ability of the global economy safely to absorb it. For example, the Eurocurrency market has grown from $65 billion to more than $900 billion since 1970. American loans to foreign governments have grown from less than $100 billion to more than $500 billion during the same period. The world is awash in credit. The result of this has been instability in the financial markets.

All three of these problems must be solved if the American economy is to recover its global competitiveness, if our growth rate is to resume its historic level, and if our traditional fiscal and monetary tools are to regain their effectiveness in lessening the swing of the business cycle.

The first problem centers on industries like autos, steel, chemicals, rubber, appliances, and machine tools, which have reached a condition some people call mature, others call sunset, and I call stagnant. To understand just what stagnation is and why it is important, let me distinguish among entrepreneurial, growth, and stagnant industries.

Entrepreneurial industries typically consist of small companies created to exploit a new idea. They are usually run by the inventor and are backed by risk-taking capitalists. Their efforts are directed primarily at improving quality and expanding the market. If their products are successful, others will enter the field, competition will be keen, and the variety of products will be great as all companies try different means of improving the quality and performance of their existing lines. Prices will initially be high, but variable, since the production runs are small and the primitive manufacturing technology can differ widely from firm to firm. Winners will be the best innovators and market strategists. Entrepreneurial industries are, therefore, characterized by rapid change in product lines, a wide variety of competing products, a commitment to quality, a major concern for customer satisfaction, and cost flexibility. This is how the auto industry began in the

1890s. Televisions in the 1950s and home computers today are other examples.

Growth industries arise when a new product is not a fad and "winners" emerge from intense entrepreneurial competition. These successful companies begin to expand production and to use mass marketing techniques. The industrial engineer replaces the inventor as the central figure in the company's efforts. Winners are those firms which finance expansion rapidly and which can develop the most efficient production technologies. Less effort is put into radically new products, more into rapid improvements in manufacturing. Flexibility is sacrificed to achieve this efficiency, and a smaller variety of products is produced. Production costs fall, prices follow, and the market expands. Companies grow, financing expansion out of increased sales and the promise of future growth. Fewer firms remain, but those which do are highly efficient producers of quality products.

Following a period of growth, some industries enter a period of stagnation. What happens? The production technology becomes fully streamlined, and large improvements in costs no longer seem possible. Prices, therefore, cannot easily fall. With steady prices, the market fills out and the rate of growth slows. It may not disappear altogether since some people will buy second cars or third television sets, but rapid market expansion is no longer possible unless the product is changed significantly or new production breakthroughs enable companies once more to cut prices.

At this point the industry typically becomes more concentrated and market shares are established. As these happen, companies soon discover that they have a large vested interest in their existing plants and equipment. They have sacrificed flexibility to achieve efficiency, and they depend on large predictable production runs for survival. They are reluctant to make major innovative changes in their manufacturing methods because their capital investment in the status quo is very great. They resist opportunities to develop a radically new product or even radically new means of producing the same product because these would make the existing production process obsolete, destroy the high value of their capital plant, and perhaps even encourage upstart competitors.* New technologies are suppressed because they are a threat to the current value of existing technologies.

Changes in both product and process therefore tend to be incremental. Productivity gains tend to be small. Advertising becomes increasingly important, as image and impulse seem more significant than real product or price differences. Money for research and development, therefore, gets channeled into market research, style changes, and minor, although not necessarily cheap, improvements in the production process. Fundamental change is resisted. The industry is stagnant.

Soon new factors emerge to keep it stagnant. Bureaucracy sets in. When industries are growing, they create large management structures to control the extensive production, marketing, and financial aspects of each company. Bureaucracies, however, take on lives of their own. They expand. They resist change. Soon people find their route to advancement by manipulating the system, not by improving it. Blame becomes easy to shift, responsibility difficult to fix, and problems are readily ignored.

Moreover, people become part of the standardized process of production. Work rules are established. These often become contractually fixed. Wages become upwardly flexible and downwardly rigid except in times of great crisis. Soon there is resistance not only to falling wages but also to any decline in the rate of wage increases. Further rigidities result.

As markets become more static, production techniques more routine, and companies more bureaucratic, values change. The excitement and challenge of innovation are lost. Style overcomes

---

* There is an interesting historical analogy. In 1906 the British launched a new battleship, the *Dreadnought*, which totally revolutionized naval warfare. No existing ship could challenge it. The British, who built the ship, had the largest fleet in the world by far. But the *Dreadnought* rendered their entire existing fleet obsolete and wiped out the value of their investment in it. The new battleship design enabled everyone to enter the competition without reference to past fleet sizes. The Germans took advantage of this, and the result was an extraordinary naval competition between Britain and Germany, leading to World War I, with both countries starting almost even.

substance in determining who will advance up the corporate ladder. Managers spin their mental wheels and lose their sense of curiosity and imagination. They look at the future in terms of the past.

As this happens, the industry finds it difficult to attract new bright, dynamic, inventive, and potentially entrepreneurial people. Why should a creative and ambitious young person want to enter an established industry where advancement is slow, new ideas are regarded as threats, "group think" prevails, and success comes from maneuver? Is it any wonder that many of our brightest graduates, seeking to retain their individuality yet facing such prospects, became academics in the 1960s, attorneys in the 1970s, and consultants in the 1980s?

Furthermore, as managers replace owners in established industries, earnings supersede growth prospects as the company's prime objective. Earnings are usually computed on a quarterly basis. Managers, therefore, are very sensitive to the short-term performance of the firm. They are hired to ensure a steady flow of dividends so that the stock performs well. If it doesn't, the directors may get inquisitive or the company can become ripe for a predatory takeover. Long-term considerations tend to be neglected or postponed. It is not surprising, therefore, that the accountant and financial manager become the most important figures in the stagnant enterprise, replacing production people who were key when the company was growing and developing its technology. The Chrysler Corporation in the 1960s is but one example.

How do the accountants produce results for the stockholders? They have three basic options: Sell more items, increase prices, or cut costs.

Selling more items in a static market must come at the expense of other companies' market shares. This can happen. It was certainly true of General Motors in the auto industry. But there are limits. Because products tend to be similar throughout the industry, existing companies can stiffly resist an expanding newcomer. The more successful the expansion, the greater the resistance. It is easier to double your market share if you have 4 percent than if you have 40 percent. Antitrust laws, or the threat to use them, can intervene if your market expansion strategy proves too successful.

Raising prices is more promising. With a fully streamlined technology and a rounded-out market, increased costs are typically passed on as increased prices. Furthermore, when production is concentrated in a few firms, these price increases are easier. "Price leadership" practices often develop, with one company raising its prices and others following after a brief pause to avoid price-fixing charges. This means that industries as a whole can find it easy to raise prices, especially if demand for the product is relatively stable over time, as it is in most stagnant industries.

Cutting costs may be an even more promising strategy for the manager with an eye on short-term profits. Big cuts in production costs are difficult if there is a large fixed investment, but some reduction in costs can always be made. It is very tempting to cut corners. Cheaper materials may be used. The assembly line can be sped up to squeeze as much as possible out of the worker. Design can become more routine. Quality controls can be relaxed. The most experienced and expensive engineers can be replaced by neophytes willing to start at a lower salary.

For a time such strategies may work. Reputation for quality falls more slowly than quality itself. Brand loyalty may persist. Advertising emphasizes style and attempts to divert people from considerations of quality. In the short run, costs fall, sales continue, and quarterly profits explode.

However, people working for the company begin to sense the new direction. If management isn't interested in quality, why should they be concerned? If managers cut corners, why shouldn't they? Morale falls. People begin to lose their sense of pride in the product they are making. The loss of quality accelerates. Management now must take expensive countermeasures, but it may be too late. The word is out: What used to be a good company now produces a sleazy product. Advertising slogans won't change the growing public skepticism. Meanwhile, the managers responsible for a large part of this have probably moved to another company, where they are currently producing spectacular quarterly earnings reports.

It is not difficult to see how an industry can become stagnant, producing products which increase in price, fall in quality, and diminish in variety. Organizations change most easily through growth. When growth slows down, resistance to change intensifies because change becomes costly, not only in financial terms but in bureaucratic, managerial, and personal terms as well.

Faced with the prospect of slow growth, managers try to break out of stagnation by joining the acquisition game. It is a lot easier to purchase a new company than to revive an existing one. Flexibility, diversity, and growth are sought by acquiring companies that produce different products. Bold breakthroughs and daring acts which were impossible within the confines of an existing industry are consummated. The rise of the conglomerate in many respects is a product of widespread economic stagnation. Du Pont buys Conoco. United States Steel buys Marathon Oil. William Agee tries to buy everything.

These opportunities for exciting action may temporarily solve the problems of executive frustration, but they do not necessarily contribute to the overall well-being of the American economy. The new high-wire performers may have a flair for creative financing, but they often have little concern for what happens on the factory floor. The performance record of the newly acquired company can therefore quickly deteriorate. The short-term profit seekers, however, will not be daunted. They will just play the tax laws, milk the company dry, sell it, use the money to buy another company, and repeat the process.

This shuffling of existing firms back and forth between companies often adds little or nothing to long-term national economic health. It diverts management talent which could be used to better ends. "Golden parachutes" to protect executive salaries in the face of takeover threats contribute little to a more efficient production process.

The problem of stagnation is severe. The supply-side policies of the Reagan administration, which were widely advertised as remedies for our industrial ills, unfortunately do not help much at all. Investment tax credits will not produce bold and innovative investments by a stagnant company which is structured to protect its existing investment in aging capital. Tax credits for research and development will produce cosmetic changes in the products of stagnant industries, not revolutionary new breakthroughs. Tax leasing provisions and other tax breaks will not generate new state-of-the-art growth but will be passed right through to the share-holder. Good use of these tax provisions may be made by lively companies and growth industries, but not by stagnant firms. Nor will these tax incentives by themselves induce a stagnant company to cast off its bureaucratic rigidities and become lively. The only Reagan-endorsed policy that has encouraged industry restructuring is tight money, which produced bankruptcies. But such medicine is not good policy, and the threat of bankruptcy has induced stagnant industries to cut back on investment, not to increase it.

The traditional demand stimulus advocated by Reagan's Democratic opposition is by itself also inadequate. It does not address the problem of stagnation. It does encourage new investment, but it is a blunt instrument to improve the quality of investment. To the degree that it produces inflation, it hurts, not helps. And it can weaken the credit structure.

Industrial bailout schemes, such as those contained in the Democrats' industrial policy proposals, will probably lock in the stagnant practices of existing companies, rather than produce real change. The Atari Democrats' solution of throwing technology at stagnant industries will also fail; it will bounce right off them. They are simply not structured to make good use of the opportunities new technologies present.

The solution is to shake these companies up, bring in good management, and restructure. For the government to encourage this process, it must have a sophisticated grasp of the problem and a set of solutions that go beyond the palliatives offered by the majority wings of the two major parties.

There is nothing inevitable about stagnation. Nor does it have anything to do with the size or the age of a company. To be sure, stagnant industries include many of the large old "smokestack" enterprises which have been operating since Carnegie, Mellon, Ford, Firestone, and Rockefeller laid claim to the fruits of our Industrial Revolution, but size and age have little to do with a

27

firm's stagnant condition. There are lively giants in the American economy. Many old industries have rejuvenated themselves through conscious commitments to innovation. Autos are stagnant here, but not in Japan. A rapid advance in technology (which companies may or may not control) can help. Production methods can keep an industry from becoming highly concentrated. Competitive conditions can mitigate or offset the effects of a slow growth in technology.

Polaroid's technological breakthroughs certainly kept Eastman Kodak on its toes. Corning Glass, a family-owned concern with a long-range perspective, has produced technological revolutions in glassmaking every five or ten years since the Second World War. In the health care field, Baxter Travenol's aggressive use of new technology and concentration on research and development have given it a steadily expanding product line.

Commercial aircraft is an industry in which development costs are so high that corporate executives must "bet the company" every time they bring out a major new line. This concentrates the productive mind wonderfully.

The communications industry, dominated by a few lively giants for most of the century, also never became stagnant. Here a commitment by management to continued technological development produced cost-cutting revolutions of extraordinary magnitude: the dial telephone, the long-distance direct-dialing system, the use of satellites, and now the use of optical fibers.

Computer technology advances so rapidly that there is little opportunity for companies of any size to milk existing production lines because they rapidly become obsolete anyway.

Why do some industries become stagnant and others not? What is the variable? It is tempting to cite technology. When it develops rapidly, stagnation seems not to occur. Yet who is responsible for rapid technological development? It certainly doesn't develop itself. It is also tempting to blame labor, with its wage demands and work rules. But the central role seems to be played by management.

Management takes over from the owners and employs short-term expedients. It expands. It seems progressively more inflexible. It becomes unwilling to take the risks assumed when companies were in an entrepreneurial stage. With so much invested, management tries to protect the status quo rather than to change it. It hoards and defends, rather than upgrades, the company's capital, its plant, its patents, its market share, its own staff. In many industries the company's machinery, resources, and workers, instead of being improved or encouraged, are simply manipulated, consumed, and ignored. Reinvestment ceases. The system is milked by management, but it is not fed. A form of managerial cannibalism takes place. This is certainly not true in all companies, but the practice is widespread enough for us to conclude that measures designed only to encourage the manager are insufficient to cure our supply difficulties. We need more entrepreneurs.

Many major American industries today are stagnant, and they exercise a formidable influence on the entire economy. Because stagnant industries are characterized by a relatively stable demand for their product and by prices that cannot (or will not) fall significantly, they tend to cut production temporarily in an economic downturn and maintain price levels. In a traditional market situation, a fall in demand should result in a fall in prices as companies try to restore the level of sales—at least that's what we were taught in Economics 101. However, in stagnant industries with stable long-term demand, there are fewer incentives to cut prices because companies expect that "pent-up" demand will come roaring back when a recession is over. There may be exceptions if the recession is deep, but usually the company just hunkers down, keeps its prices steady, lays off production workers, and awaits the recovery. Steel in 1983, operating at 40 percent capacity, even raised its prices. As a result, a fall in demand is quickly turned into unemployment but not into a fall in prices.

Alternatively, when demand is rising rapidly in the short run, stagnant companies will tend to raise prices to moderate this demand (rather than expand their capacity) because they know that their long-term demand is relatively static. The new capacity would soon become redundant. Increased demand after a point, therefore, can quickly result in inflation, but not so easily in increased employment. When an economy consists of a large number of stagnant industries, it is not surprising to see stagflation, a condition in which market rigidities can simultaneously produce both inflation and unemployment.

Stagnant industries can influence the economy in many other ways. Any industry that can successfully increase its prices while maintaining the demand for its product can put downward price pressures on the more flexible sectors of the economy. Conservative economists are quick to point out that when the money supply is kept constant and prices rise in one sector, they must fall in other sectors. What they fail to add is that if demand in one sector is less elastic than demand in a second sector and market imperfections in the first sector create price rigidities, the result is a downward pressure on sales and prices in the second sector.

How this works is illustrated by the oil crises of 1973 and 1979. In these two episodes the short-term demand for gasoline remained relatively constant. People had to buy it because they simply needed it. They paid the price and were left with less money to buy other goods. The result was deep recession as demand plummeted for products other than oil and as oil revenues, in part, went overseas. The oil producers, by their ability to increase prices and make them stick, wreaked havoc on other sectors of the economy, both industrial and agricultural.

In the 1973 oil debacle the government inflated the currency to ease this pressure. In 1979 the government refused to inflate for a long time, and the downward pressure was injurious to the more flexible sectors of the economy until the oil market eased. Stagnant industries can impose this same downward pressure, although it is seldom quite so dramatic, as long as demand for their products is relatively stable over time.

Furthermore, stagnant industries can pass their rigid prices along to other industries that buy their products, as the oil companies did in 1973 and 1979. When the price of steel rises, can the price of cars and buildings be far behind?

Small business, farmers, publishers, restaurant owners, deregulated airlines, entrepreneurial firms, many service companies, and even growth industries can, therefore, be put in a classic squeeze by the stagnant industries: Their costs will rise to the extent that they buy from stagnant industries, and either their sales or their prices of necessity will fall. In times of recession, especially a recession accompanied by tight money, these businesses in the flexible sectors will go broke by the thousands. They therefore add their unemployment to that of the stagnant sectors. This, in part, is what happened in the Great Recession.

It is not surprising that faced with such pressures, these sectors fight back and try to establish their own ability to control prices. If they have political clout, which agriculture still does, they lobby the government to intervene in the marketplace. Regulated industries, complaining for years about government control over their business, often find themselves fighting deregulation so that they, too, can resist a fall in prices.

This whole process can be very harmful because it tends to reward those who produce for stable markets and penalize those who produce for flexible markets. Since the former tend to be stagnant industries and the latter tend to be our more lively, entrepreneurial, and growth-oriented companies, the result is generally to reward stagnation and penalize those enterprises which are highly competitive and have the most potential for growth. This is not healthy for an economy.

Adjustment will, of course, eventually occur, but at a terrible cost. Cartels and stagnant industries can persist in their pricing policies for a while in the hope that demand patterns will remain stable over time, but fundamental market forces will reassert their sovereignty. If the industry persists in holding its prices above what the market will bear, basic changes in demand patterns will occur. People will buy wood stoves and insulate their houses. They will run their cars a year or two longer. They will make do with less. Markets will shrink. This process can be ruinous to industries which have structured their often massive investment in capital plant around expectations of stable patterns of demand. Chronic overcapacity and chronic unemployment result. Great and gaping holes can then be torn in the economic, political, and social fabric of our industrial society.

The effects of stagnation are felt far beyond the industries themselves. Macroeconomic policies operating on an economy with large numbers of stagnant industries are not apt to operate well. If price rigidities are widespread, they will tend to reduce the efficacy of those fiscal and monetary policies which assume relatively flexible market pricing conditions for their proper functioning. In America today not only will expansionary fiscal and monetary policies produce inflation before they produce full employment, but tight fiscal and monetary policies will produce unemployment before they produce price stability. The causes of this condition reside deep within the supply structure of the economy, where in many industries the behavior of management, the level of technology, the organization of the firm, the industrial relationship between employer and employee, and the nature of each market combine to create severe price rigidities and products of diminishing quality and variety.

I shall always remember a breakfast meeting with Fed chairman Arthur Burns in the spring of 1973. We were witnessing the onset of what was then to be the worst recession of the postwar period before the Great Recession. Clouds of smoke came from his celebrated pipe amid somber professorial pauses. As I leaned eagerly forward for his revealed truth, it came abruptly in what was to be a much-quoted sentence: "John, I just don't believe the old rules are working anymore." They still are not.

Stagnation does not stand alone. Our second great supply problem is an economic structure that tends to discourage the making of quality real investments. This situation has served to reduce our global competitiveness and retard our growth rate. A lack of perceived investment opportunities is one source of our difficulties, but there are many others.

The government shares a large part of the blame. Inflation has been a major villain. It has lowered the savings rate. It has raised interest rates. It has created uncertainty. All these discourage investment. Equally important, inflation has encouraged speculation in commodities, collectibles, currencies, gold, real estate, and similar items rather than investment in real productive capacity. Russell Baker said we were becoming a nation of loan sharks, and he may have a point.

Furthermore, during the 1970s the tax laws tended to discourage real investment, and the venture capital market dried up until Congressman William Steiger set in motion a reduction in capital gains taxes, a much-needed reform which I aggressively supported.

The Reagan administration, despite its tax cuts, has also discouraged real investment. The supply-siders predicted that the personal tax cut would lead to a higher savings rate, but savings fell instead. The deficit made credit tight and kept interest rates high. During the Great Recession business confidence was shaken and companies scaled back their investments for an extended period. As the deficit is accommodated by the monetary authorities, we will see a new round of investment-discouraging inflation.

Furthermore, Reagan's personal income tax cut altered existing circumstances by putting more money into people's pockets while forcing the government to borrow that money from the credit markets and pile up debt. This encouraged consumption and discouraged investment. It is my recollection that even George McGovern did not envision federal borrowing to finance his $1,000 demogrant. Most important, the Reagan administration has cut back on investments in human beings.

The private sector also shares the blame. Many stagnant industries, resisting the introduction of truly innovative processes of manufacture, simply patch up their obsolete equipment instead. This means that the rate of return on their investments tends to fall, discouraging further investment even more. This is why acquisitions are so attractive, but the opportunity to buy another company can itself tend to discourage real investment in plant and equipment. Witness steel.

Furthermore, piecemeal investments can be a total waste of capital under certain conditions. If a competitor, perhaps from overseas, can introduce a revolutionary new process or can even establish a more competitive production system, then piecemeal investments may not enable the older firm to catch up. If it can't, improvements to the old equipment will be a case of throwing good money after bad because the competition's new production

33

process will quickly render the old capital plant totally obsolete. Capital is not like a pair of shoes or an automobile that will still have use after new models have been produced. It becomes worthless when other capital can do the job better, unless it is protected by nonmarket means.

Given the large number of stagnant industries in the American economy, it is no wonder that our national rate of return to capital has been falling. Moreover, the large, established stagnant sector tends to crowd out the more flexible, entrepreneurial, and innovative investment-oriented companies which must compete with it in the credit markets and which often stand behind it at the loan windows. Thus the quality of new investments in the economy as a whole is significantly less than it should be, retarding productivity increases and reinforcing stagflation.

Stagnant industries are not the only major sector of the American economy that has been making bad investments. The banks are not doing very well these days either, especially with their overseas loans. Making bad loans to foreign countries for the purpose of consumption, instead of to American companies for the purpose of real investment, has not been a wise use of American capital. The banks are only partly to blame for this, but in their haste to lend money overseas and to play the oil intermediation game, they disassociated themselves from the fate of the American manufacturing sector. Large quantities of our liquid capital were frivolously squandered instead of being used to replace our capital plant. The obsolescence of this plant, in turn, may soon put at risk those banks which have large obligations from many stagnant industries.

This is a sorry record, but there is more. If you add the money spent in Vietnam and the money about to be spent for an excessive military build-up to the money permanently tied up in non-repayable overseas loans, you can account for a waste of about $1 trillion before you begin to look at the investment money misused by stagnant industries. Even America can't keep on wasting this kind of money.

Compare this record to that of Japan, which has created an economic system designed primarily to encourage the making of strategic long-term investments, with the banking system backing up the industrial sector and vice versa. This is one reason why Japan is prospering. The future strength of an economy is best measured by the quality of its current investments and the way in which it manages them.

As the quality of our investments has declined and our borrowing for both investment and consumption has increased, the quality of credit has weakened. Our national portfolio has deteriorated from sound and secure arrangements, fully hedged, to speculative arrangements less fully secured. In some cases speculative finance has given way to what Hyman Minsky has woundingly called Ponzi finance, in which debtors had to borrow more money just to service their debt payments and creditors felt obliged to facilitate such arrangements to avoid going under themselves. One reason why many people want to keep interest rates high in America is to prevent a flight of currency out of U.S. banks which would add to their shaky financial situation. A bubble has been created. This dramatic extension of credit is the third supply-side crisis we face.

When an economy expands, credit can be expected to expand with it. Indeed, the expansion of credit for investment purposes is a major factor in making economic expansion possible. But if credit grows faster than the economy can absorb it or if credit is extended to large numbers of borrowers who use it unwisely, then the result is instability which can lead to financial panic and financial collapse.

When expansion stops or when major defaults occur, the risk of collapse increases, and the government is asked to intervene. It was the threat of such a collapse that induced the Federal Reserve to permit an expansion of the money supply during the Great Recession. This solution, however, threatens to reinflate the currency so that we all pay for the folly of the bankers, the folly of unwise investors, and the earlier folly of the government. Inflation, however, provides no lasting solution because it can produce an even larger bubble in the future.

A major financial panic would wipe out an enormous quantity of American liquid capital and inflict a grievous wound upon the

American international banking position. We recovered from the crash of 1929 because our manufacturing base was the world's strongest to begin with and because it became even more dominant when the Second World War destroyed the capital plant of nearly everybody else. Our current global banking position was established after the war, when we became the world's major exporter of manufactured products and real capital. Today, with our deteriorating manufacturing base and our inattention to the production of state-of-the-art real capital, it would be much more difficult to rebuild our global banking position after a crash than it was a generation ago. There is only one lasting way out of the credit mess we are in, and that is to improve the quality of our paper portfolio by substantially improving the quality of our real investments. To do anything else is to play with mirrors.

If remedies are not forthcoming, if investments do not improve, and if stagnant industries collapse, America's social and political geography will experience great changes. These industries, located primarily in the middle Atlantic and midwestern states, have been the heart of the American economy for nearly a century. The people who work in them form the center of both traditional political parties.

The Democrats are feeling the effects first. If these industries fail, organized labor will no longer be able to deliver higher wages and job security to its own people. Political support for labor will diminish. Labor may even be blamed for the collapse. The economics of contraction will weaken its role within the Democratic party. The party itself will become weaker within the country.

Equally important, if the stagnant industries go under, the Democratic party will lose a large segment of its rank-and-file core. The middle-class working families, who are the heart of the party, will face declining prospects for themselves and their children. Their standard of living will fall. The traditional demand-side policies of the Democratic party will no longer work to save them. If the Democrats are in power, they will try to care for these people with far more humanity than Republicans do, but they will not find it easy to hold out hope for them. The Democrats will become a party of supplicants. When you divide Middle America, you deeply wound the Democratic party.

It is therefore easy to understand why protectionism and large corporate bailouts disguised as industrial policy are becoming crucial to the Democrats.

The decline of stagnant industries and the credit crisis will affect the Republican party as well. The managerial employees of the great industrial enterprises in the mid-Atlantic and mid-western states, together with the small-business people whose life-blood depends on the prosperity of these regions, form the backbone of the Republican traditionalists, the very center of the party. They believe in laissez faire, in political moderation, and in fiscal integrity. Their representatives in Congress are privately appalled by Reagan's deficits, but they have been politically out-maneuvered by him and will not openly oppose his fiscal heresy. As the economy of their region declines, Republican traditionalists will also become supplicants, in this case within the party, as protectionism, bailouts, and defense contracts become the perceived vehicle for regional recovery.

The establishment wing of the party, with its international interests and its close connections to the banking community, has been antiprotectionist for more than a generation. It does, however, have a compelling need to prevent the financial community's portfolio of stagnant industry stocks from becoming worthless over the next decade as large industries are destroyed by foreign competition. It will have to balance these two interests nicely.

The right wing, which is mistrustful of the establishment to the point of paranoia, is also traditionally skeptical of protectionism. The ideologues oppose it on principle. Right-wing money comes mainly from the defense industries and the oil companies, neither of which is subject to the kind of competition that protection will restrict. The right wing, however, cannot win presidential elections without some midwestern support. It will have to find a solution for stagnation, embrace protectionism, or lose the Midwest. Since it has no solution to stagnation, it will try to embrace a milder form of protectionism than that advocated by the Democrats, support bailouts where necessary, and increase defense spending in economically threatened regions. It is clear that both the right wing and the establishment will be forced to become more protectionist as each bids for midwestern support in its attempt to control the party.

Unless the problems of stagnation are overcome, they will realign American politics during the next decade as the old parties are forced for internal reasons to move in a protectionist direction or adopt some form of industrial planning (labor-based in the Democratic party and defense-based in the Republican party). Both parties will, therefore, rapidly become parties representing stagnation, committed to protecting vested interests in existing industrial relationships and existing firms that can no longer compete globally. These are stratagems of despair. They hold out no hope for a dynamic economic future. If the two old parties remain parties of the past, as it seems they will, then we will need new political forces to represent the future.

Since many traditional remedies for stagnation have been ineffective, some Americans and a lot of Europeans are heralding the decline of capitalism. Were it not for the success of the Japanese, these cries would be louder. The socialists, the corporatists, and the protectionists, each from a different vantage point, hold that economic stagnation is inevitable and that America must adapt to this new reality.

But they are wrong. There is nothing inevitable about economic stagnation. An economy is not an organism that grows old and dies. It can be rejuvenated or rebuilt or restructured. It can change, and it can be made to change.

There is, however, nothing inevitable about rejuvenation either. Capitalism *can* die. The prophets of doom are right about that. It is not a perpetual motion machine. If nothing goes in, nothing will come out.

Capitalism can die in many ways. It can die by becoming a form of socialism in which the temptation for government or organized labor to milk the stagnant production lines becomes too great for business to resist. It can die by becoming a form of corporatism in which government, labor, and business cooperate collusively to preserve vested interests and discourage the introduction of new ideas and methods. It can die by becoming a form of protectionist mercantilism in which stagnant companies are allowed to slumber behind escalating trade barriers that protect the value of their otherwise worthless capital plant. And it can also die when stagnation and the lack of new investment opportunities induce promoters to speculate primarily on the price fluctuations of land, commodities, and currencies. Such an economy, based on speculation, might be called a market economy, but it certainly is not capitalism.

If stagnation is the problem, then liveliness is the answer. Change and movement are the antidotes to decay. We need a dynamic economy, one in which business competes with imagination, flair, and panache. Quality and variety must replace shoddiness and routine. Risk must be rediscovered. So must creative individuality. We must use our wits to make new opportunities. We must look to the future.

3

THE NEW
TECHNOLOGY

INDUSTRIAL stagnation occurs when production lines are
fully established, products are standardized, the market is
stabilized, and the promise of new technology is at least temporarily exhausted. It stands to reason, therefore, that new technological
breakthroughs can play a significant role in alleviating the problems of stagnation. New products and new methods of production
can liven things up and help reestablish a vigorous and productive
economy with expanding opportunities for real investment.

There is no space wars magic to this. Throwing technology at
the system will not by itself rejuvenate it. The Atari Democrats
are just as wrong to focus on a single factor of supply as the
Reaganites are to concentrate on two of them. But technology is
important, and its rapid advancement has created new global realities that any program for economic vitality must recognize.

Technological changes have played a central role in our cap-
italist system in the past. In the late nineteenth century not only
were there many entrepreneurs, vast resources, cheap farm and

immigrant labor, skilled artisans, literate consumers, and an adequate process of capital formation, but there was also a technological revolution. The full development of the steam engine, the electric generator and motor, the gasoline engine, and the new advances in metallurgy revolutionized the labor and resource aspects of supply and gave industrialists the opportunities to invest in the manufacture and distribution of enormous numbers of new products made by new production methods. The Reaganite supply-siders often forget that it was not just laissez-faire promotion but also rapid technological innovation that fueled the expansion of the American economy between the Civil War and the First World War.

We are today experiencing major technological breakthroughs that are bound to affect the structure of our economy in important ways. Laser technology and chemical engineering are active fields. Genetic engineering will make astounding changes in the decades ahead. We are experiencing a revolution in health care technology, with the artificial heart and self-administered kidney dialysis being only two spectacular examples. Still to be realized, but coming, are the commercial possibilities of space and the seabed. But the development of the last two decades that is ripe for today and crucial for our immediate future is the computer chip, known to experts as the microprocessor.

What is the computer chip? It is a tiny flake of silicon, the primary ingredient of ordinary sand. It costs a few dollars (expensive ones may cost a couple of hundred dollars), but it can perform a vast number of switching operations in controlled sequence almost immediately. In other words, it can make decisions. Only a few years ago such operations required a multimillion-dollar computer. The chip is therefore unbelievably important not only because of what it can do but because it is tiny, cheap, and simple. It can be easily wired into almost anything. Its potential for industry is revolutionary. Just as the end of the nineteenth century saw human and animal muscle replaced by fossil fuels and mechanical energy, so will the end of the twentieth century probably see the computer chip replace the routine, structured, and well-understood activities of the human mind.

41

All this is not science fiction. Computer chips are the business today of firms located in "Silicon Valley," California, in Texas, around Route 128 outside Boston, and in many other locations around the country. These futuristic industrial communities, many of which I visited during the 1980 campaign, are fascinating monuments to creativity and variety.

Computer chips are also made in Japan, Taiwan, Hong Kong, and Singapore. They were invented in America, but the Japanese are closing fast on our position. The Europeans are interested; the Russians, among others, are pirating. The chip has already penetrated world technology, and the revolution is just about upon us despite many economic and social forces that can be expected to resist its impact. It is now a truly global phenomenon, and the international nature of this revolution is one of the realities we must face.

What will be the impact of computer chips on our stagnant economy? Not surprisingly, it will depend on the use we make of them.

Small business will soon be able to afford cost-cutting services available today only to large firms. As a result, there should be more highly successful small companies.

Growth industries will be encouraged as new products are developed. They will compete with the established giants. If they are successful, the result will be a more flexible market economy. For example, we can easily predict that the home computer will extend to about half the families in America by the end of the decade and that there will be revolutionary possibilities, such as electronic mail, electronic newspapers, and electronic library access, to accompany this development. Revolutions in education, health care, and transportation are also in the offing. Computer design, animation, musical composition, and other aesthetic capabilities are in sight. Highly automated and sophisticated home appliances, digital televisions, energy-saving control devices, and even more highly developed audio equipment are near-term possibilities, if not already accomplished facts.

New consumer goods, such as these, can be a major antidote to stagnation, but they are not a panacea. The industries producing them can themselves become stagnant quickly. Rapid turnover of consumer items can also foster a throwaway society and can be as unsound economically as growth simply for the sake of growth. Rags-to-riches-to-rags can easily be the fate of people and companies in times of rapid technological changes, just as in the nineteenth century. Nevertheless, the new technology, as it spreads throughout the marketplace, can create a more flexible, less stagnant, and more entrepreneurial economy.

All factors of production will be affected by the microprocessor revolution. *Entrepreneurship* will be in great demand and short supply. Many opportunities will present themselves to people and firms that behave imaginatively and boldly. Entrepreneurs will find it easier to set up shop, but to succeed in business, they will have to revolutionize marketing. Retailing in America is dominated today by marketing chains which are structured around the sales of large quantities of standardized products. Selling for stagnant industries, they are not always interested in smaller quantities or in rich variety. Market entry for smaller firms is thereby stifled. Interestingly it is also through these large networks that Japan was able to penetrate the America marketplace with inexpensive standardized products.

If flexibility and variety are to be restored, it will be necessary to devise new means of selling this variety to the consumer on a national basis. The electronics revolution, through the use of cable and home terminals, can supply a creative combination of functions now provided by television advertising, mail-order catalogues, and the Yellow Pages. Electronic shopping can enable entrepreneurs to enter the marketplace much more easily as long as that market is not controlled and dominated by giant networks. As people become more attracted to customized retailing, the Japanese advantage gained through the mass production of standardized products may diminish. The marketing revolution will create a whole new communications and distribution industry.

Capital will be affected by the new technology. Liquid capital will become more liquid as the world financial structure becomes even more unified than it is today. The stock market, the money markets, and the commodities markets will be subject to a vast electronic-based transformation in the near future. As new investment opportunities are created, venture capital will be in greater demand. Trained venture capitalists will become much more important in the financial world than they are even now.

The nature of real capital will also change. The assembly line will become increasingly automated. The age of robotics is upon us. Any routine operation is subject to robotization. This will cut costs, affect the location of factories, and make quality control easier. In the short run the computer chip will help offset the overseas advantages of cheap labor. The new technology may even enable us to recapture markets. For example, laser cloth-cutting devices, programmed by microprocessors, can bring back some of the garment industry that we have lost to Asia. GM has repatriated some of its electronics manufacturing from Mexico. Detroit is also beginning to use robots in its competition with Japan. Japan's advantages, however, are no longer primarily those of cheap labor.

Yet cost-cutting robots will not be a full answer to the woes of Detroit or to the woes of other stagnant industries facing stiff foreign competition. Cost is only one part of the picture. Flexibility is equally important. If Detroit believes that it can simply look at the assembly line, pluck out people, and plug in robots, it may find that it has achieved only a short-term solution. The basic assembly-line method of production will remain, and with it, the inflexibilities and high capital costs which contribute to stagnation. If the use of robots creates a deeper commitment to the status quo, the result will be greater rigidities. Besides, others can buy the same robots—or better ones.

The true strategic advantage of the revolution in real capital does not lie in its cost-cutting potential, or even in its quality-control potential, but in its ability to revolutionize the entire concept of the assembly line. There will come a time when computer-controlled machinery can provide the factory manager with such extraordinary flexibility that he or she will be able to compete with any overseas rival in almost any product line. The day of "Xeroxing" products is in sight. This is a bold claim, and it needs explaining.

With current manufacturing procedures, there is a negative relationship between efficiency and flexibility. The more efficient the process, the more standardized it is, the more investment it requires, and the more resistant to change it becomes. Alternatively, the more flexible the process, the less standardized, the more labor-intensive, and the less efficient it is. It becomes a batching, or a piecework, operation. The computer chip creates the possibility of a robotics revolution that can increase efficiency *and* flexibility simultaneously, so that smaller numbers of a larger variety of products can be produced as cheaply, item for item, as large quantities of a single product. Once a factory is equipped with this machinery, the assembly line will be reprogrammed, not retooled, and the computer itself will play the major role in the reprogramming.

It may be a long time before a team of engineers can sit down at computer terminals, design an automobile, press a button, and watch the finished car roll out of the factory door an hour later, but we are not far from the time when an engineer can sit at a terminal, design a basic automotive component, such as an engine block, and see it roll off the line unaided by the touch of human hands.

This "smart robot" revolution can help solve many of the problems of industrial stagnation. Computer-aided design and computer-aided manufacture will enable companies to produce a wide variety of products. The same assembly line will be used to produce a car, a jeep, and a pickup truck. Firms will be able to introduce these products quickly and test market variations cheaply. They will be highly responsive to changes in demand. Pricing will be flexible; the market, competitive. As production costs fall, as flexibility increases, and as design becomes the key to success, market entry will be easier. Efficiency will no longer require inflexibility, standardization, and enormous capital investments. Economies of scope will replace economies of scale. The consumer, therefore, will also be in a much stronger bargaining position. The economic system will regain some of its liveliness.

With this robotics revolution and the new capacity to store and distribute information, several major developments will occur. First, much existing capital will become rapidly obsolete—just as fast as the capital goods industry can undergo the radical changes necessary to take full advantage of the microchip. This will mean that the chip will destroy the value of existing capital just as fast as it creates vast new investment opportunities.

Second, competitive forces will therefore mandate that the world be retooled. A major growth industry will be created. Another growth industry will be formed to develop the systems which will train people to use the new automated machinery. The ability to design and produce flexible capital systems—and to do so quickly and cheaply—will soon become a key factor in global comparative advantage. Those countries that are leaders in producing the capital systems of the future will be the leaders in the world economy of the future.

Third, real capital will become cheaper and more productive. To the degree that it makes operations routine, it will also be globally more mobile. Fourth, the fall in costs of real capital will be matched by a rise in the importance of those people who "operate" that capital. Comparative advantage in the production of products will come primarily from skilled engineers, designers, and operatives who program and repair the equipment and who are trained to take full advantage of the flexibility it affords.

Knowledge, therefore, will be profoundly affected by the new technology as its role in the production process increases. It will be made widely available through electronic means to those who have the skills to take advantage of it. The need for systems to make this knowledge available will create another major growth industry.

One result of these developments will be that a nation's level of knowledge and skills will become at least as important as its level of capital investment. Software is already more expensive than hardware in many industries. Capital systems, composed of both machines and their programmers, will replace capital goods at the heart of the productive process. Unlike now, the people will be more difficult to replace than the machine. In the industries of the future, capital systems may become less mobile and less vulnerable to rapid obsolescence because hardware flexibility and programmer skills will be paramount.

The company's most valuable "capital" assets will be its collection of highly trained professionals. This "human capital," however, will not be "manageable" the way traditional capital has been. It will bargain; it will often quit; it will sometimes go into competition against the company. People will have a greater proprietary right to their own knowledge and skills. Furthermore, the government, through the school system and advanced training centers, will be heavily involved in the process of forming this kind of capital. This publicly created knowledge-based capital will profoundly affect the economic balance of power between employer and employee.

Resources will also be revolutionized by the computer chip. Information will be substituted for energy. The GNP will grow apart from the growth of energy. More fuel-efficient vehicles, furnaces, lighting systems, and appliances will be produced. In the long term the computer chip should reduce our dependence on imported resources and profoundly alter the nature of the energy market. It will also enable producers to substitute knowledge for other scarce resources.

The impact of the new technology on *labor*, however, will be mixed at best. Many people will come to regard the chip as a scab. In the air controllers' strike, for example, the new equipment made it easier for initially less well-trained people to perform the job. The new technology will create a more differentiated work force, less subject to unionization than today's work force. It will create greater opportunities for firms to enter the marketplace, so that unions will not as easily dominate whole industries. To the degree that unions contribute to production rigidities, they will increase the chances that unionized companies will fail more frequently than nonunionized companies. Unions, like management, can adapt, but some will look with fear at the chips. This is one reason why the neoliberals who have enthusiastically embraced the new technology may fare poorly in the presidential politics of their party.

The job market itself will become knowledge-intensive and highly technical. The number of workers needed to produce a given product may decline precipitously. Many young people are now training for jobs that will not exist when they are ready to begin work. During the next twenty years, by one estimate, about 4 million out of 8 million American machine operators will be replaced; most of the remainder could be eliminated by 2025. The Midwest will suffer special hardship.

These are mere statistics. It is something else to look at the real thing. My hometown of Rockford, Illinois, was hard hit during the Great Recession. It makes machine tools, and that industry was one of the most depressed in America. Unemployment in Rockford hit 20 percent. This was not technology-induced unemployment but the result of recession and stagflation. I spent some time in Rockford during the summer of 1982. It is not an experience that I shall forget. It is deeply affecting to talk to unemployed men and women who are frightened of the future and who fear for their families, people who cannot understand why their whole lives have been shattered, why they seem to have no more opportunities. Yet these are the very same people who will suffer even more when the new technology rapidly invades the machine tool industry, as it will, unless something is done.

It is argued that the new technology will create as many jobs as it destroys. This was true in the nineteenth century, yet the Industrial Revolution was accompanied by a reduction in the work week from sixty hours to forty hours, and it saw many women moving from the workplace and the farm into the home as single-wage-earner families became the norm.

Moreover, it is not at all certain that "high tech," at least in the short run, will produce stable well-paying jobs for Middle America. Employment to date in many of the new industries has been erratic. Compensation also has tended to be divided between very well-paying jobs at the top and low-paying jobs at the bottom, with little in between.

Furthermore, even if the new technology produces a net gain in jobs, there is no guarantee that the new jobs will go to those who lost the old ones. More likely the jobs will go to younger people or to people already employed who will move up into better positions as their own jobs are eliminated. Part of the problem is that those who are laid off will not have the required skills. Even more important, they might not have the motivation to try; they may simply give up.

When people in their fifties and sixties are thrown permanently out of work in one industry, they seldom find equivalent jobs in any industry. When the textile mills of Massachusetts shut down during the early 1950s, the workers in those mills did not find equivalent jobs. Their children entered the high-technology industry for which Massachusetts is famous today. But the parents did not.

It is glib to talk about retraining, but a serious approach to this problem goes far beyond retraining in the traditional sense. It is a problem of pride and initiative, of jobs available in a specific location, of resources to make retraining possible, of convincing employers that it is worth their while to invest in people who are forty-five or fifty years of age, and of persuading people that they should try to rebuild shattered lives when the new employment itself may not last for long. A person's job is often that person's measure of self-worth. We must approach retraining with this in mind, and we must now train young people to expect several careers in their lifetimes.

Even if these problems are overcome, there is still a danger that the evolving technology will create what many call a dual economy. The first economy would consist of the technology-oriented industries, and it would be peopled largely by highly trained professionals—executives, accountants, engineers, designers, programmers, researchers, marketing experts, communication experts, laboratory technicians, specialized clerical workers, and very skilled operatives to keep the machinery repaired and maintained.

The untrained, those who are computer-illiterate, those who lose their jobs in middle life, those who had poor educations to begin with, would be consigned to truly menial jobs, part-time employment, the welfare rolls, and make-work government jobs with no future. Divisions between young and old would deepen.

There is nothing at all inevitable about a two-caste development, but it will be a challenge to all of us to see that this travesty of the American system does not develop. The long-term answer is not to devise schemes of redistributing the newly created wealth but to engage in the most ambitious education and training programs that any nation has ever undertaken so that all people can participate directly in the economy of the future.

We must never forget that all Americans have an interest in a unified economy. The faster the level of skills rises for everybody, the more competitive the whole economy will be, and the faster everyone's standard of living will rise.

Management will be affected by the new technology even more than labor because decision making has been a management prerogative, and decisions are what the chip is designed to make. The information revolution made possible by the chip will give management powerful new tools to monitor and control the activities of the company, but the imperatives of flexibility and the human requirements of the new capital systems will at the same time force management to develop different skills.

The office itself will be revolutionized—a process now well under way. Lower-level management will be decimated because its routine decision-making functions can be replaced by sophisticated computers. Middle-level management in successful firms will need to develop skills for inspiring and directing its valuable human capital, for directing a creative and lively production process, and for promoting its products. It will require hands-on familiarity with the new technology as well as imagination and drive. Good middle-level managers in large firms will be the kind of entrepreneurial people who could run their own companies successfully, and many will leave to do so, taking their engineers and programmers with them.

Top-level management, which in the last couple of decades in many companies has tended to ignore the production process and run its business like a counting house, will be even less equipped than it is today to make good investment decisions. The accountant mentality will be no substitute for firsthand experience with technology and its possibilities in a rapidly changing and highly competitive market. The skills developed to milk existing product lines will be obsolete. Smart boards of directors will recognize this as they mandate a decentralized approach to manufacturing and as they find new people to make the system work.

Such developments will radically change American business. If we take full advantage of the microprocessor, great industrial upheavals will occur. Those companies which try to fit the new technology into existing bureaucratic arrangements built around the old system of standardized products will be defeated by those which restructure themselves to take full advantage of the strategic flexibilities offered by the new technology. Many large corporations will invest heavily in robotics and never fully understand why they went broke anyway. The casualty list will be long because corporate bureaucracies and unions are very resistant to change.

The impact of the microprocessor will be felt far beyond the realm of economics. It will probably affect the social structure of America as much in the decades ahead as the automobile affected it in decades past. On the positive side, the chip can be used to extend the reach of knowledge to a wide range of people. It can create liberating opportunities in the areas of education and self-betterment. It can enhance and intensify communication. It can be used to raise our standard of living. It will give people access to information that otherwise would never have been available. It can be used to provide better health care and to fight disease. It can become a vehicle of social advancement because its "objective" qualities can give people access to jobs and positions in society that would otherwise have been closed to them by culture-based discriminatory practices. Furthermore, it can encourage pluralism by enhancing the role of design and marketing in the economic system and by creating new opportunities for product variety. It can become a humanizing force.

Alternatively, the computer chip can produce massive economic dislocation. It can, in fact, create a dual economy and thereby accelerate the division of the middle class. It can create a superclass of cognoscenti who will control access to knowledge and undermine the democratic process. It can be used to centralize information and abuse the privacy of citizens. It can be used by government to spy on people, limit their movements, and destroy their freedoms. It can be used to manipulate and control. It can be used to create vast new weapons of destruction which undermine the fragile international balance. It can enslave the human race just as easily as it can liberate it.

The relationship between the new technology and the American political system, therefore, will be profoundly important to our future. We must learn to master the computer chip and not be mastered by it. We must design new rules to prevent abuse of the power it will bring, just as we create new opportunities for it to spread benefits widely throughout the country.

Politics per se will both shape and be shaped by the new technology. The Republican Right, quite predictably, will want it kept under strict control. Right-wingers will try to divert it to military purposes in the way they have tried to divert the space program. They will try to help their large industrial constituents monopolize the new research.

The Reagan Right has already sought to limit the public's access to information, thereby establishing a model for the future control of knowledge. It asserts that special knowledge conveys special privilege: "We know; therefore, we decide." The corollary, "We decide; therefore, you need not know," seems to be another assertion which has a future.

From the standpoint of those who already have access to knowledge, restricting the access of others may be advantageous, as it was to the medieval guild masters who limited the spread of skills to a very narrow circle. But from the standpoint of the economy as a whole, such limitations are bad. The success of the new technology will depend upon our ability to disseminate it rapidly throughout the economy in an uncontrolled and undirected way. We can regulate the effects of knowledge if they are harmful to people or to the environment, but we must not regulate or control the spread of knowledge itself (except for security purposes very narrowly construed). Equally important, the training of professionals and their access to information must be encouraged on a broad basis. The point is to expand the skills of society, not to restrict them for the purpose of creating a position of privilege.

The Democratic party is split on the technology issue. Democrats have a more commendable attitude than Republicans toward information control. The neoliberals favor a high-tech strategy. Many Democratic "Industrial Policy" advocates wish to target the chip (although their suggestions for doing so have received a cool reception throughout the computer industry). The unions, however, are understandably reluctant to let automation spread with rapidity throughout basic industry, and their power within the party is sufficiently strong to ensure that effective measures to encourage the quick dissemination of the new technology will not be enacted by a Democratic administration.

The new technology, however, may pass both parties by, despite their attempts to control it. It is already widespread, and it will be difficult to cork it back into the bottle. Furthermore, it is encouraging the growth of a new professional class, whose voice someday will demand attention in Washington. Professionals have different perceptions and different interests from those found in many traditional business and labor constituencies. In economic issues they are generally conservative, fiscally responsible, and market-oriented. They are opposed to wasteful government spending and share with the non-Reagan Republicans a moderate viewpoint on the role of government in society. They are, however, generally well educated, performance-oriented, respectful of skills, and therefore liberal in construing the rights of individuals. By the nature of their professional experience they are trained to discriminate on the basis of a person's abilities, not on his or her sex, age, race, or ethnic origin. They tend to be forward-looking, future-oriented, and aware. They will vote for moderates of either party, but they have no party home. In 1980 many of them voted for our National Unity party ticket, despite its poor prospects of electoral success, because they were looking for new alternatives to the business/labor parties of the Depression era.

The emergence of the professional class will change the nature of American politics because these people do not easily relate to the old Left-Right division. Nor are they a group whose interests are formed in opposition to those of another group, as was the case with business and labor. They represent a complete repudiation of

Marxist principles, being neither thesis, antithesis, nor synthesis. They can truly become a vehicle of the center, reaching out widely to all levels of society. They are a force around which a new economy and a new politics can be built.

We need a new political force in America that can represent the interests of this group as well as the interests of other groups in society that feel disenfranchised by the parties of the past. We need a political movement that understands the new technology, its possibilities and its dangers. We need people in government who are neither afraid of the new technology nor slavish in their admiration of it. We need people who can adapt it to human purposes and human aspirations. We need people who recognize that the future needs representation.

The technological revolution will not be an unmitigated blessing. It holds out much promise for overcoming stagnation and rejuvenating America, but we must not forget that it is a revolution we face—one as massive and disruptive as that which occurred in the late nineteenth century, when agrarian, small-town, and merchant America was forever transformed by the rise of giant industry and the urban culture it created. The Gilded Age, after all, was not the idyllic era that right-wing mythology claims it was. Mark Twain, Lincoln Steffens, Henry Adams, Jane Addams, and Louis Brandeis all attest to its economic, social, and ethical costs.

Yet if we do not undergo this revolution, it will be forced on us from abroad. Our stagnation will accelerate, and our economic system will cease to function effectively. Those countries which do embrace the new technology will export their unemployment to us along with their superior products. We have no other choice. Nevertheless, as we raze the economic and social barriers to its adoption and let it flourish, we must have the vision and the commitment to minimize the human costs such a revolution will bring. We must have the wisdom to prevent its use by the few to control the fate of the many.

4

JAPAN—THE
STRATEGIC
CHALLENGE

J APAN, not America, has made the best use of the microchip by quickly adapting it to new products and processes of manufacture. With some exceptions, American management has been much more cautious in exploiting its potential. The chip may be an American invention, but Japan has embarked on its own ambitious research program. If current trends continue, it will move ahead of us in basic computer chip development in a very few years. The Japanese understand why it is important for them to do so.

The real Japanese challenge, however, is not simply technological; it is much more broadly based. Japan has created a superb economic support system, and it has mounted a brilliant strategy of market penetration that poses an extraordinary threat to many American industries. Without the microchip, this would still be true. With it, the threat is vastly increased.

It is easy to conclude that the Japanese challenge is a product of cheap labor, or of good industrial relations which motivate workers, or of quality-control programs, or of government support and subsidies. All these do play a major role, and in Japan manufacturing has become a national obsession, a form of cultural affirmation to compensate for the humiliation of wartime defeat. But there is more to the story.

Some observers have correctly suggested that the war gave Japan an opportunity to begin with a tabula rasa and create a modern industrial base, superior to an aging American plant which American management was reluctant to rebuild. Others suggest that the war destroyed the old social and economic structure which tended to retard economic growth.

There is a ring of plausibility to these arguments, but they could apply to West Germany just as easily. Both countries were regarded as the economic miracles of the postwar era, but one very awesome fact is rapidly emerging: The West German miracle is disintegrating. Its economy is faltering. Its unemployment has rapidly mounted. Its products are less competitive globally than they were a decade ago. Its industry has become stagnant, and its whole economic structure is no longer Ludwig Erhard's *Wirtschaft Wunder*.

Japan, in contrast, is performing remarkably well for an exporting country in the middle of a global recession. The major reason for Japan's sustained performance is that it has developed a sophisticated series of economic policies which encourage all six factors of supply. Entrepreneurship and innovation are rewarded. Capital is formed and distributed through a unique system that encourages savings and rational investment decisions. The acquisition and development of technical knowledge are a very high priority. Resources are carefully managed and conserved in this resource-poor nation. People are well trained and educated, while workers are treated like human beings and are given special encouragement by management. Management itself is highly trained and concentrates on improving investments, not on milking them. The government has provided a comprehensive economic support system to ensure that all factors of supply are present in quantity and quality. In this respect Japan leads the world. The system works.

West Germany has also performed well in many of these areas, but it has neglected a key factor: knowledge. It has been far less sensitive to the new technology. As a result, its capital is increasingly non-competitive and obsolete. Lacking protection, much of it soon will be worthless.

In addition to making its system work, Japan has developed a sophisticated commercial strategy that sets it apart from all the industrialized powers except for those countries on the rim of Asia that are adopting the Japanese model of development.

Let us examine this strategy more closely. Japan has few resources aside from its people. To sustain a modern economy, it must export to pay for necessary imports. Indeed, it must export or die. Exports, however, are not only the condition for Japan's survival but also the vehicle for Japan's success. The more Japan exports, the faster it raises its level of employment, its standard of living, and its rate of growth. Profits from exports help pay for the imported technology needed to sustain its economic miracle and help generate even more capital than its own high rate of savings provides. A sophisticated export strategy, therefore, has always been at the center of Japan's whole planning effort.

Many firms fail to understand the truly lethal nature of this strategy and the fundamental threat the Japanese pose to any stagnant American industry they choose to target. They rush off to study the Japanese production methods; they analyze the worker-management relationship, the product quality circles, the lifetime employment, the good inventory management, the use of robotics, the company loyalty, and even the calisthenics that Japanese workers and managers perform together every day. They often miss the essential point about factory organization—that management's function is as much to encourage as it is to control—and they always neglect the market penetration strategy that turns excellent Japanese production methods into impressive instruments of international economic competition.

If Japanese manufacturers had simply launched a frontal assault upon major American industries, they would have been defeated before they established a market foothold. They would thus have had no leverage to raise the large amounts of capital necessary for a sustained assault. Instead, they have proceeded along the following lines:

1. *Select a stagnant industry with a high value-added product.* This means that a market for the product is already in place and the American companies cannot cut production costs significantly.
2. *Master the technology.* This has traditionally been done in many ways: joint ventures, reverse engineering, industrial espionage, and development research.
3. *Enter the foreign market at the lower end of the product line.* By *lower end,* I mean with smaller, less complex, and cheaper products. One advantage of this strategy is that it provides an opportunity to perfect the technology. Another advantage is that the Japanese company operates on a *small* profit margin. This lures the American competitor into the mistake of abandoning its share of the market, especially if the company is run by accountants who argue that the firm should concentrate on the high-profit margins at the top of the product line to make quarterly earnings look better.
4. *Establish a secure position in the market, even if it is a small position, by earning a reputation for quality and reasonable prices.* At this point the Japanese company can exploit fully the achievements of its factory system in Japan and its quality-oriented production process. With a secure position from which to operate and with diminishing American competition, it can also develop an effective marketing network to sell its products.
5. *Move up the product line to more expensive items without abandoning the cheaper products.* In this way the Japanese company takes advantage of the economics of an expanding market, even if the overall market is stagnant, because it is now selling at the expense of the giant

American firms' market share. In expanding industries the average production cost per item drops as the market increases and as companies expand their plant capacity with the most modern equipment. Expansion can easily be funded out of the increasing sales or the promise of even more sales. Once the Japanese company has reached this stage, it has established a competitive advantage that will almost surely enable it to defeat its giant American counterpart, although the American firm does not believe this yet because it still retains a larger market share than the Japanese company has. Equating power with size, the large stagnant American firms do not quickly perceive the danger of a determined competitor with a smaller market share that is nevertheless poised to take full advantage of the economics of expansion.

6. *When a secure position is established, do not undersell dramatically; undersell marginally, if at all.* This enables the Japanese company to take the highest possible profit margin on each item. The alternative strategy would be to go in for lower prices and higher production runs. The disadvantage of this approach is that it requires a very rapid expansion of the capital plant. This unduly expands corporate debt and threatens the quality of the product. Rapid expansion is also risky in the export business because protectionist sentiment can shut off your market, leaving you with debt and overcapacity.

7. *Accelerate the movement up the product line.* With its base secure the Japanese company can now openly defeat the American competition. As it moves in a determined way up the product line, it begins to eat decisively into the market shares of American companies. All the disadvantages of stagnation now cripple the American firms. They face contracting markets, inflexible production lines, bureaucratic management structures, and large overheads. Size is now a disadvantage. They often cannot get new financing, and the game can become in part a contest of relative debt burdens, especially in times of high in-

terest rates. Given the price advantage of their competitor, they desperately try to cut costs to increase cash flows. This tends to reduce quality and curtail advertising. Many are now caught in a wrenching dilemma. Should they lower prices to regain their market share, or should they maintain prices in the hope that they can still earn desperately needed profits? When they can secure financing, they try to reinvest in new plants and equipment, but they soon find that it is easier to cut average costs in an expanding industry than in a contracting one. Their debt increases rapidly, but they cannot reverse the trend. The end is near.

8. *Sacrifice profits, cut prices dramatically, and dig in.* This is the coup de grâce. The American company cannot compete with these new prices; it cannot get financing; it cannot rescue itself. It appeals to the government, or it abandons the field, claiming that the Japanese are dumping goods. In a strategic sense they are, but usually they are selling at prices above cost. Japanese companies for political reasons do not always carry the strategy to this step, although they will almost always continue to the point where it is possible.

9. *If an industry is attacked decisively from below by South Korea, Taiwan, Hong Kong, or Singapore, disinvest early in an orderly fashion, and turn the tables by exporting production technology to these competitors.* In this way, Japan is not left with surplus capacity and unemployment.

10. *If the steps in the foregoing strategy do not work, abandon it, and try another product line.*

There is nothing uniquely Japanese about this market penetration strategy. Alfred Sloan, the founding genius of General Motors, used it to defeat Henry Ford. Sloan did not start at the bottom of the product line. Instead, he perceived a hole in the middle, entered it, and established a secure base from which to operate. He took advantage of the economics of an expanding production line and Ford's inflexible commitment to his one or

two car models. Ford Motors was left far behind, facing contracting markets, shaky financing, and an uncertain future from which
it was rescued only by World War II. (In a similar fashion the
Europeans tried this strategy on Boeing with Airbus, but Boeing
reacted promptly to the threat and plugged the hole with its 757s
and 767s. This will protect Boeing's overall strategic position even
if it makes no money on the new planes.)

It is truly ironic that Japan is doing to Sloan's successors today
what Sloan did to Ford. Japan entered autos in the 1960s at the
low end of the product line, where Volkswagen had shown there
was a good market. It soon established a reputation for quality and
competitive prices, secured a market position, and moved up the
product line. By pricing its cars competitively with Detroit, Japan
then took its cost advantages in the form of profits which were
reinvested in expanded capacity, reduced production costs, higher
quality, and innovative product development. Today it makes a
car with fewer workers than Detroit does.

It also took advantage of two presumably unexpected events:
the environmental movement and the energy crisis. Japan perceived environmental regulations as a strategic opportunity to
take advantage of Detroit's inflexibility. It may be unfair to repeat
the old joke that Japan responded to the regulations by hiring
engineers while Detroit responded by hiring lawyers, but there is
an element of truth to this. General Motors created the catalytic
converter to clean up automobile exhaust emissions, but the superior flexibility of the Japanese production process gave Japan a
strategic advantage in applying the new environmental-control
technologies.

The energy crisis gave Detroit an extraordinary opportunity not
often available to stagnant industries: a completely new market in
fuel-efficient cars. Detroit, at the time, could have assembled its
best engineers, invested in new production processes with state-of-
the-art equipment, cut prices to the bone, and plowed back all
revenues into expansion. This expansion would have come, as it
turned out, more at the expense of Japanese market penetration
than at the expense of Detroit's own larger car models. Detroit
could have plugged the hole in the market and frustrated the

Japanese strategy. The accountants, however, prevailed, and Detroit continued to invest in areas with currently high profit margins and a contracting future.

Japan now has an enormous advantage, and it is easier for Japan to maintain the edge than it is for Detroit to overcome it. One reason is inflexibility. A high investment in existing assembly lines, wage and salary scales, an entrenched bureaucracy, and consumer perceptions about the product all make change difficult. Detroit's special handicap at the moment is the fact that it faces a static or declining market with seriously underutilized factory capacity. It is suffering through stage six or seven of the Japanese strategy discussed above. Unlike Japan, it cannot finance change from an expanding market in which costs drop as companies bring more efficient processes on line while financing these out of expanding profits. Detroit must bring new and efficient processes on line without expanding its total production. It must retire old capacity faster than it creates new capacity. This is a much costlier option than the one facing the Japanese.

Furthermore, Detroit has to borrow in order to do this, creating additional costs at today's high interest rates. General Motors did embark on a $40 billion capital program to improve its competitive position, but the recession forced it to cut this back. Japanese car makers, with a lighter debt load, face much less of a problem. They could probably move into the large car market and defeat Detroit even there were it not for Japan's "voluntary" export quotas, self-imposed for political reasons.

Autos are not unique. Japan now dominates the radio, television, video recorder, and stereo markets. It produces most of the microwave elements in ovens. It is cutting heavily into the machinery and machine tool markets. It has mounted a strong challenge in office copying equipment. Computers and aircraft are high on its current agenda. Home appliances and electrical equipment are additional strong possibilities. It is now entering the home computer market, characteristically at the bottom of the line. The American microelectronics industry has also fallen victim to a market penetration strategy. Japan is now the leading producer of the most advanced mass-marketed silicon memory chips. No industry can assume that it is safe from a successful attack.

Japan, however, will not attempt to enter all markets. Its centralized strategic planning process encourages selectivity. Japan began originally with textiles and other low value-added products with which it could easily penetrate overseas markets. Now it has moved up to concentrate on high value-added products which earn it the most profits overseas and on products with good growth potential. Thus it can begin to move away from the market penetration strategies of the past. It has begun to develop and sell products with wide market potential in the less developed countries so it can take advantage of economies of scale. It is also focusing on products which require the most highly advanced technologies. Japan is moving up the technology line, industry-wide, the same way it traditionally moved up the product line in a single industry.

As Japan moves up the line, it disinvests in industries such as textiles, shipbuilding, and steel. It will never totally abandon them, but it confronts problems of stagnation by rapidly upgrading its technology and products while liquidating its less profitable ventures. In this way it continually increases the quality of its capital investments.

The ability of Japan to make wise investment decisions and improve its capital is the heart of its national comparative advantage over America. It will not suffer its capital plant to become obsolete. It recognizes that turning capital equipment over rapidly —even at a loss—may make strategic sense because it increases the chances of completely defeating the competition, after which losses can be recouped.

Good investors playing against bad investors wipe out the stake of the latter over time. If a country can pursue a good investment strategy successfully, even if it starts with a relatively small amount of capital, it can eventually undermine the position of countries with much more capital if they persist in making unwise investment decisions. In effect, this is what we did to Great Britain a century ago in textiles, steel, and other areas; Japan will soon be in a position to do the same to us. It is easy to see why protection is precisely the wrong remedy for a competitive challenge like this since it locks in bad investments and reduces the relative quality of a country's capital plant.

As Japan nears the top of the manufacturing line, it is almost certain to change its basic strategy of market penetration. In fact, for the last several years Japan has been laying the foundation for its entry into a new stage of postwar economic development. Its new strategy concentrates on the technologies needed for the production of capital goods: computers, microprocessors, robots, sensing devices, industrial ceramics, lasers, optics, and other components of advanced production engineering. Japan is investing heavily in its engineering support system. Basic science is now also receiving considerable attention. Japan is attempting to open a decisive edge in many manufacturing processes so that by the end of the decade it will be the unquestioned world leader in the production of capital goods and systems.

This achievement will be strategically decisive if the new technology is used to create a kind of central flexibility, a situation in which Japan can rapidly change the nature of the products it is making so that it can quickly respond to changing demands for both products and the means of producing them. Efficiency and flexibility have tended to vary inversely in American manufacturing, as previously pointed out. Japan will use the chip to bring them together.

Japan's major commitment to the development of manufacturing technologies will bring it four obvious initial advantages.

First, it can speed up the strategy of careful penetration into the markets of stagnant industries and mount a relatively direct attack. The American civilian aircraft industry is one example of where this might happen. The industry today remains innovative and vigorous. Japan, however, has decided to enter the market and challenge American supremacy. It is starting at the low end of the product line with small executive jets. It is acquiring the American technology, using joint ventures with Pratt & Whitney, for example, (which needed the business because of the Great Recession). Admittedly aircraft will be a more difficult area for Japan than autos. Aircraft design is an art; institutional experience and intuition born of that experience count heavily. It will be several years before Japan can compete with America in top-of-the-line aircraft design. Japan, however, will persist. Its commitment to the development of a fifth-generation computer, if unmatched by America, will eventually give it a decisive edge over American aircraft designers. This is one of the major reasons why Japan is building that computer.

Even if Japan lags momentarily in the *design* of aircraft, its commitment to new manufacturing techniques may soon give it an edge in aircraft *manufacture*. It is already making F-15 fighter planes under license from McDonnell Douglas. As this practice takes hold, Japan can finance its aeronautic research and development programs and hasten the day when it can defeat America in the design area as well.

Second, advanced and flexible capital systems will enable Japan to enter new markets, especially in high technology, simultaneously with or in advance of the United States and other potential competitors.

Third, the new technology will enable Japan to make further advances in solving its basic problem of energy and resource dependence. The chip is energy-efficient. Advances in robotics and sensing devices also should give Japan an excellent opportunity to exploit the resources of the seabed.

Fourth, Japan's development of aerospace technology, robotics, and the fifth-generation computer will enable it to establish a dominant position in space manufacturing.

The new technology will give Japan the opportunity to compete in almost any manufacturing area it wants, but the tradition of careful planning will dictate a strategy of selectivity. Japan is simply not large enough to produce all the world's manufactured goods, or even half of them, as we used to.

I would expect that Japan will try to dominate a number of very high value-added product markets for a few years to come. Then, once dominance has been established, it will concentrate on the production of capital goods and systems. This is an area which Japan is large enough to dominate utterly. Japan will cut back on the sale of goods and will market the means of making goods. To be effective, it will remain in the business of producing the goods themselves so that it stays on top of manufacturing techniques and market requirements. However, its decisive advantage will be in capital goods and systems, in which it is even now opening a competitive lead over American and European manufacturers. This new strategy will bring enormous advantages to Japan. Dominating the capital systems market for a wide range of industries will give it the flexibility to choose its own manufacturing areas, retain a competitive edge, and thereby maintain its trade surplus.

Such domination will also enable Japan to defend itself from the competition of the newly industrialized countries of Asia. It can confront this challenge from beneath and meet it by divesting some of its own manufacturing capacity as it exports capital goods to these countries. If Taiwan or South Korea wants to engage in a market penetration strategy on the Japanese model, then Japan can export real capital to them to make this possible and thereby share in the returns. This way Japan minimizes its own risks, makes a profit, continues to dominate an industry, and escapes part of the onus that any country receives when it competes effectively in the markets of another. Thus Japan can continue by proxy to play the market penetration game without committing its own resources. It, for example, might decide not to enter the American consumer-durable market of refrigerators, washing machines, dishwashers, and the like. It might, however, let South Korea or Taiwan penetrate these markets and sell South Korea or Taiwan the advanced machinery and technology to do so.

Furthermore, a shift into the production and export of capital systems can give Japan one means of circumventing the rise of protectionist sentiment that is fast becoming a global economic reality. There is somewhat less resistance to the importation of capital systems than to the importation of manufactured goods because it is easy to make the argument that capital systems create jobs in the importing country.

Dominance of the capital systems market is highly advantageous in other ways. Capital systems are high value-added, and there will be an extraordinary market for them. Unless America gets its act together and enters in a major way, Japan will have the field to itself. There are enormous profits to be made in the recapitalizing of the American and European automotive, steel, rubber, electronics, textile, machine tool, appliance, and aircraft industries.

Furthermore, if Japan can establish itself as the leader in the production of capital goods and systems, it can create a very strong global financial position during the 1990s. If the economies of the United States and Europe remain relatively stagnant, if our liquid capital remains tied up in overseas loans to bankrupt countries or in the commercial paper of stagnant American corporations, and if the problems associated with our credit bubble are not solved, then the Japanese will become world bankers to finance their own exports. The export of capital systems, of course, creates special advantages not only because they are valuable but also because they create value. They earn a return. Leasing and financing arrangements will become attractive means by which Japan can create a much larger international banking and insurance business to serve the export of its capital systems to both the developed and developing world. If Japan packages its exporting and financing arrangements together, there is no reason why its banking and insurance services will be in less demand than America's.

If the Japanese do it right, they will not disassociate the interests of the banking community from those of the manufacturing community as Britain did early in the century and as America has done in the last two decades. Although international banking services can certainly take on a life of their own when they are not tied to a system of producing and exporting goods and other services, they become especially vulnerable to basic shocks in the international system and to attack by other banking systems that are more closely linked to real capital investments.

The Japanese banking system may in a decade mount a fundamental challenge to the American banking system. To be sure, the dollar, as the key reserve currency, still plays a central role in world finance, and this gives American banks many advantages. But the dollar's current strong position was created in the early postwar era, when most advanced countries in the world sought dollars to buy American capital goods and related services to rebuild their war-devastated economies. Unless the world still desires American exports in a sustained way, however, the dollar will remain central only by convention.

There is always a time lag between the establishment of a mercantile or manufacturing position and the establishment of a dominant banking position. London replaced Amsterdam by the early eighteenth century, when British exports began to dominate the Continent. New York replaced London in the early twentieth century, when the American economy was fully established as the world's most dynamic. It is reasonable to assume that if current trends continue, Tokyo will eventually replace New York. New York, of course, will continue to be an important center of world finance, as London and even Amsterdam are today, but Tokyo will be in a position to move ahead if Japan becomes the world's principal exporter of capital systems to Europe, America, the emerging economies of Asia, and the Third World. It is the obvious strategic goal for the Japanese; it is truly top-of-the-line.

This is a story of remarkable accomplishment and enormous potential which are worthy of great respect. Japan's achievements have not been without cost in human and environmental terms. Its route is not one we should mindlessly replicate, but it is one from which we can learn.

The jingoistic presidential candidates who try to make political points by excoriating Japan while calling for protection are wrong. They completely misunderstand the situation and hence advocate the wrong solution. The problem is in America, not in Japan.

We are faced with a challenge far more fundamental than any the Soviets are likely to offer. Our respect for the power and brilliance of this challenge must be matched by our resolution to respond. Those who resent Japan's success are wrong. Those who are willing to accept the challenge are the ones to whom America's future belongs.

5

REBUILDING THE
ECONOMY

Eᴠᴇɴ with recovery, our economy is in trouble. Large segments continue to be stagnant. Millions of our citizens remain unemployed. Industry is still losing its markets to superior imported goods. A large part of our capital plant is becoming obsolete. And we face a massive technological revolution which will transform society.

We have time to do something, but the politicians are wasting it. Short-term economic recoveries provide no lasting solutions. The Reagan administration has no plan for reducing stagnation. It has no plan for improving the quality of our investments—public or private. It has not dealt adequately with the credit crisis. Photo opportunities at which the president assures Lee Iacocca and hurriedly assembled Chrysler workers that "America is on the mend" will not suffice.

Moreover, the administration has met the technological challenge by reducing federal support for education, science, research, and development. With the future of our whole manufacturing industry and international financial position at stake, it is meeting the Japanese challenge by bludgeoning Japan to import more metal baseball bats. It would seem that the administration does not even begin to understand the deadly nature of the international game in which it is playing.

The answers from the majority of Democrats have been equally unimpressive: Bail out the stagnant industries, ignore the technological challenge, and respond to the Japanese by protecting the American marketplace with import quotas and domestic-content legislation, which requires most components in a product to be made in America. Those Democrats who wisely embrace the new technology and reject protectionism are a small, if occasionally vocal, minority in their party.

The current debate over America's economic future centers on three alternatives to Reagan's trickle-down laissez faire philosophy: protectionism, postindustrialism, and neoliberalism, the latter now often defined in terms of an industrial policy.

Protectionism is simply wrong. It is the best recipe for economic decline that I know of. It locks in stagnation. It removes price competition. It hurts consumers. It rewards bad management. It retards the use of new technology by removing a strong incentive to employ it. It obstructs the importation of technology from abroad. It resists the future. With it, we can look forward to becoming the Albania of the West, sweating out an everlasting "me decade."

Even with no foreign retaliation, protectionism penalizes the small-business and growth sectors of the economy since these must compete for the investor's and consumer's dollar against the protected industries, which in turn can impose higher costs and lower prices on them. *With* foreign retaliation, we would see a contracting economy, higher prices, and more unemployment in the export sector. By one estimate, the proposed domestic-content legislation would cost American consumers $160,000 in higher auto prices per job created. Protectionism may temporarily insulate our stagnant corporations and preserve the value of their capital plants, but the price will be a lower standard of living for all of us. It is a policy of surrender.

Moreover, if we are locked in global competition to determine who will shape the future world economy, the Maginot Line mentality of protectionism will not enhance America's prospects. It will leave us with decaying production facilities, while others modernize theirs. On balance, we will become less competitive. Japan, not America, will retool the world, while our existing capital investments soon become globally obsolete.

Companies urge temporary protection so that they can have time to upgrade their facilities. This seldom happens. Temporary arrangements become permanent because few politicians, I can assure you, have the courage to remove them. Companies, knowing this, forget about modernization. Consider Big Steel. Jimmy Carter gave it protection to let it modernize. Instead, it cut back on investments and United States Steel bought Marathon Oil.

I am not doctrinaire about this. I would not suggest that we rush in and instantly dismantle all existing arrangements—especially when the industries to which they apply are globally efficient and are increasing their productivity. It is permissible to use the threat of retaliation as a bargaining tool to reduce informal barriers to trade, to open protected overseas markets to American exports, or to counter industrial piracy and unlicensed copies, popularly called knockoffs. Some economists argue convincingly about protecting infant industries. Too often, however, these reasons are used to justify protectionism, not to encourage free trade. Let us be honest with ourselves and with our economic partners. Protectionism will not restore the muscle of the U.S. economy. Let's compete.

If protectionism is not the answer, is postindustrialism? Should we accept the liquidation of major sectors of the American industrial base, make this as painless as possible for the people involved, and become primarily an agricultural, mining, and service economy, expanding in such areas as communications, banking, transportation, health, advertising, insurance, education, science, technology, consulting, and personal services such as those provided by restaurants, beauty salons, and health spas?

People who support this view argue forcefully that economies pass from an agricultural phase through a manufacturing phase to a service or postindustrial phase, which they call a higher stage of development. I do not accept this argument. Postindustrialism does not describe what is happening in America. It is a cop-out to excuse our deteriorating manufacturing base.

If we were entering a new dynamic postindustrial era when services would replace manufacturing the way manufacturing replaced agriculture, then we would see the service industry straining at full employment, pulling people away from manufacturing, as manufacturing pulled people away from agriculture a century ago. This is not happening. Services have grown, but so has unemployment.

Nor do services themselves represent any higher stage of economic development. Goods and services compete in the marketplace for the consumer's dollar. When the goods-producing sector of the economy becomes stagnant, when prices rise and quality falls, is it at all surprising that people buy services instead of goods? If Detroit could produce fuel-efficient cars at significantly lower prices, Americans would buy more cars and eat fewer restaurant meals. Unless we accept the inevitability of stagnation, we need not accept the inevitability of postindustrialism.

Moreover, the distinction between goods and services is breaking down. We are witnessing the growth of marketable systems that are composed of both. Communications is a complex system in which satellites, computers, and optical fibers play as important a role as the friendly newscaster. Medicine has become as dependent upon expensive chemistry and hospital equipment as it has upon Trapper John. Complex office equipment requires constant servicing. The military refers no longer to weapons but to weapons systems. Capital systems, rather than capital goods, will fill the factories of the future. If we do not play a role in supplying the goods required in these systems, if we become only a service economy, then we will indeed become a nation of servants.

If by *postindustrial*, people mean that the knowledge component of the manufacturing process will be vastly extended and production will thereby by revolutionized, then I accept the concept. But this is a transformation, not an elimination, of the industrial economy.

If America needs quality goods, must we produce them? Can we not participate in an international division of labor, according to which we import our televisions, home appliances, computers, aircraft, and service support equipment? Perhaps, but how will we pay for them? Other countries will not always be content to take the dollars we print unless they can use them to buy something from us that they want. What will we export?

Commodities such as soybeans, wheat, and coal just won't do by themselves. Markets fluctuate widely; terms of trade can shift. Ask Argentina, Ghana, and even the oil exporters. Commodities provide no secure basis for an economy that must import most of its manufactured goods. Half the world is trying to escape such arrangements because they are ruinous.

A service economy can export technology. But how can we develop marketable technologies apart from the manufacturing processes to which they are relevant? For how long can we export computer technology if we are not making computers? For how long can we export communications technology if we are not involved with the production of communications equipment? Technology divorced from hands-on experience will not remain globally competitive.

We can expand our export of services themselves, but this is risky and has many political and cultural side effects. Services are potentially more personalized than goods. They emphatically require a larger social or political context in which they are delivered. The Russians may be willing to buy parts for a pipeline from us, but are they ready to let us run their telephone system, no matter how well ours works? Are the Japanese? Are the British?

In service delivery, cultural barriers are important, and protection, formal and informal, is much easier. With many goods you can still pay your money, say thanks at the customshouse, and return home with no strings attached. This is not always the case with services. They usually require political stability and social interconnectedness. They can be the first casualty in any international crisis.

Furthermore, no matter what the economists may suggest, a service economy smacks of clean-hands gentility—a rather Edwardian vision inevitably linked to charges of social prejudice and overseas imperialism. Services raise the specter of neocolonialism far more visibly than goods. They are more vulnerable to political demagoguery and upheaval in other countries.

Equally important, can we really be sure that we have a comparative advantage in services? Even assuming one, how long can we maintain it? London and New York may have a comparative advantage in banking, but what does this mean? Today modern communications make location less important than ever before. The facilities we provide certainly can be copied by other countries. Are American bankers smarter than others?

Importing most of our manufactured goods from overseas can also threaten our security. First, we will depend on a narrowing circle of defense industries for the production of our weapons systems. It will be difficult to expand this circle rapidly in times of emergency. The defense industries will be unable to draw by example on the usually more innovative and dynamic private commercial sector. Second, we will feel constrained to mount a large defense operation to protect the sources of supply, as we are now doing to protect the oil supply in the Persian Gulf. Thus our defense capabilities will diminish while the demand for them will increase. Furthermore, in the spirit of "no more Irans," we might feel compelled to take a very great interest in maintaining the regimes in those countries which produce our manufactured goods, with all the added problems this would entail. The likelihood that these overseas production facilities would be owned by American multinational corporations does not alter any of these security problems.

Postindustrialism is an excuse for failure which we must reject. We should indeed expand our exports of commodities, technology, and services, but to contain the risks and ensure stability, we need a strong manufacturing component in our export base and a manufacturing sector producing for the home market.

The third alternative is neoliberalism. Bet on the winners. Ax the losers. Face the sunrise. Divest.

Impressed by the Japanese experience of moving quickly up the value-added line by expanding in growth areas while contracting in stagnant areas, the neoliberals argue for disinvestment. For an economy to become more efficient overall, it must rid itself of the old and support the new. In this way productivity rises. The problem of stagnation is solved by eliminating the stagnant. One of those tough decisions, but smart.

There are five problems. First, who are the winners? People don't always back winners on the stock market. Can they score better with the national economy? It's one thing to lose money playing the ponies; it's another to lose the American economy on a bad guess the way the British lost theirs. The word *sunset*, employed by the neo-liberals to categorize industrial candidates for elimination, is invidious. It judges in advance that industries are beyond repair. Despite my Calvinist upbringing, I reject a concept of economic predestination—the industrially elect and the industrially damned. I sense that among neoliberals virtually all manufacturing industries, even those that are doing quite well, are considered sunset unless they produce high-technology products.

Moreover, the new technology, which provides the means of designating an industry as sunset, is itself creating new realities that render the term useless. Technology can make it possible for industries which left America to return again. It can also reduce the length of the product cycle from decades to months. Is the production of the 64K RAM chip a sunset industry? Will the home computer industry, now a sunrise industry, see that sun set in three years if other countries enter the marketplace from beneath?

As the new technology makes design more important, the result will be a larger variety of products and a much swifter change in the nature of those products. When this happens, advance judgments of product success will be very difficult for the government to make.

Second, if government is really going to make life-and-death decisions about industries, those people truly on the inside stand to profit immensely from such power and knowledge. If Congress makes the decisions, the result will reflect its power structure and the influence of the increasingly ubiquitous PACs. If the White House does, the policy will reflect the president's reelection strategy. If august boards are set up to represent industry and the "public," they will soon become captives of stagnant industrial forces, the way regulatory agencies usually become captive of those industries they regulate. In all cases the insider will maneuver to gain. Insider profits on Wall Street are bad enough. In government they are simply intolerable.

Third, there are strategic problems. What happens to a sunrise industry when it finds suddenly that all its necessary components have been axed as sunset? This is the standard bureaucratic snafu. Also, if a specific strategy is developed to invest in certain industries and disinvest in others, then knowledge of this strategy would make it easier for the overseas competition. A narrow and predictable range of industries is strategically very vulnerable to shrewd market penetration attacks by other countries. Furthermore, a national economy that aspires to be on the cutting edge of the world economy, as ours does, should be able to grow in unplanned directions. A broad industrial base makes this possible.

Fourth, there is something to be said for the marketplace. If unfettered, it can provide an efficient means of allocating resources. Furthermore, its legitimacy is more widely recognized by economic actors than is the legitimacy of governmental fiat: Companies don't fight the marketplace (in the short run) the way they fight the government.

Finally, politics is certain to intervene and defeat the neoliberal agenda. The willingness of politicians to ax losers is problematical. A striking illustration of this is the emergence of Democratic industrial policy schemes from the old neoliberal winners/losers proposals.

There are many versions of what an industrial policy should be. The Democrats envision a centralized body, either a bank or a public corporation, to lend money to prospective industrial winners and to those "losers" who can be rescued by a large infusion of capital. Although this rhetoric pays lip service to the winners/losers objective, the proposals are little more than plans for direct government subsidies to stagnant industries to keep them afloat in perpetuity at the taxpayers' expense. Pious assertions that the funds would be used to modernize the industry remain unconvincing. In this way, through the vehicle of industrial policy, neoliberalism in putative practice is giving way to a version of unimaginative state capitalism.

In rejecting the arguments of the authentic neoliberals, however, let me pay tribute to their analytic contribution. They are in many respects pointing us in the proper direction: We must not subsidize inefficiency, we must not lock in the rigidities of stagnation, we must help those people who are suffering from economic dislocation, and we must have a sense of strategy if we are to restore health to the economy and meet the challenge posed by others.

Even though these three alternatives have problems, Reaganomics is worse. Hundred-billion-dollar deficits for the privilege of trickle-down policies are regenerating hostility and recriminations that will last for decades. They have not enhanced the prospects for industrial cooperation. They have not encouraged peace between labor and management. Rather, they have left a residue of bitterness that does not bode well for the industrial future.

If all these approaches are unattractive, then what must we do? How do we get the economy moving again? How do we liven it up and defeat stagnation? How do we improve the quality of our investments and overcome the credit crisis? How do we turn the new technology to our advantage and meet the overseas challenge? How do we put people back to work again?

Common sense dictates that the government must take an active role in rebuilding the American economy, but common sense also suggests that the government cannot accomplish this task by itself. If we are to remain a market-based economy, and I believe we should, then the market must be the principal vehicle through which the government works. Government policies should be designed to support the market, not to work against it.

But the "magic of the marketplace" is no panacea for economic stagnation. Relying on it alone to rejuvenate our economy is to misunderstand the problems we have and to abdicate the government's responsibility for solving them. The reason for this is that the marketplace in contemporary America is basically flawed in three important ways.

First, in many sectors of the economy we do not have a free marketplace because rigid pricing practices are widespread, because the price is controlled by cartels, or because governments here and overseas simply set prices. Energy is an obvious example. Second, the marketplace often creates a short-term perspective which may lead people to neglect long-term interests. Managers looking at next quarter's earnings are an example here. Third, the marketplace itself often cannot ensure that our basic factors of supply are adequately developed to make a modern market economy work properly. Our first task, then, must be to overcome these deficiencies by repairing and extending the support system of our market-based economy.

It has long been recognized that all economies depend upon a support system which is often called by that grotesque name infrastructure. Ours is no exception. In the early days of the Republic this system was quite simple and consisted of such activities as creating currency, building roads, granting patents, chartering banks and corporations, establishing courts, and collecting the taxes to pay for them. Later on both private and public sectors collaborated in the creation of vast and efficient transportation and communications systems. Canals and railroads were often built with government grants and subsidies. Utilities benefited from "natural monopoly" legislation.

The highly complex economy of today requires a much more extensive and comprehensive support system than the one which was fully adequate a century ago. The creation of a favorable climate for enterprise, the stimulation of new savings, the conduct of basic research, the education and training of people, and the policing of the marketplace all are economic requirements that neither individual companies nor the business community as a whole can fully provide. If the economy is to flourish, it needs to have an adequate support system designed to make it do so.

The Japanese understand this. Their economic miracle is the product of a unique and highly effective support system underneath a vigorous and effective free enterprise system. Contrary to some popular American myths, the Japanese economy is not collusive; it is highly competitive, much more competitive in many respects than are some American industries. As mentioned above, Japan has developed a sophisticated support system for all six factors of supply. It has also developed such traditional support systems as effective transportation and communications networks. The heart of its support system, however, is an extraordinary financial and planning structure that is designed to encourage wise investments and to discourage the waste of capital.

This structure centers on the Ministry of International Trade and Industry, which works closely with the Japanese Development Bank and with a national banking system which uses the vehicle of equity ownership to encourage investments in real capital. Centralized investment planning is thereby made possible by these institutions, which underwrite and support the investment policies of the Japanese private sector. This arrangement makes possible the enormous strategic flexibility that I outlined in the previous chapter, while Japan still enjoys a vigorous economy oriented to free enterprise.

With an investment planning facility, a banking system designed primarily to underwrite and monitor real investments, and a savings ethos, it is not at all surprising that Japan's investment record over the last few decades has been excellent. The fact that it has had relatively stationary targets against which to pursue its market penetration strategy has been a major advantage, but this should not disguise the fact that Japan has created an effective investment support system that will continue to give it great flexibility in choosing how to make those investments that will maintain its own position in the future and defeat the investments of its competitors.

A second example of an excellent support system, in this case a decentralized one, is found in the American agricultural sector. Our farm economy on the supply side is probably the most successful in world history. It is entrepreneurial, investment-oriented, flexible, and very efficient. For more than a century this system has centered on the land-grant colleges and the widely based, democratically controlled Extension Service of the Department of Agriculture. These two systems, working very closely together, have provided the means for developing new varieties of seeds, new technologies for planting and harvesting them, and new business practices for marketing them. These innovations have been disseminated widely throughout the agricultural economy by universities and government field representatives. The Department of Agriculture has also created numerous lending institutions. In these ways an effective support system has helped create an effective supply system. The farming community as a whole, despite occasional gripes, would not wish to part with this governmental activity.

To solve our long-term economic problems, our first need is to create a sophisticated and flexible support system for the entire economy. The crisis in supply, associated with the stagnation of our industry, is in part the product of an inadequate and malfunctioning support system that has not kept pace with the growth, complexity, and needs of a modern economy.

We should not create a centralized system on the Japanese model. This is the winners and losers strategy. It would only discourage the kind of innovative change we need to regain our flexibility and to achieve the rapid dissemination of the new technology. It would be a mistake to run the economy from above in a controlled way. Rather, we must support it from beneath. Just as a county agent does not tell a farmer what to plant or what tractor to buy, the government should not tell business what to produce or what to sell. That should remain the function of the marketplace. There are, however, measures the government can take to support the economy and to encourage the private supply sector to operate more vigorously.

An effective support system must address all six factors of supply: entrepreneurship, capital, knowledge, resources, labor, and management. It is the responsibility of government to see that these factors operate in an equitable and stable fashion that is dependable and accountable. It is also necessary for the government to ensure that the traditional infrastructural systems are adequate and functioning properly.

It is easy to outline why we must pay attention to all six factors of supply, how the factors logically relate to one another, and what strategies we would adopt. Briefly, then, what must we do?

To begin, we must design policies to encourage entrepreneurship. Entrepreneurs and promoters contribute flexibility and variety to the economy. They are the source of new enterprise and the force behind growth industries. They create most of our new jobs. They are customer-oriented and understand the need to market quality products. They are generally lively and not afraid of price competition. They are our best vehicle for spreading new technology. They are the means by which the new will defeat the stagnant, to the advantage of the whole economy—unless the stagnant, too, become entrepreneurial. They are the key to our economic survival.

How do we encourage entrepreneurship? In one sense, we cannot; entrepreneurs are born, not made. Yet we can train people in the skills of operating a business. We can acquaint many more people with manufacturing techniques and with the possibilities of new technologies. We can create a business climate in which entrepreneurs will flourish. We can give them strong tax incentives to invest. We can ensure the creation of broad marketing opportunities to give them ready access to a wide range of customers. We can give them the means of resisting the cannibalism of the stagnant sectors. And we can make sure that they have easy access to the other relevant factors of supply, such as capital, technology, resources, and skilled people. In sum, we can make new opportunities available to them as part of an overall strategy of entrepreneurial encouragement.

An entrepreneurial economy, however, cannot operate effectively without an adequate supply of venture and growth capital. Capital formation is a high priority, especially since new ventures must compete with the capital demands of government deficits, stagnant industries, infrastructural repairs, and consumer credit. A much higher savings rate is needed in normal economic times to create this capital.

Capital formation, however, is a waste of effort and a needless sacrifice unless the financial community is structured to distribute that capital efficiently, responsibly, and strategically. The soundness of the banks must be reestablished. The specialized needs of small business, growth industries, and stagnant industries must also be met. We need both local development banks and new investment banks with trained venture specialists whose sole function is to evaluate the quality of real investments. These investment-oriented lending institutions should be decentralized, unlike their Japanese counterparts, to guarantee flexibility in the system.

Creating a climate for entrepreneurial promotion, forming capital, and making it rationally available are not alone sufficient to rejuvenate our economy. We need to make potential investments in American enterprises more attractive than loans overseas. Investors need investment opportunities. These are best created by generating knowledge and disseminating it widely. New invention and innovation are key components of a healthy market economy. They form the basis of real capital, and it is by creating revolutionary real capital that we can both compete with Japan and earn an increased return on our investments. The unfettered supply of science and technology and the ability to apply them to manufacturing are as important as the supply of finance capital.

We must extend our support for research and development. We must rebuild our scientific plant. We need new institutions specifically designed to support the development of real capital and to train people in ways to use it. As with liquid capital distribution, this system should emphatically remain decentralized if flexibility is to be preserved. It ought to be a resource for the private sector to draw upon, in terms of both technology and people. Special attention needs to be given to the problem of technology transfer, so that newly created knowledge can spread quickly. This is best done through the training of people themselves. The model of the land-grant college in agriculture is a compelling one. With a system specifically designed to support the creation and distribution of technology, we should be able to regain our lost lead in the techniques of manufacturing.

These strategies, however, will not be fully effective if the economy is denied access to resources, especially energy resources. The government has a responsibility to ensure that the development and distribution of resources are rational, fair, and in conformity with free market principles. It should, therefore, guarantee that the resource sector is not dominated by cartels or monopolies or by the politically motivated actions of foreign powers. The government must also fashion policies designed to minimize the chance of major supply interruptions. Without such measures, the economy (or parts of it) can still be held hostage by resource landlords, and its long-term health seriously impaired.

Even these measures by themselves will not be adequate to create a globally competitive American economy. As the new technology takes hold, the nature of work will change and the level of needed skills will rise. As new jobs are created, many more people will be required to fill the enterprises of the future. The government must ensure that our education and training systems are vastly improved to perform this task.

These exercises in building and rebuilding, if properly carried out, will together be sufficient to support the small-business and growth sectors of the economy. They are, however, inadequate to effect a needed restructuring of stagnant industries. Companies in such industries must be encouraged to restructure themselves so that they can compete again. This will not be easy. The traditional pattern of industrial change is for the old to fail as the new succeeds. For existing companies to escape stagnation, they must be willing to adopt not only new technology but new management practices as well. They must build flexibility into the production process and put in charge people who know something about it. They must draw upon the ideas and skills of those on the production line. They must rediscover the virtues of quality and variety. They must be able to regain price flexibility.

This is a tall order for an established company. Entrenched management and corporate bureaucracies are often powerful enough to prevent rejuvenation from occurring. If good management practices are difficult to develop within an existing firm, the best strategy for the very top management in most cases is to create whole new divisions almost completely apart from the existing company and let them be run independently by new management teams with incentives to act entrepreneurially and competitively. Such new divisions, built around new products, new production technologies, or just new management practices, can pursue a market penetration strategy similar to that of Japan. They can take advantage of the dynamics of expanding markets even if the parent company itself faces a static market. The new divisions can grow and eventually replace the old divisions.

This radical restructuring may be necessary if many traditional industries are to survive. Governmental policies should be aimed at encouraging it as well as the entry of completely new companies into established markets. One way to do so is to alleviate the human costs involved when such restructuring takes place. Another way is to provide capital incentives to make it possible for companies to create new divisions which can operate at the frontiers of technology and which can expand to replace the old divisions of the company. A third way is to enact policies which encourage profit sharing and other such vehicles which highlight the interests of both management and labor in increasing productivity. Stagnant industries are special. They require special attention.

Rebuilding the supply base will give the marketplace a chance to operate effectively once more. But to rebuild the supply base successfully, we must have a comprehensive and coordinated approach. Single-factor solutions will not work. It is at this level that economic planning is an important and necessary governmental function.

We must set goals and devise strategies to achieve them. We should have an economic master plan for rebuilding the supply base. We must coordinate government policies to conform to the plan. We must streamline government operations themselves to make the plan work.

Where we should *not* plan is in the noninfrastructural parts of the economy. We should not tell firms what to make. We should not set industry production goals. We should not plan to target one industry at the expense of another. We should not set wages and prices (except in times of emergency). These decisions must be left to the marketplace.

Nor should we go the mixed economy route that many European countries have adopted. Our basic industries should remain in private hands, together with our transportation, communications, and banking systems. These hands may change over the years, from distant stockholders to managers or to workers, but they should remain private. Even in the support system area itself, we should take the maximum advantage of contributions by the private sector. The government must assiduously avoid new schemes which will lead to corporatism or to state ownership of industrial enterprise. Let us use the market where it can be made to work.

But the price we must pay to preserve the private enterprise system and to give it the opportunity to function optimally is more government attention to the support system. Here the marketplace genuinely needs strategically coordinated help.

If we succeed in rebuilding the economic support system of the American economy—and the task will not be easy—then we will have made a good beginning toward solving many of the supply-side problems that plague us today.

First, America can make significant steps toward overcoming stagnation. We will help surround the stagnant sector with new and flourishing growth industries. We will make easier the creation of new capital systems that will give the stagnant industries a chance to compete. We will encourage the restructuring of those industries. We will contribute to the goal of a more harmonious labor-management relationship in stagnant companies. We will assist the spread of new technology to them and hasten the turnover of their capital investments. This attack on stagnation will not be easy. It will succeed only as companies themselves see the advantages of restructuring, but determined government action can help.

Second, this program should encourage the making of quality investments. The new entrepreneurs will provide variety to our investment patterns. The new banking systems will be structured so that their success is tied to the quality of the investments they underwrite. The new technology will create investment opportunities. Upgrading the skills of the American people will itself provide an opportunity for investments with genuine payoffs. The restructuring of stagnant industries will improve the quality of our investment portfolio.

Third, as the quality of our investments improves, we will ease the credit bubble in a noninflationary way.

Fourth, this program will enable us to meet the technological challenge by creating the means of generating and distributing technology, while we minimize its negative effects on people's employment prospects by making major commitments to education and training programs.

Fifth, we will be able to accept the Japanese challenge. The creation of new growth industries and the rejuvenation of stagnant ones will be a start. We will be able to deny Japan and others a stationary dartboard for their market penetration policies. As new enterprises spread, we will present a moving and confusing commercial target. We will play to our strengths and take full advantage of our freedom, openness, pluralism, and cultural richness, together with our present advantages in software and design capabilities. We will encourage quality, variety, and change. The marriage of efficiency and flexibility promised by the new technology will help us keep one step ahead of the competition.

This program is also designed to meet the Japanese challenge directly in the production of capital goods and capital systems. We may even have the opportunity to pursue our own market penetration strategies. In short, we can begin to recognize the dynamics of capital investments and the economics of expansion and thereby meet the Japanese challenge before the competitiveness of our machinery is lost, the value of our capital is wiped away, and the security of our financial position is undermined.

Sixth, and most important, as we succeed in mastering these problems, we will lay the foundation of a full-employment economy. A rebuilt supply base will give us a good handle to attack the unemployment problem. We will be able to maintain our standard of living because we will remain globally competitive and will develop the relevant skills in our work force to keep good, high-paying jobs in America. We will earn our way to global economic survival, not manipulate our way through inflationary practices that temporarily and artificially prop up a decaying position. With growth industries proliferating and stagnation on the run, we should be able to restore price flexibility to the system. This will enable us to master stagflation and retreat from stop-and-go oscillations between unemployment and rising prices. I present the details of such a strategy and how it can work in the next six chapters.

The supply side, however, is not enough. Demand must often be stimulated for the system to work efficiently. Intelligent fiscal and monetary policies are needed if a sustained economic recovery is to occur. As we defeat stagnation and restore price flexibility, such policies should regain some of their potency.

To begin, it is difficult to overstate the importance of dismantling the structure of Reaganomics before it wreaks more havoc on American investment patterns, generates high trade deficits, destroys our chances for future global competitiveness, and keeps people on the unemployment lines. When the deficit is brought under real control, not just symbolic control, we will be able to lower interest rates, make more money available for investment, and restore some stability to government fiscal and monetary policy. We can then ease away from measures that have tended to shock the system.

But these are negatives. We also need a new and positive approach to demand stimulus. First, we must recognize the realities of a debt-imposed austerity and the bloated credit structure of speculative investments. We will have to live in a world of monetary restraint, eased by a tax-based incomes policy.

Demand stimulus to fight recessions, therefore, can no longer take the form of routine deficit spending because when it does, the result is liable to be either an inflation of the currency or a severe pressure on the credit market, leading to high interest rates and renewed recession. Still, there are times when the government must stimulate demand while running deficits. To remove the long-term negatives associated with demand stimulus, the government should adopt an investment approach, rather than a consumption approach, to spending. There is nothing revolutionary about this, but it is not being done.

The budget as a whole should move in an investment direction. Not only are there traditional infrastructural needs, but the imperative to rebuild the support base for the supply system presents a wide range of investment opportunities. Unlike the transfer policies of the Reagan administration, these investments can benefit all levels of society, not just the rich. Education, nutritional, and job-training programs for the poor should take their rightful place in the supply pantheon, alongside tax credits for business and expenditures for research and technology (which will tend to benefit the middle class). To work, these investments must be real, not phony, and they must be closely monitored to ensure that the government and the people involved are getting their money's worth.

We can begin to put this program in place as we ease our deficit position. In addition, we must create new anticyclical trust funds and purchasing policies to deal with recessions in noninflationary ways. They must be designed to respond quickly in downturns and must receive a predictable flow of tax revenues, some of which they can bank in prosperous times and spend when times are bad.

To make all this work, we need new federal budgeting, accounting, and monitoring procedures.

Finally, to restore a healthy American economy, we must also cooperate with other countries to help solve the problems of global depression. We must build our export position as part of a strategy for global economic expansion. But we cannot simply export our unemployment. Rather, we must invest overseas in real terms, aid the economies of other countries, help expand the global economy, and with it, our trade.

These basic strategies—rebuilding the support system of supply, wisely managing demand, and expanding world trade—can be used as an integrated approach to resolving our economic difficulties and to breaking the cycle of stagflation. There is no magic to them, no quick fix, no wave of the wand, no rabbit out of the hat. But they are sound, and they will work. They provide a sensible alternative to Reaganomics, protectionism, postindustrialism, neoliberalism, and current industrial policy schemes. The economy will be rebuilt. Demand will be sustained. The market will choose.

But more is needed than mere economic policies. The economy cannot be divorced from the larger value system of which it is rightfully a part. An economy is not an abstraction. An economy is people—their preferences and choices; their aspirations; their willingness to work and to sacrifice; their commitments to themselves, to each other, and to the country. This is why for our economy to work, we must pay more attention to our basic values. The Japanese know what they want—the restoration of their national pride —and they will work for it. What do we want?

We want our freedoms. The ability to move and grow and change with new circumstances is vital to Americans. Our economic policies must reflect this value. Freedom is the source of our flexibility and variety. Tie down the economy, and Americans will not perform. Inflexible direction, either public or private, will not work in America.

We also need fair play. Whatever we do to cure our economy must be equitable. It must be fair across the board, open and honorable in intent. Break faith with Americans, turn them into cynics, give them reasons to believe that the system is rigged, and you destroy the economy as well as the polity. A government of the rich, by the rich, and for the rich will not work any more than a government of the poor, by the poor, and for the poor.

We also respond to impulses of basic decency. Americans won't support a system that they think hurts other Americans or fails to give them a chance. The economy must be dependable. People must know that they will be protected as well as possible against a sudden economic catastrophe. Business also has a right to expect stable conditions. We face great changes, and change can be good. But Americans will not allow these changes to occur when they know that people who are hurt by change will not be taken care of. A safety net is not sufficient. Anyone who jumps into a net from a burning building is glad to be alive, but the net will not restore the charred structure left behind. Americans, if they can help it, won't stand for an economy that tells a fifty-year-old unemployed worker to go sit in a rocking chair until he or she is old enough to draw retirement benefits.

We do not need to sacrifice our basic American values to achieve our economic objectives. Indeed, if we do sacrifice them, we will not achieve those objectives. If we rebuild our economic support structure and employ intelligent demand-side investment-oriented policies, we can remain at the leading edge of economic development and change. The world economy still needs a point of reference. During the foreseeable future we can fulfill this role better than anyone else. We are big enough in population, land-mass, resources, and market to decide for ourselves how we wish to live and what products to produce. Our own life-style, standard of living, and quality of life can therefore continue to help shape the patterns of world production. We are indeed still very lucky.

It will not be easy to put this plan into operation. It is one thing to set forth an economic program. It is another to have it enacted and administered well. To do both involves politics.

One reason why we have not built an adequate support system in the past is that special-interest groups are prying us apart. Business spends millions lobbying for its interests. Capital has its lobby —with the bankers buzzing all over Washington during these days of financial upheaval. The knowledge sector and related interests make themselves heard. The resource lobby—principally oil and gas—is very powerful. Education and labor are both well organized and well entrenched. The stagnant industries, attempting to protect their markets, their capital plants, and their set ways of doing things, have some of the highest-paid and most effective advocates in Washington.

Our economy simply will not work when banking and energy interests war with the manufacturing interests, stagnant industries war with farmers and entrepreneurs, labor wars with management, everyone makes life hard for the unemployed and the unskilled, and the government plays an armchair game of divide and conquer. We have lost our sense of wholeness. We have lost our commitment as Americans to help ourselves by helping each other. We have to put it back together again so that the system can run properly and humanely, with both its supply- and demand-side elements being used to ensure a dynamic market-based equilibrium. It makes no sense to have a party system with one party committed to supply-side policies and the other committed to demand-side policies when both are needed for economic rejuvenation. It also makes no sense to have a party system structured around an outmoded fight between business and labor. The real division of interest in American society, I believe, is not between supply and demand, or between business and labor, but between the stagnant and the lively. Even this division need not be debilitating since the interests of the lively are not to curb the stagnant but to enliven them.

We must put the economy back together again, not collusively in the corporatist image but openly in terms of traditional market categories, backed up by honest and fair government. Yet neither major party, given its ideology and its constituency base, can support the unified program of national economic recovery that we need.

The majority of the Republican party, now more than ever, is suspicious of knowledge, captured by energy resources, misunderstanding of labor, and unlikely to change. Its right wing has even narrower perspectives. With the failure of supply-side economics, the party is intellectually bankrupt.

The majority of the Democratic party has a short-term vested interest in preserving the existing system. It will support science, education, and labor, but it remains suspicious of capital and many types of entrepreneurs. Its industrial policy proposals show that Democrats will resist the restructuring of stagnant industries and, like Republicans, will cling to the solutions of the now-distant past. These demand-side, consumption-oriented policies are inflationary and contribute to the deterioration of our credit structure. This the economy can no longer afford.

The character of the two major parties was shaped in the Great Depression. They hold to a past that is gone. Rhetoric aside, their majorities have no solutions, and their minorities, some of which do, stand little chance of success within the old party structure.

There is a future to be won. It will be won only if we work together to win it. We need a new national unity. We need a new economics. We need a new politics. We need a new political party.

II

*The Supply Side:
Rebuilding the
Support System*

6

ENTREPRENEURSHIP

To succeed in rebuilding the supply base, we must devise a coherent plan to encourage the six factors of supply. Entrepreneurship is the first of these. America needs a more entrepreneurial economy.

Our industry is too concentrated. Two hundred companies control half our productive capacity. Many people say we should break this system apart, but a more practical solution is to let new companies grow up around the existing ones while we discourage the giants from devouring the newcomers.

Ideally the American economy should consist of a wide variety of businesses and professionals providing goods and services in both private and public sectors. There should be small individualistic enterprises and cottage industries, entrepreneurial ventures, growth industries, and large established producers that constantly upgrade their lines and improve their production techniques. We need flexibility in our firms (with decentralized operations), flexibility in our industries (with many firms competing), and flexibility in our whole economy (with a broad range of industries).

The economy should change continually. There should be a flood of new entrants. There should be many companies expanding rapidly to replace older ones, taking full advantage of the dynamics of growing markets and creative financing. There should be new firms splitting off from others as people leave to start their own ventures. There should be losers as well as winners because only through both failure and success can the system try everything, preserve its flexibility, and create the incentives for quality and efficiency that enable it to develop.

Such an economy will be unpredictable in its growth patterns, open to change, receptive to new technology, oriented toward customers, and tough to beat. It will not be a dense pack vulnerable to first strikes. It will be competitive in the traditional sense of the word. It will enjoy price flexibility. It will not be controlled by the government in any of its guises, or by the banks, or by the large corporations themselves. It will be alive.

To create an economy like this in America again, we need entrepreneurs—and lots of them. What are they? Visionaries. Gamblers. Risk takers. Optimists. Builders. Innovators. Some are pirates and magicians. All are promoters who have more fun. In a lively economy they, not the managers, will set the pace.

Managers tend to be cautious and pessimistic, the trustees of past accomplishments. Efficiency and control are their games. They are trained to protect their bureaucratic posteriors. Entrepreneurs do not always make good managers. Bureaucratic managers seldom make good entrepreneurs. We need them both, but today it is the entrepreneur who is in scarce supply and great demand.

Where do they come from? The day may be past when a blacksmith can invent a bicycle, two persons in a bicycle shop can invent an airplane, and a mechanic can set up an assembly line and make a fortune. But some are still trying. Hewlett-Packard, after all, did start in a home, with Mrs. Packard baking components in her kitchen oven. Twenty-five-year-old millionaire programming geniuses, while not common, do exist.

Today's successful entrepreneur is typically not the inventor of a Hula-Hoop or a surfboard but a scientist or engineer with advanced training in a technical discipline who builds a business around a newly patented process or, perhaps, a business person with a degree in business administration who leaves an established company to start his or her own firm. These innovators are usually trained either in engineering or in commerce. Often they operate as teams. Established firms may also have their entrepreneurs, men and women or management groups that make bold proposals, but they get snuffed out all too often by experts in bureaucratic maneuvering who have mastered the managerial style.

Why are entrepreneurs so important? Because in large numbers they provide an economy with its variety, flexibility, and dynamism. They invest. They usually stake their own money. They closely supervise their own enterprises. They will try almost anything. We need them today because the new technology can best be created and disseminated rapidly throughout the economy by people who are willing to take risks. Entrepreneurs will create the growth industries of the future. It is they who will defeat stagnation.

Entrepreneurs will play a special role in the next two decades because we need them to help rebuild the support system of the entire economy. For example, we need entrepreneurs to develop the new marketing techniques and electronic marketing systems that will enable the producers of the future to emphasize variety in their sales and help the economy escape the problems associated with standardization. We need entrepreneurs with an understanding of the new technology to help build an equity investment banking system which will underwrite the expansion of the new economy. We need entrepreneurs in the capital goods industry to apply the new technology to the capital systems of the future upon which our manufacturing base and export position will depend. We need entrepreneurs to develop the software that will educate and train people in the future as the electronic revolution is brought to the home, the classroom, and the retraining center. We need entrepreneurs to develop the management systems of the future that will enable businesses to regain their flexibility and competitiveness.

These emerging businesses, which will support the development of the entire new economy, will be exploding growth industries in the future—like the railroads in the nineteenth century. They will take advantage of the economics of expansion, they will be sources of new employment, and they will make the whole system possible. The government will also play a role in the development of the economic supply base. But the support system will grow quickly, effectively, and efficiently if the entrepreneur takes a leading role. Because we all have an interest in rebuilding this system, the entrepreneurs engaged in these activities will be serving more than just a narrow interest.

How do you create a "supply" of entrepreneurs to build the businesses of the future if entrepreneurship is a state of mind, an "animal spirit," as Lord Keynes styled it? One strategy is to ensure that they are not snuffed out prematurely. But we can take more positive steps than this.

We can educate more scientists, engineers, technicians, managers, marketing persons, and others who are familiar with technology, or with systems sciences, or with business practices. These people will form a pool of expertise from which the entrepreneurs of the future can come.

We can establish an extension service for small-business people on the scale of that for farmers. This service could advise business people on such matters as inventory control, accounting, billing, advertising, office equipment, and strategic decision making. It might be especially useful to newcomers, and it might provide an opportunity for retired business people to share their knowledge, as many are doing today voluntarily. This whole project could be run in close cooperation with community leaders and with the school and university systems.

We can also establish an environment in which entrepreneurs can operate effectively and profitably. As some succeed, others will follow. For example, government, if it wants steady growth, must create a stable climate so that investment decisions can be made in an atmosphere of rationality. Unpredictable monetary policy, rapidly changing tax laws, arbitrary regulations, inflation, fluctuations in the value of the dollar, and the failure to enforce the laws effectively all tend to discourage investment. Shell games to convince people that budget deficits are harmless are not what business needs.

A good environment for entrepreneurship, however, goes beyond just fiscal and monetary policy. Classically the function of entrepreneurs was to bring capital, knowledge, resources, labor, and management together to create an enterprise. In the nineteenth century they often could find, acquire, create, or train all these from scratch by themselves. Reagan thinks they still can. In most cases, however, he is wrong. In an advanced modern economy successful entrepreneurs rely upon the existence of all these in the larger economic marketplace. They cannot assemble them if they are not there to begin with, if access to them is controlled, or if they are poorly distributed.

If capital is not available because the banks are too interested in Argentina, if the technology is not accessible because the government has classified it, if people with appropriate skills cannot be found because the schools are no good, then the entrepreneur quite literally cannot put it all together. The idea that entrepreneurs, lacking resources, can simply start their own banks, set up their own research laboratories, develop their own energy sources, and build their own school systems is simply ridiculous. Unfettered access to all factors of supply is essential to business in a modern economy, and the government must help provide it.

The government must also ensure access to a free and honest marketplace. Competitive fairness is especially crucial to entrepreneurial firms in growth industries in which their whole business is built around a new idea. This is a complex area. For example, the patent process needs substantial overhauling to ensure that most patents can be granted quickly and infringements can be prosecuted rapidly. Software programs need better patent protection. The opportunities for piracy created by new technology may require innovative antidotes to guarantee that inventors reap the fruits of their efforts. The growing practice of making unlicensed copies, commonly called knockoffs, should also be curbed. At the very least, the Customs Service should have the equipment and personnel to halt the entry of such imitations into the country. Our whole economic policing machinery needs overhauling in light of rapid technological change.

Even more important will be the ability of small and medium-sized firms to obtain access to the electronic markets of the future. These markets will enable customers in their homes to shop for a wide variety of products displayed, demonstrated, or modeled at their request from producers anywhere in the country. The ability of small firms to plug into this system will bring lively competition and great variety to the marketplace. Coupled with flexible production methods, this system will create an economy so oriented to the consumer's unique tastes that overseas producers of standardized products may find themselves at a serious disadvantage when competing with decentralized American entrepreneurial companies. Other marketing systems will be developed to serve the professional, commercial, and industrial customer.

These systems, which will essentially be information systems, may grow into idea banks at which entrepreneurs can exchange new ideas in a national marketplace. All this should energize the economy. But if the electronic markets are controlled by a few giants that shut out the small producer, then different results will occur. The marketing systems themselves must remain decentralized and entrepreneurial with open access. The government, through its communications-licensing function, should ensure that this is the case.

Entrepreneurs need not only access but also a favorable tax environment to support innovation and growth. It is important to maintain and extend tax incentives which encourage business to take investment risks. The laws today are considerably better than they were in the early 1970s before the Steiger reforms began a process of tax liberalization for investors. This trend must be maintained. Tax liberalization itself is no guarantee of economic expansion, as the painful lesson of Reaganomics has shown us. But taken together with other measures, liberalization will make a major contribution. I favor several further reforms, especially to encourage small business and growth industries.

First, I recommend that the capital gains tax on the sale of businesses up to a specified size be changed. The maximum rate is now at 20 percent. The effective rate should be reduced on a sliding scale determined by the length of time the company was held. Thus, if the company was owned for one year, the maximum tax would be 20 percent. It would fall over time, and if the company was owned for more than twenty years, there would be no capital gains tax. This would give people the long-term incentive to create, build, and hold their own enterprises.

Second, I would favor liberalized dividend reinvestment tax regulations. Congress in the 1981 tax law provided a dividend reinvestment feature for those who invested in utility stocks. Under this plan shareholders who elected to reinvest cash dividends in stock were allowed (until the provision's repeal in 1982) to treat each dividend as a stock dividend for tax purposes. They therefore paid no tax until they sold the stock. I would apply this tax provision to small and medium-sized businesses. It would encourage investors to reinvest their dividends in the company and thereby provide additional capital for expansion.

Third, I recommend, as an additional aid to growth industries, that the tax laws be changed to enable certain categories of new companies to opt for a substantially lower corporate income tax. They would be subject, however, to a surtax on the dividends they paid out. For example, under this provision, a new company might for fifteen years have a maximum tax rate of 20 percent but a surcharge of 25 percent on its dividends. This would be another powerful incentive to retain earnings and reinvest them in the company. The investors would know in advance that their reward would come primarily in the appreciation of their capital over the long term. A stiff recapture clause would be written into the law to discourage the use of these funds to acquire other companies.

In addition, I would recommend further changes in the federal estate and gift tax laws so that they are more generous to the heirs of individuals and families who were majority stockholders in small and medium-sized companies and who passed stock on to their children. This provision, too, should encourage a longer-term perspective in the growth sector. It would obviously require appropriate safeguards against the creation of companies simply designed to circumvent the inheritance tax laws.

We also need to encourage the rapid turnover of capital equipment. I would further liberalize for small and medium-sized firms the existing allowance for "expensing" investments in the year the investment was made.

I would retain the investment tax credit for all companies. Furthermore, when the current tax leasing provisions expire, I would make this credit fully refundable. If a company operating in the red made a new investment, it would still receive the credit, even though it had no tax liability. This credit could be either refunded immediately or carried forward by the company. Hence companies operating in the red would still have an incentive to invest. This credit, together with existing depreciation allowances, gives business the ability to write off capital investments very quickly and encourages the rapid turnover of real capital. Further liberalization would actually create a subsidy for capital investment. I do not think that is warranted at present.

I would also retain the 25 percent investment tax credit on research and development and would extend it to the salaries of many research and development workers so that companies can be encouraged more fully to develop software.

Added to existing law, these tax provisions will create very strong incentives to invest and to replace capital rapidly, thereby contributing to the strategic objectives of a rapid growth in the number of small businesses, the rapid expansion of growth industries, and the rapid turnover of their capital stock by companies of all sizes. These measures will mitigate *some* of the problems of stagnation.

In addition to a favorable tax environment, entrepreneurs, as well as managers, need a more predictable regulatory environment. This is not an easy goal to achieve. If a federal agency wishes to be fully specific in promulgating its regulations, the result can be an absurdly long list of minute details which can become totally arbitrary and often self-defeating. (How many portable toilets do you need on a construction site?) If, on the other hand, the agency promulgates regulations that are vague, then a company lacks clear guidelines. Often agencies are purposefully vague because vagueness can be a deterrent. Not knowing what ultimately might be permissible, some companies stay away from the entire area, while others barge ahead, hire lawyers, and use delaying tactics to circumvent all regulatory restraint as long as possible.

Deterrence is a technique that heightens the conflictive atmosphere of the relationship between government and business. It leads to lengthy litigation and encourages the growth of political lobbying. A whole industry has been created in Washington to intermediate the conflict between business and the regulatory agencies. The intermediators have an enormous vested interest in exacerbating conflict. Hence they advise their clients to fight by means of formal proceedings and to resist attempts at informal solutions of the regulatory objectives. This creates an irrational atmosphere for business decision making. The situation must change.

Let me be clear about my own record in the area of regulation. I have been a strong supporter of many areas of regulation because I believe that the objectives are worthwhile. I have coauthored, cosponsored, or supported virtually all the environmental legislation that came before Congress during the twenty years I served there. I consistently supported the legislation creating the Occupational Safety and Health Administration (OSHA) and opposed the legislation attempting to dismantle it or reduce its powers. I believed then, and I believe now, that the environment and human health and safety need strong regulatory protection. The agencies designed to provide that protection should be staffed by professionals, and they should operate according to statute, not according to the ideological whims of the White House. The constitutional mandate to enforce the law should preclude presidential game playing with regulatory agencies. It is against the law and the Constitution to appoint people to agencies for the purpose of liquidating or destroying them. It is truly regrettable that the spirit of Nixon was revived in Reagan's approach to regulation.

It is neither the objective of regulation nor the content of the law that is usually the problem. It is the *process*. A rational regulatory environment should consist of clear and reasonable guidelines, a procedure by which answers can be obtained quickly, and a vehicle by which disputes can be resolved.

There are ways of achieving these objectives. J. R. Fox, writing recently in the *Harvard Business Review*, cites the National Coal Policy Project, among others, as an example in which industry, government, environmentalists, and interested parties came together in an attempt to find common ground among their various points of view. He suggests that many disputes can be resolved before they reach the litigation stage.

I would recommend that the government create a mediating service to try to resolve regulatory disputes before they require formal action. This would be small, nonbureaucratic, and streamlined. It would operate on the model of the Federal Mediation and Conciliation Service. The mediating groups would try to establish a climate of cooperation and problem solving. They would try to develop trust between the parties, and above all, they would try to find the means of ensuring rapid resolution of disputes without litigation and other adversarial activities. The threat of legal action from both sides would hang over the mediation process and give the mediators some bargaining leverage with both parties. The whole process would be informal. The legal recourse of neither company nor agency would be impaired. If this process was successful, both business and government would save enormous amounts of money, and the basic regulatory objectives would be preserved.

Entrepreneurs need not only a defense against governmental arbitrariness but also a defense against the cannibalism of giant corporations.

Predatory acquisitions hurt both entrepreneurs and managers.

If companies in growth industries can easily be acquired against their will by predatory stagnant firms, the incentive for entrepreneurs to create companies is diminished. Stagnant firms should not have a warrant for returning to the robber baron practices of the late nineteenth and early twentieth centuries.

The merger mania has been spectacular. In 1981 costs for acquisitions by major corporations reached $82.6 billion. There were 113 acquisitions of companies for which more than $100 million was paid. The Great Recession dampened the game somewhat, and the 1982 tax law removed some tax incentives to mergers; but the carnival will soon resume. This development is not good for America. The celebrated attempt by William Agee to take over Martin Marietta should illustrate why.

Mergers absorb corporate talent that could be better used elsewhere. They cost money and time. The enormous lines of credit extended for them can put upward pressure on interest rates. The fear of hostile acquisitions forces managers to produce quick profits and dividends to keep the stock price high and to ignore long-term considerations. There also is very little evidence that conglomerate mergers, taken as a whole, increase productivity or efficiency. The result too often is to put people in charge who know nothing about running the business.

There are several ways of addressing the problem. One is to extend the scope of the antitrust laws to make it more difficult for large firms to acquire others. This I favor. Secondly, we also need a much more vigorous enforcement of the existing laws and the staff to make this possible. A third measure is to put a stiff tax on the acquisitions of large publicly held corporations by other corporations. This also makes sense. It would serve as a deterrent, but it would not eliminate the threat of takeover altogether, so managers would still have to stay on their toes. In putting a tax on mergers, I would not favor a tax on the sale of assets by one company to another. This, in effect, would make friendly takeovers exempt from the tax and preserve the incentive of people to build up their companies, knowing that the assets of those companies could be sold to others with the approval of the owners.

A fourth proposal would be to limit severely the extension of large lines of credit to companies for the acquisition of others. When small businesses were failing by the thousands in 1981 and 1982, it was incomprehensible that in a credit crunch, multi-billion-dollar lines of credit were available to corporate giants such as Du Pont and United States Steel so that they could buy oil companies. I expressed this idea in 1981 to Beryl Sprinkel, under-secretary of the treasury for monetary affairs, one of the most dedicated monetarists in the Reagan administration. He fairly bristled at the suggestion and went off into a denunciation of overregulation in the banking industry. In 1983 there would not be as many takers as there were then for the idea that the lending practices of banks should be immune from scrutiny.

Together with the tax law changes proposed above and the equity investment banking system outlined in the next chapter, these measures should enable growth industries to compete with less fear of predatory takeovers. Some business people may protest that this is a policy of undue intervention, but I believe that most owners of small and medium-sized businesses and most managers of all but the largest corporations would agree that this is not interference. It is maintenance of a competitive and rational marketplace to attain important national objectives.

My proposals for creating a more entrepreneurial environment are suggestions that could be put quickly into practice. No doubt other possibilities will arise in the future. The point is that government must begin to pay attention to the needs of entrepreneurial business (of whatever size) if our economy is to become lively again. Government is not doing so today despite the presence in Washington of a "probusiness" administration.

Small businesses, entrepreneurial firms, and growth industries still labor under disadvantages they have had for years. They have less access than the stagnant sector to capital. They pay higher interest rates. They pay a higher effective tax rate. They get less business from the government. They are the early victims of tight money. They suffer from the price repression unwittingly imposed upon them by industry giants. Yet they produce most of the new jobs in America and a disproportionate share of America's new inventions. I suspect that their investment decisions, taken as a whole, are better than those of most stagnant companies. If we are to have a lively economy structured with variety, something has to be done about this.

Surprisingly we cannot look to the Republican Right for answers, its assertions to the contrary. Its tax cuts for business aided large companies more than small. Its cuts in the technology supply base hurt everybody, but especially the small entrepreneur who cannot afford to build an extensive research facility. Its pledge to get the government off the backs of business put a recession on the backs of business far more devastating than anything else the government was ever likely to concoct. This fell disproportionately upon the small firm. The high interest rates and tight credit which Reagan's deficits sustain bode ill for the future of small business. The Republican party today gives its rhetoric to the entrepreneur and its tangible support to industry giants.

But even these industry giants must wonder at times whether or not the Reagan administration has taken leave of its economic senses. It must seem more than passing strange to the captains of large corporations that the "most conservative administration since Calvin Coolidge" should undertake to leave America with the most massive burden of federal debt in its history. This is rather un-Coolidge-like behavior. Nor does it bear any resemblance to the conduct of William Howard Taft or Dwight Eisenhower.

To be sure, the Republicans have given Big Business billions in tax breaks, but they took a lot of this windfall right away again with both recession and high interest rates. The administration also gave Big Business friendly access to the regulatory process, such as to the Environmental Protection Agency (EPA), but that blew up in everybody's face. Former Interior Secretary James Watt did a land office business at the land office, but this helped only a select few in the business community (while harming the environment and giving all of business some bad publicity). Of course, business has received bushels of favorable rhetoric from the Reagan White House, but what good is rhetoric when profits plummet?

Where it really counts—on the bottom line—the administration has performed miserably. Federal deficits, high interest rates, the overvalued dollar, and the exploding money supply: Does business really want these? How much longer will business find it comfortable to be in a party of right-wing ideologues who create economic upheavals for the sake of their crackpot theories and their fifty-year-old vendettas?

Moreover, how much longer will business find it advantageous to be in a party that is cutting back on federal support for public education just at the time business itself has rightly discovered the importance of improving the school system? How much longer will business want to remain in a party that is decimating federal support for higher education, science, technology, research, and engineering just at the time when business needs all the technology and expertise it can muster to compete with Japan?

How much longer? Quite a while, in fact, if the Democratic party is the only alternative. Nobody believes that the Democrats can bring the budget under control or contain inflation. Business is not inspired by the recollection of Jimmy Carter's stop-and-go pseudo-Keynesianism. Ted Kennedy's industrial planning may rescue some large stagnant companies, but it will not help most of big business and certainly will not help the entrepreneur and the average business person.

Even the neoliberal Atari Democrats have the wrong approach. They want somehow to "target" high technology, support it through subsidies, grants, government purchases, and even protectionist measures. This is not what entrepreneurs want. They want a well-policed open market; access to venture capital; a supply of computer scientists or engineers, workers, and customers who can read and write; and a political system that leaves them alone. The purpose of government should be not to subsidize entrepreneurs but to give everyone access to the new "raw material" of the coming era and let them put these together in the million ingenious ways that innovators will devise.

Moreover, the Democrats remain largely under the sway of Big Labor. In view of their constituencies, this is understandable but is hardly reassuring to business as long as we have an economic system structured around the business/labor division. With rhetoric like Jack Kennedy's "My father told me, all businessmen are S.O.B.'s," is it surprising that business will not happily jump ship to the Democrats, even though business profits have been better under Democratic administrations than under Republican ones ever since President Eisenhower left the White House?

We need a new political party in America. A party which, among other things, can take a sane, sober, and detached attitude toward the needs of the business community. A party (unlike the Republicans) which is willing to raise taxes and cut spending to balance the federal budget, lower interest rates, revalue the dollar appropriately, police the marketplace against predators, and emphasize education and the development of scientific and technical knowledge. We also need a party (unlike the Democrats) that understands the need for capital formation, business tax incentives, and an entrepreneurial climate. A party that is willing to defend these positions against the politics of the moment.

But we do not need another "party of business" or of labor or of professionals. We need a party that represents the national interest. A party that is unashamed to say that a strong, healthy, decentralized, and private enterprise system is central to our economic well-being, but a party that is also not afraid to say to business that it must play by the rules of modern America. There are laws on the books about safety in the workplace, about job discrimination, and about environmental damage. These laws, too, are in the national interest. They must be enforced in a predictable, effective, and fair way. Most business people understand this. We have to start being honest with ourselves once again and work together to achieve valid national objectives. That is why we need a new political party.

7

CAPITAL

Entrepreneurs need capital. Growth industries must finance expansion. Forward-thinking established companies need money to keep ahead. The American economy needs large amounts of finance capital over the next decade to undertake the revolutionary developments that are necessary for its long-term survival.

This capital must be generated on a sustained basis. The most obvious and immediate way to create it is to cut Reagan's deficits and relieve the pressure they put on the financial market. In 1982, for example, the federal deficit devoured 60 percent of all new savings generated in America. Halve the deficit and we would increase the amount of credit available in America by $100 billion.

We must also increase the national savings rate. Holding down inflation is a first step because a steady dollar makes savings more rational; in times of inflation, when the price of goods goes up and the value of the dollar goes down, people buy goods and hold fewer dollars in savings accounts.

More is needed. For example, Congress should restore the tax exemption for the first $200 earned by individuals from dividends ($400 for couples). This level might be gradually increased. It would encourage capital formation.

Although these measures will help, we need a truly powerful instrument for stimulating savings. I would extend the principle of the Individual Retirement Account (IRA) to permit individuals to deposit money in special savings accounts or investment accounts up to a limit based on a percentage of their annual incomes. This money and its interest would remain tax-exempt until it was withdrawn, at which time it would be subject to tax at the rate it would have been taxed when it was put into the account. There would be roll-over provisions so that the money could be transferred among different forms of investment. The government would have the authority to raise and lower the percentage of income that individuals could set aside this way each year, depending on the desired national savings rate. Once the money was in the account, there would be no restrictions on the length of time it could stay there. This would create a strong incentive to save. It would be the equivalent of a consumption tax, but it would have the additional advantage that it could easily be adjusted to reflect the capital requirements of the country and the occasional need to encourage consumption during recessions.

These measures by themselves are sufficiently powerful to create enough savings to provide much of the capital needed over the next decade. But what good does it do to create savings if those savings are going to be wasted by an economic system that makes unwise investments? Capital must not only be generated but also be made available to borrowers through a sound, efficient, investment-savvy, and well-managed financial system.

Today the financial system is unstable. Henry Kaufman, whose prediction of lower interest rates helped trigger the great bull market of 1982, stated in early 1983 that the chances of a world financial collapse occurring that year were "one in six." He did not add that these are the odds in Russian roulette—with stakes nearly as high. Rimmer de Vries of the Morgan Guaranty Trust Company expressed this same concern to me directly in the fall of 1982. Other people were telling me in mid-1983, "If the price of oil goes up, it will bust Brazil; if it goes down, it will bust Mexico; in either case, it will bust the banks." We have been lurching from postponed crisis to postponed crisis for months.

There are many reasons for the financial system's instability. One is a fragile international structure. There are "offshore" countries, such as the Cayman Islands, with effectively no banking regulations, where international banks can open branches and play games. Just about anything goes. The system as a whole has a series of weak links whereby local failures can cause global shocks. The *Wall Street Journal* late in 1982 ran a major article presenting a scenario for world financial collapse stemming from the troubles of a small bank in Hong Kong. I suspect that it was trying to tell us something.

More dangerous than the faulty structure of the system is the awesome expansion of global credit that has occurred over the last decade and a half, fueled by American balance of payments deficits and especially by the oil price explosions.

The oil contretemps is a central factor in the current financial mess, just as the World War I reparations payments were a central factor in the instabilities that led to the crash in 1929. How did this situation arise? When OPEC raised the price of oil in 1973 and 1979, American dollars went overseas to pay for it. The OPEC countries then deposited many of these dollars back in the American banking system. The banks, which had to pay interest on the deposits, were under great pressure to lend the money out. Normally it might have been invested in American corporations. But the American economy, shocked by the oil crisis, was not expanding, and investment opportunities were lacking.

Meanwhile, the rise in the cost of oil fell harshly upon those developing countries which did not themselves produce oil. They were even less able to adjust than we were. Therefore, they needed the cash to pay their oil bills at the same time the banks were in the market to make loans. They got the money.

Normally bankers are supposed to be conservative people to

whom we entrust our savings in the expectation that they will be wisely used. But the oil carnival created a new breed of buccaneer banker, especially in many of our large international banks. Suddenly, dashing young loan officers were jetting around the world with basketfuls of cash, dumping them liberally on oil-thirsty recipients. A London lender, quoted in *Time*, explained: "Bankers like travel and exotic locations. It was certainly more exciting than Cleveland or Pittsburgh, and an easier way to make money than nursing along a $100,000 loan to some scrap metal smelter."

The cause of our current difficulties is not that the banks made large loans or even that they made them to developing countries. The problem is that the loans were made primarily for consumption, not for investment. This need not have been the case. There were many investment opportunities, even in the developing countries. Prudence required that the loans be designed to carry out reasonable goals of economic development. Instead, they were used to pay for oil imports and to raise temporarily the standard of living of politically powerful people in the borrowing country, typically the urban middle class and the elite.

This was the largest "foreign aid" program in history—and one of the worst. The "collateral" for these loans in many cases was the ability of Third World governments to keep paying the interest on them and to keep rolling them over. This, in turn, depended upon those governments' ability to raise revenues. And that in turn depended in most cases upon the country's exports—usually commodities. The banking system, as a result, found itself effectively dependent for the security of its loans upon the tender mercies of the commodity markets. And in the Great Recession, many commodity markets collapsed.

The oil price rise effectively put a tax on the American consumer which was paid to OPEC, deposited in American banks, and lent to Third World countries, which consumed it. The money flowed rapidly, but the debts remained and grew, together with the deposits of OPEC countries, which could always threaten to withdraw them from the American banks.

No amount of sophisticated argument can disguise one simple fact: The American banking system has squandered hundreds of billions of dollars on bad loans. The money is gone. It will never be recovered. Fancy schemes will be devised to make it seem as if this is not true. But it is true. The debtor countries cannot pay, in the absence of global inflation, and no amount of frantic rescheduling will conceal this. Real wealth has been lost, and the system remains vulnerable to collapse. Everyone pays when banks make bad investments with their depositors' money.

There is an even more serious crisis gathering on the horizon. This involves the future viability of stagnant industries with enormous debts which are held by the banks and other lending institutions. If the traditional enterprises of industrial America go broke over the next decade, their failures will dwarf in importance the defaults of Argentina, Mexico, and Brazil. This is not just a problem for the banks. It is a problem for literally millions of small stockholders and bondholders and for anyone who expects to receive a pension from a major private pension fund.

These developments are grave. All nations would be devastated by a financial panic. But one nation would suffer far more than any other: the United States. We are, to use an increasingly familiar term, more exposed than anyone else. It is we who have more invested in the global economy than any other nation has. It is we whose overseas corporations are most vulnerable to upheavals. It is our capital that is principally at risk. It is our banks that would suffer most. It is our international economic arrangements that would collapse.

It is imperative that we reduce this exposure to disaster—be that disaster war, protracted depression, or financial panic.

But to reduce exposure is not easy. Washington's response has been to increase the money supply in the hope that this will ease the pressure on the banks. A rapidly expanding money supply, however, is bound to be inflationary. In effect, Washington's policy is to inflate the currency so that the banks' loss of real wealth is assumed by everyone. This strategy may ease the pressure on the banks, but its effects on the economy are negative. Inflation is not the answer.

The banks themselves have sought relief through high interest rates. These have not helped the borrowing countries, the U.S. Treasury, or the U.S. economy, but they have enabled the banks to widen their profit margins enough to increase reserves against the threat of default. The banks also need high interest rates to attract money to America to help cover the Treasury deficit. The flow of capital into the country, however, has created a strong dollar and has discouraged exports. The banks, to create a temporary respite from the mess created by the oil intermediation and to handle Reagan's deficit, are pursuing policies that severely hurt the American manufacturing sector by reducing overseas sales and by discouraging domestic real investment. There is no easy short-run quick-fix answer to these problems. We must prop things up, cut the federal deficit, get off the commodities kick, and restructure the system to encourage wiser banking practices in the future.

Stopgap measures are needed. First, we must strengthen the International Monetary Fund (IMF), expand its lending authority, and ensure that its oversight mechanisms are not subverted by political pressures. This will increase the international margin of safety.

Second, we should seek rapid agreement to give the IMF the authority to create an agency with broadly recognized powers to intervene in a financial crisis at the national or subnational level in countries where there are no lenders of last resort. This will prevent a domino effect when financial institutions collapse. The Bank of International Settlements, as presently constituted, is simply not adequately equipped to play this role.

Third, the Organization for Economic Cooperation and Development (OECD), which consists of the world's major industrial countries outside the Soviet bloc, should establish stand-by emergency procedures to quarantine the international effects of either a large default or a major bank failure since either could trigger chaos. Each country should have the power to grant emergency loans, to assume the operating functions of banks in failure, and to intervene in financial markets to isolate panic responses. In some cases joint OECD action would be necessary. For the duration of the emergency we need a supranational OECD coordinating group based on the example of our military coordinating and planning groups.

Fourth, by agreement with the other OECD members, if the IMF cannot do so, we must curb the practice of offshore banking. No bank should be permitted to do business in an OECD country if it has a branch in another country that fails to require safe banking practices as agreed upon by OECD members. If the OECD itself cannot reach agreement on such a principle, Congress should forbid banks to transact business in America if they have branches in countries which fail to enforce safe banking practices as specified by American law. Thus American law could in effect create a regulatory environment for the offshore bank to which it would have to conform.

These are only interim measures. Fundamental reform is needed. The United States and the OECD countries should begin immediately to consult regularly among themselves and with the IMF to establish a procedure for overhauling the world financial system. A new Bretton Woods Conference is needed. If the world recedes from the brink of financial collapse, it is all the more necessary to repair the system before a new recession begins.

On the agenda of such a conference would be the problems of exchange rates, international liquidity, the control of the Euro-dollar market, the international credit structure, the evolving role of the IMF, and the long-range stability of the international financial system.

These proposals will address the technical problems of international finance. They will not, however, fully rescue the international banks unless there is a true global economic recovery, fueled by vastly improved investment patterns here and overseas.

Even if the international financial structure is stabilized, the American lending industry will experience great changes during the 1980s. Deregulation is proceeding. Banks are rapidly entering new financial areas hitherto denied them. The next few years will see the savings and loan institutions become commercial banks, their unique mortgage-taking function drastically altered. The banking industry as a whole will also undergo a major consolidation. Interstate ownership is now growing rapidly. Acquisitions are soaring Pac-Man style; the small local banks are being eaten by the giants. Instead of 14,000 commercial banks, we may soon have just a few hundred large networks, if that many. Citibank chairman Walter Wriston expects only a handful of national full service financial institutions will survive the consolidation. (I hope that I may be pardoned for the speculation that in some cases the assets of well-managed small banks are sounder than the assets of the larger banks and that the latter buy them to keep one jump ahead of the sheriff.)

Furthermore, as the banking system is consolidating, the financial system itself is diversifying. Institutions other than banks are becoming major sources of finance capital. Large corporations, such as General Motors and General Electric, have moved into the venture capital business in an impressive way. They set up joint ventures with small businesses, usually in areas of their own expertise, carefully monitor them, and thereby provide new avenues of finance. Insurance companies, pension funds, and even stock brokerage firms are now major actors in the finance capital industry. Venture capital companies are proliferating.

As banking itself becomes more consolidated, decision making will become more centralized. Concern for the local economy will lessen. Concern for the needs of specialized industries may disappear. Small loans, carefully negotiated, will become less attractive to many banks as they operate on the national and international level, just as small cars became unattractive to Detroit. Bankers, in short, will cease to be bankers in the traditional sense of the word. Careful evaluation of investment risks will take too much management time and effort.

Banks will concentrate on two types of loans. The first will be consumer loans for which computers will make the decisions on the basis of customer profiles. The other will be large loans to governments and giant corporations, principally to roll over their paper. The hard-headed function of carefully nurturing hundreds of thousands of medium-sized loans to small and expanding industries, so necessary for our economic development, will become relatively more expensive and less attractive to banks. But computers are no substitute for good loan management. Investing in consumer loans and treasury notes contributes only indirectly at best to improving the quality of American investments. The banking system, if it continues in this direction, will be forced to rely for its long-term survival on the investment successes of others but itself will not contribute to that investment success. When banks that fill this function today are absorbed by the larger international combines, the quality of investment decisions will decline. Other lending institutions will try to fill the gap, but they can never fully replace proper banks.

Furthermore, deregulation and consolidation will mean that many parts of the country will see a capital flight as the fully consolidated banking system looks upon some regions as "cash cows" to be milked for the benefit of other regions or other countries. The local branches will remain a receptacle for local savings but will no longer be an adequate source of local finance.

One approach to these difficulties would be to legislate a halt to interstate acquisitions. This deserves some attention. Another approach would be to reregulate and use the vehicle of portfolio requirements or credit requirements to ensure that regions are not milked, that small businesses are not neglected, that industries are not ignored, and that sound banking practices are not abandoned. In view of the still-shaky condition of many banks, some additional safeguards may prove necessary.

A better alternative to massive reregulation, however, may be to create two specialty banking systems that will fill the functions we can expect the large consolidated banks to abandon and then to permit the large banks to lend money to them. In this way, good investment decisions can still be made at the local level. That scrap smelter in Cleveland can get its financing, and the large banks will have the incentive to invest in rebuilding America. One of these new systems should be targeted at small-business and community development, the other specifically at growth industries.

First, to encourage the growth of small business, we should create a system of independent local development banks. Chartered by either states or the federal government, these institutions would have a local board of directors on which would sit representatives of government, agents of local financial institutions, and local business, labor, and community leaders. They would have the authority to issue bonds in large and small denominations so that financial institutions and citizens could invest in the bank. Indeed, this would provide the opportunity for public-spirited citizens to become involved with community development in the same way that patriots bought bonds during World War II. Federal and state governments would participate in the initial capital funding and might also play a supplementary role in the bank's financing. The banks would be permitted to accept deposits. The federal government would have auditing and inspection rights and authority to set portfolio requirements. This would ensure the integrity and proper functioning of the system. The government might even guarantee the equity of the investors in these institutions. If it did so, state and local pension funds could be permitted to invest in the banks.

The banks would have several lending windows. One would be for small and medium-sized businesses. Others would include community development projects, as set forth in Chapter XIII. A final window would be for unrestricted lending. Large communities might have many such banks.

The use of several lending windows and the attendant portfolio requirements would spread the risk over several kinds of loans. It would enable the banks to extend a percentage of their loans at lower interest rates, which could be balanced by high-yield loans through the unrestricted window. Aside from the unrestricted category, all loans would be made to local people and businesses.

This system of banks, which might become as large as the savings and loan system is today, would be designed primarily to finance the expansion of small business ventures and to provide a vehicle whereby the increasingly consolidated commercial banking system would have a convenient means of investing indirectly in small businesses and in community development.

Concurrent with the creation of this local development banking system, I would envision a significant expansion of the Small Business Administration (SBA). It should be permitted to offer more favorable interest rates and more flexible repayment schedules. A standardized commercial loan should be developed to facilitate lending procedures. More offices should be opened. The staff should be upgraded, and the system energized.

Growth industries have their own capital needs. To meet them, we should charter a network of venture and capital investment banks. These would be permitted to own equity in corporations as well as to lend money secured by equity. I envision a large number of these banks serving as the financial support system for the growth industries of the future until those industries became so large that they could easily tap the resources of the major consolidated banks. This investment banking system could serve the same function as that of the Japanese investment banking system, but it would be entirely private and decentralized to provide flexibility, geographic distribution, and market responsiveness. The banks would grow with the new industries and be tied to their fortunes. They would provide the money needed to underwrite the rapid introduction of new products and the retooling of the American capital plant which are so necessary to keep ahead of our foreign competition. Many of the banks would be expected to specialize in specific industries so that they could develop expertise in those areas. Deposits would be insured on a percentage basis tied to portfolio requirements. The opportunity for equity investment provides a sufficient incentive for people to start such banks.

Because the banks would be permitted to own stock in businesses and thereby expand the capital bases of those businesses, the entrepreneurs would not be forced to "go public" at an early date to finance expansion. The expanding companies, therefore, would be less susceptible to takeover threats than they are now. This, too, imitates Japanese practice.

Moreover, because the large consolidated commercial banking system would be permitted to lend money to these banks (although not to own them outright), the banks would serve as a vehicle for attracting capital from the international money markets back into real investments for the expansion of the American productive base. This would encourage the international banks to begin investing more in the rebuilding of American industry and thereby harmonize financial and manufacturing interests to a greater degree than they are today.

Furthermore, this system should encourage the training and development of investment bankers who are experts in real investments and growth ventures. As the system develops, the quality of our investments should improve. The loan officers will be close to the loans they make, and the banks can be expected to monitor closely the management performance of the companies in which they own stock.

These banks would function in an analogous way to the venture capital operations of large corporations and would provide more depth and flexibility to the system. They would also supplement the activities of venture capital companies, many of which might reincorporate as investment banks. Moreover, they would be permitted and encouraged to make loans to expanding companies with a lower degree of equity than is now customary. Unlike the venture capital companies, the banks could accept deposits and become excellent receptacles for the sheltered savings accounts outlined earlier in this chapter. In this way, small savers could make a direct contribution to industrial rejuvenation.

There would be appropriate safeguards to protect the integrity of the system, including portfolio distribution requirements and adequate reserves against bad loans. The banks would not be permitted to make consumer loans. There might be restrictions on the size of holdings in a single company and on the extent to which the banks' fortunes were linked to the performance of a single industry. The object, however, would be not to regulate these banks to death but to give them latitude.

This investment banking system could grow in due time to rival in importance the current commercial banking system. Its opportunity to expand would be directly tied to its ability to make quality investments in growing industries. Its existence should force the rapidly consolidating commercial banking system to pay more attention to industrial development in America and to the quality of its own loans. Like the Japanese car makers, the investment bankers should be able to enter an emerging hole in the financial market, provide a unique and quality service, take full advantage of the economics of expansion, and grow to rival their more stagnant cousins.

Under these arrangements the American banking system would consist of four major categories of banks: the local development banks, the small and medium-sized commercial banks not absorbed through consolidation by the larger international banks, the new equity investment banks, and the large international banks themselves.

The soundness of the local development banks would be ensured by federal audit and supervision, together with portfolio requirements. State and local governments would have a stake in ensuring their success.

The soundness of the nonconsolidated commercial banks would be ensured through slightly expanded existing arrangements. These would also be permitted to recharter as equity investment banks.

The soundness of the investment banks themselves would be ensured through federal audit and portfolio requirements.

The soundness of the large, increasingly consolidated international banks would be ensured by federal regulation, by existing and new international arrangements, and by a federal commitment to monetary and fiscal probity. In addition to these, the consolidated system's ability to lend to the equity investment banks would enable them to benefit from the closely watched investments these banks would make in the American growth sector. As the new technology develops, great opportunities will arise for the international banks to finance the export of new capital goods and systems. Participating in government programs (explained in Chapter XI) to rejuvenate and energize the stagnant sector will give them the opportunity to help rescue their large investments in stagnant industries. In these ways the portfolios of the large international banks can become more secure, and the entire banking system can be put on a much more stable and solid footing. We can begin to invest our way out of the credit bubble. In this way the interests of the banking industry can once again be tied to the interests of the American manufacturing and service-producing industries to the advantage of everyone.

Many people wish to go beyond these proposals and impose strict regulations upon the international banks. Certainly I would not approve of a banking bailout unless the banks paid a substantial penalty for their folly. But to heap new regulations upon the banks beyond those suggested here is not wise and will not help the system in the long run. The better alternative is to create positive vehicles through which the banks can begin to improve the quality of their investments.

The solution to our capital problems lies beyond the old arguments between Right and Left. The Republicans say, "Deregulate, and leave the system alone." But this policy has led to instability, dangerous consolidation, and a departure from traditional investment-oriented banking practices. The Democrats say, "Regulate, and tie the system down." But regulations will not provide bankers with incentives to make quality loans to an expanding growth sector. More likely, regulation will encourage stagnation and investments in "sound" government paper.

We need new approaches. The answer is to restructure in such a way that the system as a whole supports itself and has powerful incentives to underwrite wisely the rejuvenation of the American and global economies, but the present party system is unlikely to produce such an outcome. We need a political party that is committed to a sound private banking system in America but that is also willing to take the steps necessary to restructure that system and enliven it. Such a party, acting in the national interest, should be neither servile in its adulation of the banks nor hostile and suspicious of them in the manner of partisans from the distant Left and the distant Right. Indeed, it should honestly recognize the existence of structural problems and proceed to provide the appropriate structural remedies.

Even more important, we need a party (unlike either the Reagan Republicans or the majority Democrats) which understands the need to emphasize investment over consumption. A party that is committed to a national investment strategy to meet the Japanese investment challenge and provide the broad economic underpinnings for a rejuvenated banking community. A party committed to the real recapitalization of America.

But we must go beyond this. We need a party with an investment philosophy in the sense that it is willing to emphasize long-run solutions over short-run solutions. A party, unlike the Republicans and the Democrats, that is not just looking ahead to the next election. A party with a ten- or twenty-year time horizon. A party willing to advocate policies of saving and sacrifice today so that our future and the future of our children will be more secure and prosperous. The current two-party system does not contain such a party.

With adequate measures to encourage a high rate of savings, with strengthened commercial and international banking systems, and with two new targeted banking systems, the capital needs of a new economy will be met. But this is only a beginning. Entrepreneurship and capital by themselves are not enough. Unless there are sufficient investment opportunities, the savings we generate will find their way into commodity and currency speculation or into government and overseas paper, none of which will help our supply problem in America. Pouring money into the banking system is very destabilizing unless there are investments to be made that expand the economy. Genuine investment opportunities are just as important as investment capital. As Andrew Grove, president of Intel, said to me while reviewing the future prospects of Silicon Valley, "Venture capital is still looking for good ideas."

8

KNOWLEDGE

Bᴀɴᴋᴇʀs need investment opportunities. So do entrepreneurs and established companies. The better mousetrap may help, but it is not enough. We need widespread innovation, if we are to have a sustained economic recovery based on the proliferation of real investments.

Basic science, applied science, engineering, and systems engineering all are therefore central to America's economic recovery. They hold out promise for new quality products and better ways of making them. They also contribute to the creation of new entrepreneurs. The excitement of working at the frontiers of invention and discovery can be a good reason for starting new companies. The spirit of inquiry can be as important as the spirit of enterprise.

Given the centrality of technology to our economic future, it is unconscionable that the Reagan administration (in virtually all areas except defense) has neglected basic science, higher education, energy research, space exploration, and government-sponsored research and development programs. For example, nondefense basic research and development support is projected to fall from $15.8 billion to $14.8 billion between FY 1982 and FY 1984, while defense research and development increase from $22.9 billion to $33.0 billion. The federal government today is spending about three-quarters of what it spent in 1967 on research and development, despite our growth in GNP. We are eating the "seed corn" from which our future will sprout. As a result, the number of our science and engineering graduates is dropping, our research facilities are aging, and our campus laboratories in many cases no longer compare favorably with those of other countries. The scientific support system of our economy is deteriorating. We are going backward. It is all too reminiscent of the steel industry, which decided decades ago not to invest in new technology and now cannot compete globally. With an obsolete American technological plant, quotas won't help.

Scientific knowledge starts with basic research, the kind that will not have a payoff in a year or two but will shape the economy and the world a few decades from now. During the 1960s we created the world's finest scientific plant, but we have been letting it go to ruin ever since. We need a long-term commitment to upgrade our basic research facilities and expand the training opportunities for future scientists.

The grant-awarding authority of the National Science Foundation (NSF) should be expanded at a steady rate of about 15 percent per year over the next decade in real terms. This would reverse an extended period of decline and would emphasize our basic national commitment to a long-term scientific development program.

The Defense Department should be permitted to fund basic research in nondefense-related areas with the presumption that the results of this research would be unclassified.

The federal government should initiate an ongoing university endowment program, under the aegis of the National Science Foundation, to provide a permanent support system for scientific research, training, and instruction on the campuses. I would support a similar program to be funded by the National Endowment for the Humanities in nonscientific research areas.

I would favor endowment funds for graduate fellowships and postdoctoral fellowships, junior faculty positions, supplements to senior chairs, and senior chairs themselves. This would encourage students to become scientists and help faculty to remain teaching. We also need special endowment funds for research itself. Many of these would be on a matching grant basis. State legislatures would be expected to match federal funds for state universities. Private colleges and universities would seek matching funds from alumni and the private sector. The advantages of the endowment approach are that it creates a long-term commitment to research, makes planning possible, removes government strings, and leaves the principal invested in the economy.

Private industry (with a few notable exceptions, such as Bell Labs) primarily supports applied research, not basic research. Nevertheless, there should be an opportunity for public-spirited businesses of any size to support basic research. When a grand average is made over all fields and projects, basic research today makes a tangible profit, but the odds against financial gain for any given project may be so great that stockholders cannot realistically be expected to gamble. Transistors and lasers are not invented every day.

We should create an institution that can spread the risks and the benefits of basic research. I would create an Industrial Science Foundation (ISF) which can accept unrestricted funds from industry, award grants to researchers, and then distribute the economic benefits derived from the patents obtained by the researchers.

The ISF would work as follows: Industry would make contributions to the ISF fund. One-third of a contribution would be treated as a tax credit; the balance would be tax-deductible. These monies would go into a pool. The donor companies would not specify the projects to be funded. Scientists would apply to the ISF for research support precisely as they do now to the National Science Foundation. Their applications would be subject to peer review. Revenues from patents which were obtained from ISF-sponsored research would be divided equally among the university and the inventor, the ISF for future research, and a pool to be distributed to the ISF sponsors in proportion to their contributions.

Our national laboratories, such as Los Alamos, Livermore, Argonne, and several others, also need attention. Originally these were designed for basic research, especially in defense-related areas. During the Ford and Carter administrations, the government changed their mission and encouraged them to develop new energy-related technologies. This produced a confusion of mission which continues today. It would be difficult once again to shift signals quickly, but the primary mission of the laboratories should be basic research—good science. A gradual return to this would be the best use of these important facilities.

Multiple funding sources are strongly to be recommended in an area such as basic research, in which the fruits of each line of inquiry are difficult to predict. By using the NSF, the Defense Department, the ISF, and university endowments, we can avoid choking off promising research stemming from the biases of a single agency.

The country's applied research capabilities also need more support. Our engineering schools are losing faculty members to private industry faster than they can replace them. Engineering students are being bid away quickly after college graduation by the private sector. The defense build-up has made the problem worse. We need to rebuild the depth and the breadth of our engineering schools and to support the process of training in the engineering sciences. As with basic research, it is imperative that we endow graduate fellowships, scholarships, junior and senior faculty positions. Endowments for new equipment should be part of the program. In addition, we need either a National Applied Research Institute with generous funding to serve the same function as the NSF does in basic research or an expanded applied research function within the NSF.

In addition to these funds at the graduate level, there should be continued federal support of undergraduate education. Federal student guaranteed loans and Pell grants for the disadvantaged should be continued so that no qualified student is denied a college education because he or she cannot afford it.

Efforts to support teaching and research, both basic and applied, should strengthen our colleges and universities and help increase the number of trained scientists and engineers who graduate in the future. Rebuilding the existing system is our first priority. But there is also a need to emphasize the generation of special technologies, primarily in the areas of capital goods and manufacturing systems, to provide direct support for retooling and reprogramming American industry. New technologies, once generated, must also be widely diffused throughout the economy.

We should create a large system of Regional Technology Institutes (RTIs) on the model of the land-grant college. In some cases these would be associated with existing universities; in other cases they would be autonomous. They would be centers for developing new technologies and for training people in the use of technology. Their purpose would be not to produce new products but to concentrate on new methods of production.

The technology developed by the RTIs would encompass many areas. One would be microelectronics. The RTIs would be designed to play a central role in developing a broad national support system for this industry, concentrating on design methods, production methods, and systems research. In the technology of memory chip production we are decidedly behind the Japanese, who use robotics at home while we rely upon cheap labor overseas.

Another area would be robotics and programmable capital equipment for the production of machine tools, vehicles, farm machinery, construction equipment, transportation equipment, appliances, metal fabrication, and other kinds of traditional heavy manufacturing. A third area would be new machinery to make the capital equipment itself. Backing up each of these would be research on measurement, control, and sensing devices and on materials: steel, aluminum, plastics, ceramics, glass, and others. Systems research and the advanced development of computer-aided design and manufacturing technologies would be another high priority.

The institutes could branch out into many other important fields: communications research, simulation technology, training systems, automated warehousing and inventory systems, transportation systems, laser applications, and environmental protection systems, especially those relevant to the handling and burning of coal. This is certainly not an exhaustive list.

There are also several areas in which we can experiment with radically new manufacturing technologies. One of these is shipbuilding. In America this industry is stagnant, to say the least. In 1980 only sixty-nine commercial ships of more than 1,000 tons were under construction in the United States. But the competition is also stagnant with high capital investments, increasingly rigid production processes, and a falling market. If we can develop the machinery for large-scale automatic fabrication of ships and the design systems for controlling the costs of their interior construction, we can then pursue the same kind of market penetration strategy against others that they have used against us in autos, even though the overall market is static or declining.

Another area is aircraft fabrication. We should give a high priority to developing automated manufacturing technologies to discourage companies from moving their manufacturing facilities overseas. The Defense Department has programs in support of aircraft manufacturing techniques, but more can be done, specifically with respect to cutting production costs.

Still another great opportunity for automated large-scale fabrication is modular housing. This concept has had a spotty history, but if the technology could be developed, a whole new private industry would flourish. Home ownership would then be possible for the estimated 75 percent of Americans who now can never expect to own a home at today's prices.

We should also investigate the exploration and development of the seabed should this prove to be economically feasible and environmentally acceptable. Alternative energy research would be a very high priority.

In all these endeavors, research should be conducted not only on the development of the "machinery" but also on the larger production systems and the software that would program the machinery. Furthermore, the RTIs should develop systems for training people to use the equipment, from production engineers and programmers to line workers.

The institutes would have a permanent staff of engineering specialists and a much larger number of "research associates," who would be a mixture of recent engineering graduates and experienced industry specialists at the institutes on a released time basis from their companies. They would also have students. The staff would engage in teaching, training, discovering, and developing. I would envision people working on a project-oriented basis.

The logic behind the RTIs is that if companies in the past have benefited from spin-offs of defense and space technology, they certainly should benefit from technology developed with their own special needs in mind. Yet there are no guarantees that this will happen. The government, trying to be helpful, has often developed things that the private sector does not want and cannot use. Technology transfer needs as much attention as technology development. Everyone I have talked to on the subject emphasizes this point. The institutes, therefore, would be designed to transfer technology in many different ways.

First, the staff could perceive the need for a new process, develop it, publicize the results, and license it for a nominal fee to any American firm that decided to use it. Second, the RTI could engage in joint research and development with one or more private firms that would then have an exclusive right to use the results for a set time period negotiated in advance. Third, the RTIs would be permitted to engage in consulting work.

Most important, technology would be effectively transferred out into the economy through large numbers of people who had received practical training and experience. Recent graduates of the centers would bring hands-on expertise to the companies that employed them. Alternatively, they might start their own businesses. The RTIs could serve as retraining facilities for research personnel in the private sector. People on released time from their companies would bring new-found knowledge back to the private sector. Furthermore, the institutes could hire engineers laid off during a slack period in an industry who would seek retraining or would teach and work on projects between jobs. Valuable talent would thereby not go to waste.

Fifth, the institutes would be encouraged to offer joint programs with business schools or to offer business courses themselves. It is important that we marry engineering and production skills with business skills. Today we are training a generation of M.B.A.'s who are manufacturing illiterates. We need more people with hands-on production training.

Sixth, the institutes would be required to develop special programs to retrain teachers in the vocational educational system. Finally, they would have a large extension service attached to them to disseminate new techniques to small and medium-sized businesses.

The Regional Technology Institutes would be located throughout the country. In view of the emphasis on the development of machinery and capital goods, however, a large number of them should be located in the middle Atlantic and midwestern states, where they could draw upon the existing industrial base for expertise and simultaneously make a large contribution to its rejuvenation and entry into the new age of automation.

There would be no set formula for creating these institutes. They should be built as fast as possible, consistent with a growing supply of engineers as projected above. In some cases existing institutions would be given additional support and encouraged to expand their functions if they wished to participate. In other cases the RTIs would be created as part of existing university systems. Industries themselves might create and endow RTIs with government matching grants. The federal government would provide both endowment and operating support, sometimes on a matching basis, with state, local, and private participation. For the system to make a real impact, it would have to be large. I envision a major support system for the industries of the future.

States, localities, colleges, universities, and industry itself would be asked to play a major role in the planning process. The states would be given the final say in determining the relationship of this system to their existing public colleges and universities. The point is not to run around and create institutions, nor is it to "target" industries. It is to build a large, diverse, comprehensive, and effective system of technology development and dissemination to underwrite as many potential areas of manufacturing as possible.

The Regional Technology Institutes, working together with a better-funded university system, will provide a broad-based support system for the economy of tomorrow. They will respond to the market-created needs of the private sector. They will help companies of all sizes. They will give America a better opportunity to lead the coming revolution in capital goods and systems. They will create new industries for America and help old industries survive. They will underwrite a new export-based economy. Most of all, they will get people involved. The more people we have who are acquainted with the new technology, the more who study it, develop it, and play with it, the faster it will spread, and the livelier the economy will be.

The government's encouragement of science and technology, of course, should extend far beyond the universities and technology institutes. America must continue to encourage private-sector research and development by using tax credits. We should also make it easier for private corporations under certain conditions to engage in joint research efforts.

Public-sector support ought to continue and in many areas be expanded. Health sciences are one important area, although the priorities of the National Institutes of Health, like other governmental agencies, need periodic review. Support for the environmental sciences and energy research should be greatly expanded, as discussed in the next chapter.

A highly visible government scientific effort for twenty-five years has been in space, but today the program is in trouble. Reagan cut the space research budget by more than half in real terms. The Reagan administration strategy here, as elsewhere, was to augment the military and cut back on the civilian. This is a mistake.

I am reminded of sixteenth-century Spain, the country that discovered the New World but failed to exploit it commercially. The English came along, made money off America, and soon surpassed Spain, where large military expenditures put a severe strain on the economy. Within a generation the New World, despite its gold, had become a liability to Spain. Soon the Spanish economy could no longer support its military, and Spain exited the stage. Japan with advanced robotics can soon do to America in space what Britain did to Spain in the New World.

We should sharply distinguish three separate missions in space: a basic research mission, a commercial mission, and a military mission. These should be kept separate so that the aims of each do not become subordinated to the requirements of the others.

The air force should maintain its own space program apart from NASA. It should eventually have its own space shuttles, its own development programs, and its own communications systems.

The research and commercial activities should also be kept separate, either within NASA or, eventually, in two distinct agencies. Research should be supported at higher funding levels than at present. A permanent laboratory in space should soon be established, followed by a permanent base on the moon. A full program of planetary and solar probes should be reinstated. The space telescope program and other means of exploring deep space should be continued.

The commercialization of space is the ultimate means of paying for all this. To make it possible, the government must provide a support system. The private sector should be encouraged to purchase space shuttles and operate them, along with more traditional launch vehicles. Initially these should be subsidized, with the subsidies decreasing over time as economies of scale brought down costs. The government and the private sector should cooperate in designing and building manufacturing platforms. This is an area in which we can steal a march on the competition, establish our position, and create major growth industries of the future which will provide expanding employment opportunities here on earth. We can enjoy a virtual monopoly for a few years and stay ahead after that. Unfortunately we are playing space wars instead. Time is slipping away. Others are catching up. Soon our advantages will be gone.

In addition to a major effort in space, and as a support for that effort, America must extend its research in computer technology. We must build a fifth-generation computer. This technology, when fully developed, will represent an astounding breakthrough in the power of computers. It will lead to machines which can approximate many functions of the human mind that computers today cannot imitate. Reading, listening, speaking, identifying objects, and performing artificially many functions of intelligence that are now uniquely human are among the projected accomplishments of this marvel-to-be. It will vastly increase the productivity of service providers the way robots today can increase the productivity of factory workers. Medical diagnostics, teaching, writing, scholarly research, entertainment, musical composition, art, weather forecasting, and basic sciences are just a few examples of where this new technology can supplement (or replace) the efforts of many contemporary professionals.

The Japanese are making a major effort to be the first country to develop this wizard machine and diffuse it into the world economy. It is probable that they see the fifth-generation computer both as a marketable artificial intelligence tool and as a means of establishing and maintaining a decisive lead in manufacturing technology. Aeronautical design, marine architecture, genetic and molecular engineering, chemical engineering, metallurgy, ceramics, plastics, and any other field that can benefit from the capacity to engage in complex modeling procedures will benefit mightily along with such predictable endeavors as computer-aided design and manufacturing processes.

We must not only develop this technology but also ensure that it becomes widely diffused throughout the economy. The Reagan administration has shown little interest in the project. A few large companies have created a consortium to conduct research. This effort should be carefully monitored to ensure that it does not become a means of centralizing all high-technology research in America. To the degree that the research is limited to producing a fifth-generation computer, however, it should be encouraged. We need to do more. I would recommend that we fund two or three separate university projects and that we create a new national research and teaching facility specifically designed to develop advanced computer technology and to devise ways to make it widely available to the private sector. Duplicative efforts will not be wasteful because each program can become a learning and teaching experience for those involved.

These proposals, if adopted, will create an effective support system for science, engineering, and manufacturing technology in America. They will underwrite our entrance into a new economic era. The technologies developed and consciously diffused will create enormous investment opportunities and will play a central role in America's economic rejuvenation.

In our haste to embrace the virtues of scientific and technical knowledge, however, it is easy to forget that all knowledge is important. The social sciences and humanities must keep pace with the natural sciences and professions if our emerging culture is to be democratic and humane. We must understand history and culture as much as we understand the natural and mechanical world. We must pay more attention to the significance of being human. The world of technique by its nature is a narrow world characterized by the absence of underlying purpose and values. It is a world of reduced proportions where reality is codified in probabilistic laws and mathematical symbols. It lacks the richness of humanity, although it may be employed to amplify our expression of that richness. There is a world beyond the reach of the machine, beyond the reach of narrow technique. It is a world of religion, belief, ethics, arts, literature, and culture. Knowledge of this world is just as fundamental as knowledge of the natural world, not simply for its own sake or even for the pleasures of understanding but for our very survival as a species. Even at the mundane level of the economy, knowledge of our own culture and the cultures of other societies will give us the ability to set goals, to motivate people, and to compete. We must ensure adequate support for both the social sciences and the humanities at the college and university level.

. . .

The knowledge and information revolutions will create limitless opportunities for an expanding future. Yet they will not be without dangers—to our jobs, our liberties, and even our survival. We are all familiar with the Frankenstein myth. We know Big Brother can exist. Most of us have lived more than half our lives in the shadow of Hiroshima. Still, I believe—and this can only be a matter for belief—that human beings can control that which they invent and discover. I also believe that the extension of human knowledge is a noble endeavor, a fundamental purpose that gives meaning to our humanity. The awareness that there is a universe to explore is a powerful incentive to human action. Exploring that universe in all its fascinating dimensions is not a bad goal for any nation.

As America becomes an information-oriented society with a knowledge-based economy, we will need new rules of conduct to ensure the continuity of our constitutional principles, democratic traditions, deeply held beliefs, and human values. Knowledge is indeed power. Since the diffusion of power is our most fundamental constitutional principle, the diffusion of knowledge must be a guiding dictate if we are to remain a truly free society. Since broad-based access to power is our most central democratic tradition, broad-based access to knowledge must be a widespread practice if we are to remain a democracy. Since the responsible and restrained exercise of power is the heart of ethical public conduct, the responsible and restrained use of knowledge is essential if we are to remain a decent society. Since the use of power for the betterment of humanity is an important objective of representative government, the use of knowledge for the betterment of humanity must remain one of our central tenets. The benefits of knowledge are often purchased at a cost to many people. We must make the social decision to bear the costs widely. If we cannot guarantee these ends to the American public, then people will rightly resist the new technology and bend their energies to thwart its adoption.

I believe that such guarantees can be made. We need a legislative Bill of Rights for the information age based on our timeless constitutional guarantees. This should consist of four basic parts.

The first should be a *right of privacy*. People must be truly secure from the inquisitive intrusions of both government and the private sector. Electronic surveillance must be limited to criminal investigation authorized by the courts. No agency of government in pursuit of any other objective should be permitted to violate this principle. Furthermore, all public and private holders of data about individuals should be required to inform those individuals about the nature of the information held, how it is used, and who has access to it. The only exceptions to this rule should be for purposes of criminal investigation and national security very narrowly construed. Using the checks and balances system, organizations independent of government control should be created to ensure the execution of this guarantee.

Second, we must guarantee all Americans a *right of access to information*. The government should collect and make available broad categories of information. The public domain in the information sector should be widely extended. Freedom of information should not be curtailed. The right of access is more than the legal authority to obtain data. It includes the skills to use data. We should establish minimum standards of scientific and technical literacy as a national goal for all of our citizens so that they can truly have access to knowledge.

Third, we need a *right of inquiry and of dissemination*. These would include the right to research, to publish, to discuss, and to share knowledge without restriction. As part of this right, the government must be careful to refrain from attempts to control free inquiry on our campuses and to hamper the exchange of knowledge in any way, subject only to the most narrowly defined questions of public health and safety. It must be especially careful not to let its increased financial support become a means of intellectual control. This is a matter both of policy and of close monitoring of governmental agency behavior by other responsible bodies.

Recent government attempts to limit the private dissemination of knowledge are narrow, short-sighted, and counterproductive. We must not have a knowledge-classified society. We must continue to build a society of the future that can make better use of knowledge than any other society can. To restrict the dissemination of knowledge to such a society would be a self-destructive act, aimed at economic and political control, not at economic expansion.

Fourth, we need *proprietary rights.* Those private persons who produce knowledge or who assemble it creatively should have a right to the exclusive use of that knowledge for a period of time if they wish to. The knowledge explosion has led to an evasion of this right as patent infringements, industrial piracy, and the theft of new discoveries have reached astronomical proportions. We need a new enforcement system. We also need to define with more precision the boundaries between the right of access and the right of proprietorship. By establishing such rules, we can create a legal framework that will enable the new knowledge to flourish harmlessly and effectively.

In addition to securing these rights, the government must monitor the impact of knowledge upon society, not to limit that knowledge but to compensate for its effects when they are harmful to individuals, to a humane culture, and to the environment. We must know more about the psychological effects of interactive programs. We must know more about the social effects of computer networking. And we must know more about the economic effects of that knowledge—especially its impact on employment.

Congress ten years ago created the Office of Technology Assessment (OTA) to assist in evaluating the role of technology in economic growth. Its efforts to monitor developments in technology diffusion should be encouraged so that Congress can be careful to adopt federal programs that do not lead to the creation of a dual economy. The OTA concept should also be extended to the executive side, and an equivalent body attached to the Office of Management and Budget (OMB) to assess the impact of the unfolding technology on people. We all have an obligation to understand what we are doing to ourselves and to our environment as we enter an electronic age.

The two existing political parties have neglected science for more than a decade. They have recently abandoned space. They have let our universities and engineering schools wither from lack of support. They have cut back on federal funding for research and development. They have done little to give knowledge the economic emphasis it deserves. They have no workable ideas for bringing the capital revolution to America. They have not adopted the legal framework to govern the new information era. The majority in both parties has relaxed its vigil in the area of electronic surveillance.

We need a new political party in America which (unlike these Depression era parties) can lead us wisely into the coming information era. A party willing to champion science and technology, while understanding their limits and their dangers. A party unafraid to support the exploration of space, the oceans, the atom, and the gene. A party devoted to free inquiry and able to develop the rules to keep it free. A party committed to an almost unimaginable increase in the scientific and technological literacy of the American people over the next two decades in order to preserve our democracy and to give everyone the tools of direct access to the benefits of the coming age. A party also willing to use the new technology to give the American people more direct access to the governmental process. A party willing to reject a policy of trickle-down knowledge just as emphatically as it rejects a policy of trickle-down wealth.

High technology will make a major contribution to competitiveness in America. It will provide a rich field for new investment. It will help generate new wealth to sustain our standard of living. It will be the foundation of a new export strategy. It will be the source of countless jobs. It is one antidote to decline.

But new technology is no panacea. By itself it will bring no lasting advantage to America. Computers and robots are only tools, though powerful ones. They will enhance our ability to compete, but they cannot compete by themselves. Ultimately it is not just smart machines that we must look to. It is smart people.

9

RESOURCES

Eₙₜᵣₑₚᵣₑₙₑᵤᵣₛₕᵢₚ, capital, and technology by themselves are not enough. We need resources. Resource economics and resource politics have dominated the national agenda for a decade. The energy shocks of 1973 and 1979 are the most spectacular examples of this, but there are many others. Water, coal, and shale shape the politics of a dozen states. Topsoil erosion threatens the prosperity of the Farm Belt. Acid rain from coal enrages New Hampshire. Oil does not mix easily with fish in Massachusetts. Toxic wastes seem to be everywhere. The seabed controversy goes on and on. Resources are unique in the supply pantheon because many are nonrenewable and ultimately irreplaceable. In some cases they represent nothing less than the earth itself—whether to preserve it, conserve it, or carefully utilize it. They are part of the environment; their development and use change that environment.

I have always believed that we should preserve the unique and conserve the scarce. One of my proudest legislative achievements was the Anderson-Udall Alaska Lands Act, which has preserved millions of wilderness acres for future generations to explore and enjoy. My most celebrated legislative initiative was a conservation proposal—to put a tax of fifty cents on a gallon of gasoline.

I believe that it is possible in many cases to preserve the environment while using the resources of the earth, but it takes an effort to do so. The politics is complex. Great interests are at stake. Positions often seem unreconcilable. Emotions run high. People know when they are being given a line.

The only approach to these issues is to be open and honest in full recognition that you can't please everybody. Sometimes you will please nobody. I remember a campaign day in Colorado in 1980. I lunched with some of the area's leading business people who were developing western slope resources. They paid lip service to environmental concerns, but their interests lay in the rapid exploitation of coal and oil shale. They emphasized energy independence. This is a goal that I, too, strongly believe in, and I told them so. But when I added that they should pay the costs of environmental safeguards, they were unimpressed. Later that day I spoke at a rally in Boulder at the University of Colorado. In the course of the speech I stated that I favored coal and shale development but with environmental safeguards. The students were even less impressed than the business people. I was resoundingly booed.

Resources raise tough economic questions in addition to environmental ones. This is especially true when an economy becomes highly dependent on one of them. If that resource can be controlled, those who have the control either can exact a high rent for the resource or can blackmail a society for political objectives. When they do, the result can be economic chaos. This is what happened in 1973 and again in 1979, when the OPEC cartel twice tripled the price of oil.

It is difficult to overstate the negative effects of these price hikes. Two recessions hit. The banking system was expanded, destabilized, and then imperiled. Inflation soared as the monetary authorities, in effect, accommodated the 1973 price increase. Stagnant industries were hurt because they could not easily adjust. The lively sector suffered from rising costs. Millions were inconvenienced. The oil industry itself underwent a seismic boom-and-bust cycle. Real wealth was lost. (In 1980 the combined income of every person in Illinois was equivalent to the amount of money that went overseas to pay for our imported oil.) We were left with a legacy of high interest rates, unemployment, and severe economic dislocation. A major resource supply shock is probably the worst single event that can happen to a modern economy, short of total financial collapse or war.

By 1983 the energy market had begun to adjust to the new realities. Since the 1979 price increase had not been accommodated by the monetary authorities, oil became overpriced. People conserved or converted to other sources. Demand fell, a glut developed, and prices moderated. OPEC, for example, rolled back its base price from $34 to $29. The lower price levels, however, though still high, threatened even further economic dislocations as the banking system faced loan defaults from some oil producers and deposit withdrawals from others.

The oil hostage crisis is not over. Our economy remains highly vulnerable to another oil shock. Even now we rely on imports for more than a quarter of our oil. Additional conservation measures will be more expensive than those we have already taken. Our allies are more dependent than we are, and America is pledged to help them in the event of another oil crisis. As we emerge from the Great Recession, demand may increase. A political upheaval in the Middle East could trigger a new oil crisis that would throw the world into recession again.

The Reagan administration has been even less effective than the Carter administration in solving our long-term problem of excessive dependence upon a dominant energy resource controlled in part by overseas forces which we, in turn, cannot control. Reagan's energy policy has consisted of two strategies: Let the marketplace take care of the problem all by itself, and police the Persian Gulf with a permanent American military presence.

143

The first strategy has led to one positive result: the decontrol of oil prices. This has meant that domestic oil prices could rise, reducing consumption and encouraging exploration. But to rely exclusively upon the marketplace ignores the existence of OPEC. The oil cartel is neither omniscient nor immortal. When demand drops sharply, it can be broken open. But when demand firms up again, it is once more in the interests of OPEC members to come together and set prices. The oil market still does not behave as an unfettered commodities market does, nor will it as long as a few countries can control the world flow of oil.

The oil cartel must be met by strong countermeasures so that it can neither gouge its customers nor engage in cutthroat competition to deter new energy sources from coming on line. This the administration has failed to do. On the contrary, it cut back federal support for conservation measures, decimated alternative energy research programs, and put the synfuels program on stall. The private sector, meanwhile, after a year of boom, cut back its exploration efforts. Exxon's large experimental shale oil project in Colorado was one casualty. Penn Square Bank was another. The long-term vulnerabilities remain.

Reagan's second initiative, the Rapid Deployment Force, is a grand gesture. If we had to use it, however, there would probably be as much economic havoc as during an embargo, with troops, tanks, battleships, and planes fighting among the oil refineries and storage depots. The greatest danger in the Persian Gulf is internal upheaval, not foreign invasion. This force may have a stabilizing effect on area politics, but the Iranian precedent is not encouraging. We should not abandon the gulf, but we must recognize that it still can blow up in our faces anyway. There is no rational alternative to kicking the habit; we need a program to reduce our dependence and that of our allies on Middle East Oil. We must never again let our economy become dependent on a single energy source. Let us simply have done with it.

In the summer of 1979 I proposed that the United States confront the oil addiction crisis in a bold and aggressive way by imposing a tax of fifty cents on a gallon of gasoline. Most of this money was to go into the Social Security Trust Funds to bolster that system. The very large amounts of revenues raised by the gasoline tax would have permitted a deep cut in the payroll tax which now funds Social Security. The money from the gasoline tax, therefore, would have been passed back directly into the pocket of the American taxpayer. There were further provisions to return money to unemployed people and others who do not pay a payroll tax.

The purpose of this tax (in addition to supporting the Social Security system) was to raise the price of gasoline with respect to the price of other goods and services, thereby cutting demand for gasoline and, with it, our dependence on imported oil. On average, the amount taken out of the taxpayer's pocket at the gas pump would have been put back into that taxpayer's pocket in his or her payroll check. Some people would have suffered, and some would have gained; but on the average, Americans would have had as much in their pockets as they had before the tax.

What would this have done? Demand for gasoline would have dropped even more than it has during the last two or three years. As demand dropped, more price pressure would have been put on OPEC. Prices, after the initial rise of fifty cents, would have fallen, probably significantly more than they did between 1980 and 1982. It is difficult to estimate, but prices might have dropped, let us say, twenty cents instead of ten cents. This would have left gasoline at the pump about thirty cents higher, not fifty cents higher, than 1982 prices. In the meantime, however, the government would still be putting fifty cents a gallon back into the pockets of the American taxpayer. This would have been a significant gain. On average, Americans would have been ten cents per gallon better off than they are now. Such a tax might even have broken the hold of OPEC altogether. In either case virtually everyone this side of the Persian Gulf would have been ahead within a few months.

Where would that extra money have come from? There is no magic. It would have come out of the pockets of the OPEC oil cartel (more accurately, it would not have gone into those pockets in the first place). Some money would have come out of the pockets of the oil companies. But the oil companies should have been able to make a good profit at prices which would have been considerably higher than they were before the 1979 OPEC price rise.

Raising the price of gasoline relative to the prices of other commodities with a tax and then passing that money back to the taxpayer would have had a very different effect from raising it directly with the money going overseas. Americans would have had more money to spend, to the extent that they conserved on gas. This money would have been available to buy other goods and services. The downward pressures on the lively sectors would have been less. The demand for the products of stagnant industries would have dropped less. Therefore, there would have been less unemployment and a less severe set of recessions. This does not mean that there would have been no recessions at all. OPEC still would have drained billions from the economy, but the impact would have been eased.

In addition, with a lower world price for oil, the Third World countries would not have had to borrow as much. The banks, with less OPEC money to lend in the first place, would not have advanced such large loans. Their exposure to OPEC withdrawals and to Third World default would have been less. We would not today have as much instability in the international financial system.

What we failed to do through a gasoline tax has been partly done by a recession: Our dependence on oil imports has been reduced, but at a heavy price. It is time to reevaluate our situation and ask if a tax on gasoline is still a good idea. Or should we have an alternative form of energy tax? Or should we let the marketplace continue on its present course? I have thought about this a great deal, and I believe that an energy tax still makes very good sense.

A $10-a-barrel tax on imported oil would yield roughly $18 billion if import levels held to the 5-million-barrel-per-day range at which they stood as 1983 began. The conservation effect of such a tax might drive down imports to as low as 3 million barrels a day, although we must recognize that a major economic recovery would eventually raise the level again. I favor such a tax. This import fee should also be accompanied by a low-income energy-assistance plan to alleviate the effects of a rise in home heating fuel prices on our less fortunate and elderly citizens. The revenues from the tax would be set aside for a comprehensive transportation fund, as described in Chapter XIII.

Can such a tax be enacted? My 1979 proposal certainly did not get far in Congress, even with wide editoral support throughout the country. Today, however, prospects for an energy tax are brighter. Oil prices have been falling. The tax would push the base price down further. The federal government, with wide bipartisan support, raised gasoline taxes by five cents a gallon in the fall of 1982. Many states are imposing new gasoline taxes. This piecemeal approach will be less effective than a federal import fee which will discourage imports, encourage domestic production, and further the goals of conservation. Strong executive leadership in times of moderating energy prices could put through such a bill. With imports as low as they are, now is the time to do this.

A tax on energy consumption is not enough by itself to insulate the economy from an energy shock. Additional measures are needed.

First, we must accelerate our efforts to fill the strategic petroleum reserve. If prices fall, we should take advantage of this. Additional storage capacity should be created. We should have at least a year's supply.

The reserve can have many uses. Not only can it give us security against an interruption of the oil supply, but it also can give us the ability, should we wish, to stabilize the price of oil. A high American reserve would give us more bargaining leverage with the cartel and would also fulfill our alliance responsibilities.

Second, we should encourage Mexico to develop its oil fields, and we should rely principally upon Mexican oil to fill the strategic reserve. For this purpose, we could exchange some of our surplus grains for the Mexican oil, thereby solving two problems at once. The development of these fields would reduce the susceptibility of the world oil market to a Middle East oil shock.

This set of measures will provide relief and will restore flexibility. The cartel's potential for mischief will be reduced—but it can never be eliminated as long as oil is our principal energy source and realistic substitutes are lacking.

Oil used to be an exclusive American game. It was an important means by which we replaced the British in world finance. We controlled it from all angles: exploration, production, finance, and marketing. We still control exploration. We no longer fully control production. We control finance only by international convention (which can be undercut or abolished). Because we no longer control production, we cannot even maintain our position in marketing much longer. Kuwait is already buying retailing chains in Europe. The Middle East producers will soon be able to refine, ship, and market by themselves. They can undercut American companies' prices at the pump in Europe because they can give themselves preferential prices at the well. The game, as it has been played, is nearly over. We should recognize this, cut our losses, and take the necessary measures to reduce our financial system's dependence on oil.

I am not suggesting that we abandon the oil game altogether. On the contrary, oil will remain an important and convenient energy source well into the next century. American companies will still make money in oil. Oil exploration will continue to be an American-dominated industry in the foreseeable future. What I am saying is that we must invest heavily in alternative energy sources so that the possibility of substitution restores flexibility to the international energy market. Only in this way can the market function as markets are supposed to function. Only in this way can we ensure that we are not forced to play an energy game dominated by others.

One alternative is natural gas, but the gas market is in even more of a mess than the oil market. The 1978 Energy Act—against which I led the floor fight in the House of Representatives—was an extraordinarily complicated piece of legislation designed to deregulate gas slowly. It created, however, a set of perverse pricing conditions that forced many distributors to pay high prices for gas, which they then passed on to their customers. To get out of this mess, we should move swiftly toward deregulation of gas at the wellhead and eliminate the perversities of the current system.

Strong executive leadership from a president not beholden to special-interest campaign contributors could build upon the public's disgust with the situation to amend this law and let deregulation proceed in a rational way.

We must also expand the use of coal as an interim fuel. Its environmental problems, however, are not trivial. These include strip mining, acid rain, transportation side effects, and carbon dioxide build-up. There is no doubt that coal is messy, but nuclear energy, its short-term alternative, is more so.

We must spend federal money in an intense attack upon the environmental problems of coal. The basic technology of burning coal cleanly through such means as fluidized-bed combustion must be more fully developed. More efficient means of manufacturing and installing that technology are also obvious requirements. These technologies should be exported to other countries along with our coal.

All transportation of coal should be subjected to stringent environmental controls. Our ports must be upgraded to handle exports, but more attention must be given to the environmental problems of coal dust caused by loading and unloading. The railroads should be encouraged to reconvert to coal locomotives. With new microprocessor control devices, steam engines can be both economical and environmentally acceptable. We should investigate more efficient methods of converting coal into electricity, including magnetohydrodynamic processes which may increase the efficiency of coal usage significantly.

Coal presents many problems, but research money spent to solve them would be an excellent federal investment in the future. It would be returned to the Treasury many times over throughout the rest of the century.

We must also completely reevaluate the current nuclear power situation. I was an advocate of nuclear power before Three Mile Island. But the dangers and costs have become so apparent in the last few years that we cannot continue a program of expanding our nuclear generating capacity. We must cut our losses and disengage in the least costly way. We should immediately evaluate which plants have a reasonable chance of being completed in the near future, and we should complete them. We should halt the construction of any new plants. We should not complete the breeder reactor at Clinch River. We should put our attention into efforts at solving the waste problems of those plants that already exist and weigh the costs of waste disposal carefully in considering the long-term advisability of completing plants under construction. The energy situation will not permit us to phase out nuclear power quickly, but that must be our long-term goal. Frankly we have no safe and economic alternative.

I would not, however, halt research into fusion power. Its chance for commercial success seems distant; but the payoff would be enormous, and the environmental problems seem far less than those associated with fission.

With oil a recurrent problem, with nuclear energy a dying alternative, and with coal still a persistent environmental hazard, other approaches are needed even as we attack the environmental problems of coal. This will be difficult because the technologies in many instances are not yet commercially feasible. In some cases, there are simply natural limits which put a ceiling on the amount of energy we can reasonably expect to obtain or save.

Conservation is still our most promising strategy, even though the Reagan administration wants to cut back federal support for energy conservation 90 percent and virtually eliminate conservation grants to state and local governments. Industry, homeowners, and the government have made solid gains in saving energy over the last decade. During most of the postwar era GNP growth was closely associated with energy growth. Recently, however, this has changed. The GNP is now growing faster than energy consumption because we are becoming more energy-efficient. This is a positive development. Lower interest rates, policies to encourage rapid capital turnover, research on production techniques, tax credits for the rehabilitation of old plants, and the microprocessor revolution will accelerate this trend. The faster we rejuvenate our economy, the more energy-efficient it will become.

Conservation in the home will continue to make a significant contribution. The energy window at community development banks will provide a source of additional capital for this purpose. The Public Enterprise Corporations discussed in the next chapter can play a role in community conservation projects.

One idea for encouraging conservation that should be tried on a nationwide basis is to give power companies the authority to "invest" in conservation. A power company, for example, would insulate a person's home or a commercial building. The cost of this project would be built into the rate structure of the company—just like the investment cost of building new capacity. The company's stockholders would gain because the average cost of electricity would fall. The homeowner would gain because the electricity bill would be lower; he or she would be using less electricity. The principal on the investment could be made due to the electric company upon sale of the house. This practice has been successfully used in parts of California. Federal legislation could speed its adoption in other regions.

We must also encourage more companies and private individuals to become producers of electricity. Cogeneration is already beginning to take hold. Wind and low head hydropower can make a modest contribution. Every little bit helps. To encourage experimentation with different energy sources, regulatory barriers should be swept away (with federal legislation, if necessary) so that small producers of electricity can more easily sell their products to the existing power grids.

To help our long-term energy needs, the government should engage in a crash program to develop affordable solar energy technologies. This must be one of our highest national priorities. Photovoltaic energy looks especially promising. Solar energy gathered in space and transmitted to earth is a long-term possibility. The government should launch a widespread experimental effort across a broad range of promising technologies. This effort should include further research on geothermal, ocean thermal energy conversion, and tidal energy. As soon as reasonable break-even points are reached, the industry itself will take off and solar energy will diffuse rapidly throughout the economy. The private sector, commendably, is also working hard in the area. Solar is the energy of the future. It is clean and permanently renewable. Once the technology has been fully developed and diffused, this energy source will be controllable by nothing except the marketplace. The resource landlords will be the only losers.

One of the great tragedies of the Reagan administration was its decision to cut energy research nearly in half. For an administration worried about the future power of the Soviet Union, emphasizing oil and deemphasizing solar energy showed remarkable strategic stupidity. The Russians are awash in oil. If we develop solar power, it will be American technology upon which Europe and Japan will depend for their energy, not Russian oil and gas.

Energy is not the only scarce resource. There is potentially a shortage of materials as well. Rapid development and wasteful use of all the earth's resources are helping cause these shortages. For example, here in America our economy is becoming more dependent on the importation of heavy metals and other minerals.

Furthermore, the waste products produced by the usage of all resources has caused complex problems of disposal. We need to launch a major research effort to develop more efficient methods of recycling our wastes and safer means of disposing of them. Dumping the problem into our oceans where future generations will not be able to get at the mess we left behind is not an answer. Needless to say, the Reagan administration in its 1984 budget proposed a large cutback in funding for research on hazardous waste. We need a national policy for waste control that enables us to dispose of our wastes in the most environmentally safe way possible. At the same time we must preserve accurate records and scientific data of what has been done so future generations will not suffer the environmental shocks and surprises many of our citizens have already suffered.

The resource problems of today can be solved if we make our economy livelier. Entrepreneurship, capital, and technology can flush inefficiencies rapidly out of the system and develop long-term alternatives. For example, if our economy had a flexible production system, built around batching operations, we would soon see transportation vehicles proliferating in small lots, built of new materials and employing new fuel technologies such as fuel cells, ethanol, methanol, and hydrogen. We would see new fleets of battery-driven cars. Flywheels would become common energy-saving features on buses, delivery vans, taxis, and other vehicles that make frequent stops. Many of these experiments would fail, but others would succeed, some in small markets, others in larger markets. This is one reason why an industrial system keyed to produce a wide variety of products is superior to a stagnant one. Many of these ideas for vehicles are technically and commercially feasible today, but the large vehicle companies are reluctant to produce them without a guaranteed market. As the economy livens, they will be produced.

Moreover, as our knowledge develops, we will be able to substitute it for scarce materials and scarce energy. By the middle of the next century we may have an economy based primarily on silicon and solar power, the cheapest material and the most easily renewable energy resource. The structure of the American economy in such a world would certainly be different from that of today.

The political and economic power of the major energy producers is changing. Oil is losing its hold on the American economy. Lower prices would not quickly reverse this trend. People have long memories. They will continue to conserve, to substitute, and to use fuel-efficient cars. Manufacturing industries are not about to let themselves get hooked again, nor are the utilities. New England electric companies, for example, were once almost exclusively dependent on oil. Today they have almost completely shifted to other sources. They will not soon return.

Energy can become a free market again. The price of oil can be forced to fluctuate. Other sources can be substituted. Conservation can continue. Deregulation can become widespread. Unless the major oil companies can control all the energy sources, they will lose their commanding position. A truly free market in energy, with solar power on the horizon, will bring broad benefits to the American economy.

It is emphatically the duty of government to promote this open market. We must recognize, however, that great interests are at stake. Should the price of oil or gas fall significantly, then the value of oil and gas reserves would also fall. Billions in paper assets would be wiped out. The oil and gas interests are, not surprisingly, reluctant to see this happen. Policies designed to break OPEC, encourage solar energy, and free up the market will be fought by one of the most powerful lobbies in Washington, a lobby that works both sides of the aisle in contributing substantial sums of money to Democrats and Republicans alike. Until this obstacle is overcome, we will not have a free energy market. The current party system will not permit this to happen. Both parties have been trying since Nixon to achieve energy independence without much success. Neither has the courage to exercise the leadership we need to convince Americans to sacrifice in this area for an important national objective.

We need a new political party in America. A party devoted to the national interest and unafraid to reject the ministrations of special interests. A party, unlike the Republicans and Democrats, which has the courage to require its candidates to refuse all PAC money. A party willing to support basic electoral reform to break the hold of energy money and other special-interest funding on the political process.

We also need a party, unlike the Republicans and the Democrats, that is committed to adopting a coherent energy strategy that will return genuine energy independence to America. A party fully committed to an open and flexible market in energy. A party committed to breaking OPEC. A party committed to bringing the solar revolution to America. A party committed to ensuring that other resource shortages do not occur. A party willing to ask America to sacrifice to achieve these objectives.

Such a party must be fully committed to environmental sanity. To environmental research. To enforcing the law. To protecting our public lands. To protecting our water and air. To cleaning up our toxic wastes. To encouraging throughout the society an environmental ethic based on a respect for the future and on the expectation that many more generations will need the resources of the earth during that future.

Can such a party succeed in its objectives? I believe so. The energy lobby may be among the most powerful in Washington, but the source of its power is not only its current wealth but its ability to command future markets. If it loses this ability, it will also begin to lose its political power. The freer the market in energy, the more difficult it will be for the special energy interests to exercise their sway over Washington. This is why it is so important for the government to counter OPEC, to deregulate the energy markets, and to promote alternative fuels. As it begins to achieve these results, it will be politically easier to achieve further results. Nearly everyone will benefit. A great roadblock will be removed. The economy will come alive.

10

PEOPLE

S M A R T and lively people make the economy go, whether
they are running companies or working for them. It is men and
women, not machines, that compete. The skills, attitudes, values,
and health of people are just as important to America's future as
the real capital in our factories and the oil in our wells. We may
not be able to measure this "human capital," but it is the true base
of the economic pyramid. Our gross level of skills is as important
as our gross national product. The health of our school system is as
vital to America as the health of our banking system.

These are not pious platitudes. When the new technology takes
hold, competitive success will be determined by the skills of those
who use it. The new capital equipment will be different from the
old because there will be no single way to program it. Its value
will be in the range of opportunities it will create. Those who take
full advantage of the opportunities will defeat those who take only

partial advantage and those who fail to use the new equipment at all.

Skills will therefore be as important as the machinery. A word processor is great, but it gives you a competitive advantage only if you and your operators know how to get better use out of it than your rivals and their operators can. The same is true of a robot. Both are as good as the people who use them. The new technology, by extending the range of human mastery, gives individual human beings a more central role in the production process. This is what flexibility is all about.

The new technology will be mobile. Other countries will buy and develop it, too. The multinationals will shuttle it all over the world. The only way for America to remain competitive is to make better use of it than others can. This means that we must rapidly improve skills throughout the entire production process.

It will not be sufficient simply to rely upon better engineers and designers at the top. Modern communications will enable them easily to plug into overseas production processes if these are more efficient than American. To keep an integrated system in America, all parts must be competitive. If they are, American business can create production systems relying on the unique skills of American workers that cannot quickly or cheaply be duplicated overseas. Even American multinationals have an interest in developing processes which rely upon the specialized skills of American workers because their foreign competitors can quickly duplicate the whole process if production skills are easily acquired elsewhere.

Not only must the skills of our work force be improved, but they must be improved continually year after year, to take full advantage of the rapidly changing capital goods. People entering the work force from the school system must be better prepared than their predecessors. People already in the work force must continually extend their abilities. The age of perpetual education and training is at hand. We can keep industry in America, but we must constantly work at it. Business, professionals, and labor will soon find that they desperately need one another to keep ahead.

The skills of Americans are important not only to specific industries but also to the economy as a whole. The higher our national level of relevant skills, the more rapidly we can adopt the new technology, and the more rapidly our economy can advance. If competitive skills are developed widely, the economy can remain broad-based and become more integrated and efficient.

When people acquire skills, they are not the only ones who gain. The whole economy benefits through the division of labor. Adam Smith was right about this. After all, it is in your interests and mine that others know how to fix the plumbing the first time, make change at the supermarket, build the car so its wheels won't fall off, and fly the plane. The greater the level of our specialized skills, the higher is everyone's standard of living.

This is why Reagan's cleft society is not in the interest of America. If the skills of half our population are no longer relevant and these people fall into a stagnant pool of dependency, then everybody suffers. Goods and services are fewer, inferior, and more expensive. Business loses customers as well as qualified employees. Real wealth is lost. Those who say, "Go look in the want ads," do not understand that Detroit can't make a go of it just selling Buicks and Cadillacs.

People may be our most valuable resource, but they are also our most wasted resource. Every person who receives inadequate training, who does not fully develop his or her skills, who cannot find a job because of recession, discrimination, or economic stagnation, or who has been turned away from the system by whatever means is a wasted resource. The whole economy suffers.

We are today creating in our country an underclass of millions who cannot find jobs, who cannot hold jobs, who have stopped seeking jobs, or who never had jobs to begin with. Given a choice between dead-end menial work and depending on unemployment benefits or welfare, many simply drift back and forth between public assistance and private-sector employment, never making any material advancement. Their children, too, will grow up in an economically and socially deprived environment. Today youth unemployment rates in many cities exceed 40 percent; the rate among young blacks is even higher. The resulting effects of unemployment, welfare dependency, and even criminal recidivism cost society billions of dollars, amortized slowly and painfully over many lifetimes. There is no "Human Capital Cost Recovery Act" that can redeem these wasted assets.

We are destroying more than the lives of an underclass. The middle class paid a heavy forfeit during the Great Recession. People lost ground that will be tough to regain. As stagnant industries fail, jobs will disappear permanently, and more people will head downward into dependency. Discrimination still takes its ugly toll. America is slowly dividing in half.

The answer is not make-work employment, or the temporary protection of stagnant companies, or a larger system of income redistribution. Those who look in these directions should remember Great Britain, which once led all others and which now experiences the lowest standard of living in the large Western states. This must not be our future. The answer is a major long-term national commitment by both private and public sectors to upgrade the skills of Americans so that we all can compete in the world and so we all can enjoy access to the fruits of successful competition.

America must invest in the American people. I have never fully understood why we are often reluctant to do so. Japan invests in the Japanese. France invests in the French. Britain's record is poor in this respect, but that is due to its class structure. This would not explain America's reluctance. Surely it is not a lack of generosity, although Americans often are more generous to others than to themselves. Is it politics? Is it latent racism or ethnicism? Is it because we compute the sums and conclude that others would be the winners and we the losers? Is it because we have tried to invest and the investments have failed? Most parents will sacrifice for their children. Most citizens will support local expenditures for local needs. The reluctance grows as the needs become more remote, the recipients more abstract, the country more fragmented. America's willingness to invest in Americans seems to be a good measure of our unity as a country.

If our economy is to compete globally, these investments must be made. But we are today moving in the opposite direction. The degree to which the Reagan administration decided not to invest in people while it was spending more for weapons is extraordinary. It proposed massive cuts in compensatory education, in Indian education, in education block grants to the states, in education for the handicapped, in vocational education, in adult education, in higher education, and in support for students. On average, the cuts proposed exceeded 50 percent for the fiscal years 1982–85. Congress did not go along with all these, but the result was still a massive disinvestment at the federal level, largely uncompensated for at lower levels.

All this is just wrong. We have an economic battle to win, and we cannot win it with functionally illiterate people. We must rejuvenate, not liquidate, our educational and vocational systems so that people entering the work force can compete with their counterparts overseas. And we must do this now.

We need an educational revolution in America as massive in scope as the revolution of the 1960s that saw the number of students in college rise from 3.5 million to more than 10 million. The new educational revolution must be both quantitative and qualitative, embracing all levels of education from preschool through vocational, professional, and graduate training. It should also include adult education. We ought to aim at nothing short of the entire society's becoming highly literate, computer-skilled, and in many respects professionalized. We must become a nation of achievers. It is only in this way that we can create new wealth and keep enough high-paying jobs in America to enjoy a full-employment economy with a high standard of living.

We should start with the schools themselves, and the problem is staggering. It includes the fall in SAT scores, the rise of illiteracy, the high school graduates who cannot add or subtract a set of numbers, the collapse of science instruction, the dropout rate, the teachers knifed or raped in the classroom, the schools that have become detention centers to keep students off the streets for a few hours of the day, and the flight of middle-class children of all races to private and parochial school alternatives. Virtually every parent is aware of these problems. Recently I slipped into the back row of a social studies class to observe for an hour. I was struck by the fact that the young teacher spent most of that hour simply reading previously assigned material from the text. The students, with books open before them, seemed to be following along. There was only the most desultory discussion of the material by either teacher or students. When I inquired about the reason for what seemed to be a most uneconomical use of classroom time, the answer was simple. Very few of these high school juniors could read at a sufficiently advanced level to comprehend the text.

I am sure that there are many good public schools in America and many thousands of dedicated, though often underpaid, teachers. However, taken as a whole, the public school system of the United States is very far from what it should be.

Unless something is done soon about conditions in the public schools, private and religious schools or computer-based instruction in the home will soon become the principal methods of primary and even secondary education in America. We have seen the electronic church. Can the electronic classroom be far behind?

As Seymour Papert of MIT has shown, the classroom computer will do far more than teach students how to run and program computers, although that itself will be a major contribution to their future employment prospects. The computer will assist in the teaching of mathematics and science and eventually almost every other field of the traditional curriculum. Combined with audio and visual capabilities, it will help students read, to understand another language, to compose music, to design and draw, and to locate information. The electronic classroom of the future will have a large repertoire of movies and plays, taped lectures by famous people, visual encyclopedias, operas, concerts, and entire courses in geography, history, and civics.

The great advantage of electronic instruction will be its "interactive" nature. It can ask questions of the student, it can test the student, and it can move at the student's own pace. It can transcend language and cultural barriers. It can diagnose individual learning problems and proceed in ways to correct them. It can sharpen perceptions and deepen understanding. It can help motivate. People who enjoy Pac-Man can also enjoy acquiring useful skills if the program developer has sufficient imagination and expertise to make this possible. Furthermore, the electronic classroom will provide a much wider variety of course material than any school can afford to provide with just its own human resources. I have no hesitation in saying that we must bring this electronic revolution to every classroom.

The computer should not be regarded as a replacement for teachers. Good teaching will always be a human experience. Machines are not role models. Electronics should extend, not reduce, the human contribution. Indeed, computers should make teaching more important, interesting, and demanding. They will make individualized instruction easier. Classroom activities can emphasize tutorials and discussion groups. Teachers can be relieved of many dull routines.

The electronic revolution, however, *can* be used to reduce substantially the number of teachers needed per pupil. Although this situation will not provide the best education, it may still provide a better education than students are getting today in many classrooms. That is how the private sector can enter the marketplace.

Electronic equipment is relatively inexpensive. Software costs will fall as the volume of sales increases. A terminal for every student is today a possibility in many school systems. It is easy to envision a private school with a teaching staff of 25 well-paid professionals providing a good education to 1,000 or more students at a cost affordable by middle-class America. It is also easy to envision a student's getting a very good education at his or her home terminal, using programs available at reasonable prices.

Half the students in America could be in private schools by the end of the century. If this occurs, the public school system will come to serve only the poor. It will lose its middle-class constituency and thereby its local funding support. Public education will become equated with welfare and viewed with disdain. This will help divide society even more into a well-educated overclass and a poorly educated underclass.

The public primary and secondary educational systems in America today share many characteristics with stagnant industries. They face a declining clientele as the school-age population drops (the drop was 10 percent between 1970 and 1980). They are highly bureaucratic. They are resistant to change. Their costs keep rising. The public, given a choice, may decide to buy from the competition. This will further shrink their market, drive good people away, and reduce the quality of their services even more. The expanding private sector will bid the best teachers away and leave the rest. Calls for "protection" will not succeed because the private sector today is already large enough, diverse enough, and well enough established to resist.

This is unfortunate. People certainly have a right to start and operate private schools, and parents have a right to send their children to them. But the public school plays an absolutely crucial role in American society and must continue to play that role. Not only is it an institutional expression of the basic American belief that all children should have equal educational opportunities, but it is also the place where people from all social backgrounds can find a common meeting place, share experiences, and develop a modicum of mutual understanding. Education should not be thought of as something just for purchase. It is a right of all Americans, and it should be a shared experience. Most important, an educated citizenry is the heart of democracy.

I have always been a strong supporter of the public school system. I continue to be. I oppose tuition tax credits, and I will continue to do so. Yet something must be done to improve the quality of a public school education if public schools are to survive.

To begin, the public school curriculum should be designed to provide students with at least four educational experiences. First, all students as a minimum should acquire the basic skills of reading, computation, expression, and advanced computer literacy. Those who are graduated without these skills are condemned to low-paying jobs, recurrent unemployment, and the most menial of occupations.

Second, the basic liberal arts curriculum must remain at the center of the educational experience. Not only is it essential to an understanding of human values, but also it will be vocationally more relevant to students in the future than at any time in the past. Not only will mathematics and science create employment opportunities, but the humanities will also be enormously useful in preparing people for the rapidly changing demands of a flexible economy. The future will heavily reward imagination, problem solving, cultural awareness, vision, design skills, and the ability to think structurally as well as linearly. It will also reward advanced language skills and the understanding of other cultures. All these the liberal arts curriculum should offer.

Third, students should be exposed to courses on coping with modern society—how to fill out a tax form, how to deal with the government, what the basic political and legal system is like, how to run a business, how to keep books, how to fix an automobile, run a household, and solve practical problems.

Fourth, the public school curriculum should acquaint students with a wide range of vocational opportunities. Whether this is done through courses of instruction, audiovisual methods, innovative simulation equipment, released time, or whatever, it should be built into the standard school experience as a significant extension of what is now called guidance or counseling. Students should be aware that they may need several careers in their lifetime. They should understand the possibilities open to them and the training required to perform the job. An important part of this "guidance" function should be to overcome sex stereotyping and to acquaint women with the opportunities they can have in jobs not traditionally open to them.

Public school systems in areas of high dropout rates and chronic youth unemployment need to provide further services to students and their parents. We must have more trained professionals whose duty it is to encourage students to stick with their education and not to drop out early from the system. These professionals should work closely with teachers, students, parents, potential employers, and the social services network in the community to help guide students through their school experience. More attention must be paid to showing students why an education is important to their future in the coming economic era. As the age of electronics arrives, motivation will remain primarily a human exercise.

Outreach programs, activities to increase the school's social role, and closer coordination between the educational system and the social support structure of the community are needed. In addition to these, all schools should be given the resources to initiate special classes for the parents of their students. These classes should be designed to encourage parents to emphasize education at home and to give them the ability to help students with their lessons. Parents must be brought more decisively into the educational process. Indications are that such involvement can be highly successful in improving a student's achievement.

In addition to these measures, we should expand our system of adult and continuing education and make it easier for people to take advantage of it. Everyone should have the right to return to the school system in later life. Such an opportunity would go well with the special programs for parents. It could help people in their jobs. It could help motivate people with poor job prospects to widen their vocational horizons. It could provide the larger social and cultural context that would make retraining a more effective experience. It could enable us to mount an attack on the growing problem of adult illiteracy. Employers might be encouraged to provide released time to employees who wished to take advantage of these opportunities.

We have had many experiences with failure—failure to break the poverty cycle, failure to break the welfare dependency cycle, failure to break the unemployment cycle, and failure to break the motivational cycle. Our approach should be to learn from these, not to be deterred by them. The school system is where we must start.

Although the local school boards and the states must take the leading role in rejuvenating our public school systems and their curriculums, the federal government should provide vigorous support. Quality public education must become a major national priority, even though control over the content of that education must remain at the local level. For example, the federal government on a matching basis determined by a state's and school district's ability to pay should provide the following:

—Salary supplements for teachers.
—Grants for faculty development, including paid leaves of absence, to improve teaching skills and especially subject

matter skills. This program should include instruction in the use of new classroom equipment.

—Grants to schools of education to improve courses that emphasize subject matter competency and the new tools of instruction.

—Grants for staff development, including outreach and expanded vocationally oriented guidance functions in areas of high dropout rates and chronic youth unemployment.

—Grants to encourage experiments with new methods of instruction, especially to reach students with learning and motivational problems.

—Grants to establish classes of instruction for parents to involve them more in the educational process.

—Grants to institute experimental adult and continuing education programs.

—Grants to purchase hardware for classroom computer training. The goal of a computer terminal and ancillary equipment for each student is not unrealistic and could be reached within a few years.

—Grants to support the development of educational software. Because the federal government should not be directly involved in curriculum development, it must serve as a catalyst in this area.

This software proposal needs elaboration. Software development costs are high. Once developed, software can be used cheaply. I recommend that the federal government make a large number of medium-sized grants to schools of education, to states, and to local school boards for the purpose of developing and testing new electronic educational programs. Once the efficacy of the programs was demonstrated, a demand would clearly be established, and the private market would, no doubt, rapidly take off. Support for the purchase of software might continue for a longer period of time in needy school districts.

The federal government should parallel these steps in the vocational education area. Our system of vocational schools should be expanded, and its mission extended to meet the needs of the future. With new equipment and better training, many "jobs" today will become "professions" tomorrow. Vocational schools must keep abreast of these developments. They should also receive support for experimentation with simulation techniques in job training.

Professional schools themselves in many fields may also need substantial federal support to increase their enrollments as the professionalization of the American economy proceeds.

This major commitment to improving our educational system should be continually evaluated. No purpose is served by merely throwing money at a problem. The U.S. Department of Education should fill the vital function of evaluating expenditures which must quite literally be regarded as major national investments of scarce dollars.

Education is not the only investment America should make in Americans. Health care, nutrition, help for the handicapped, and many social services contribute to our national well-being. These, too, should be regarded as investments in our future. Consider nutrition. Programs to eradicate severe malnutrition have succeeded rather well in the past. They are now being cut back by the Reagan administration (which also seems to object to adequate funding for child inoculation programs). I truly fail to see how starvation and disease among our children contribute to the strength and well-being of America. It makes elemental sense that money invested in these areas will be fully paid back in the future (in Medicare and Medicaid payments alone, for example), apart from the humanitarian questions which the administration sternly steels itself to ignore and apart from the probable contributions to America's future that well-nourished and healthy people can make. This appalling nonsense must be reversed.

A human problem that involves even larger numbers of people is unemployment. This scourge touches far more than the 12 million Americans out of work at a given time during the Great Recession, far more even than the 30 million who were at some time unemployed during that period. It is not simply a case of people "between jobs" or "looking for jobs"; it is a deep and persistent economic problem that government must make a commitment to solve. What can be done?

First, the government can institute a systematic job bank information service on a nationwide basis to remove some of the imperfections in the labor market. This might find jobs for people in the tens of thousands and might reduce slightly the average time spent looking for jobs. But when people seeking jobs number in the millions, this is only a modest beginning.

Second, we must augment our facilities for retraining the structurally unemployed. A large national system of retraining centers should be built into existing school facilities. The private sector should be asked to play a major role. Opportunities for electronic instruction and simulation should be explored. The programs should stress not only skills but motivation. An outreach program to serve people in their fifties and older would be important, as would special programs for single parents. Adult illiteracy would also be a major target.

Training facilities will have a much larger impact if they are integrated with the job bank service. The job bank could provide market information to the training centers, which in turn could then actively recruit people for training in the fields that are available or that hold promise for the future. In this way the job bank system could guarantee to a potential employer either that he or she would find a person with the required skills or that such a person would be trained.

The trainee, alternatively, would better understand the job marketplace. The number of unfilled jobs should decline significantly. A voucher system to encourage employers to retrain might be a useful supplement.

Third, we must recognize that these two proposals, while helpful and needed, are inadequate. Unemployment is a problem so large that job information and even extensive retraining programs will only begin to solve it. The heart of the issue, of course, is the number of jobs available. Demand stimulus, the obvious first strategy, itself may not be sufficient to spread employment around among the chronic unemployed.

Another approach has been wage subsidies, partial or complete. The difficulty with these is that they generally tend to be for make-work or dead-end jobs which do not solve the basic problems of the structurally unemployed. The Comprehensive Employment and Training Act (CETA) programs sponsored by the Democrats in recent years have provided limited job-training opportunities and public-service work for millions of young or displaced workers. These programs, however, have not been successful in generating real economic opportunity. The public-service jobs approach used in the 1970s was a failure. Employability did not seem to increase. Skills did not improve. Congress was dissatisfied with the results. The program is being phased out.

The Republican response to the problems of CETA has been to place greater emphasis upon private-sector involvement and job training instead of on menial public-service jobs. This approach has merit, but Republicans do not want to give stipends to participants who are training. Therefore, the economically disadvantaged are deprived of the ability to participate. Moreover, stripped of their rhetoric, Republicans generally want to scale back federal involvement, not simply to change its direction. Another Republican suggestion has been to lower the minimum wage or exempt certain categories of people from it. This would increase employment to some extent—but the jobs generally would be ones without a future.

It is important, in view of the nature and costs of the modern welfare state, that the government take a dramatic new step aimed at promoting economic opportunity. We need to bring private-sector principles into the administration of public-sector services.

Private enterprise has been defined as "Economic activities carried on by private individuals with the expectation of profit." Extending this concept to the public sector, we discover a need for public enterprise, defined as "Economic activities, *serving a public purpose*, carried on by private individuals with the expectation of profit."

To facilitate the expansion of "public enterprise," the federal government should establish a Public Enterprise Board with the power to charter privately owned and operated Public Enterprise Corporations (PECs). These PECs, which would be fully taxable, would be permitted to bid on all federal, state, and local contracts and to engage in any other economic activity serving a public policy purpose, such as day care services, energy conservation, or waste recycling. The definition of *economic activity* or *public policy purpose* would be settled by statute and by regulations issued by the Public Enterprise Board.

To encourage the formation of PECs and the hiring of chronically unemployed workers, PECs would be exempt from Davis-Bacon wage requirements on any project in which 50 percent of their labor force had a Public Labor Certification (PLC). This percentage might be lowered in times of falling unemployment. A Public Labor Certification would be issued by employment offices to those individuals experiencing chronic unemployment problems according to some objective test (e.g., people unemployed for the last nine months or people who have looked for jobs but have never been employed). To encourage the hiring of unemployed workers with a PLC, the PEC would be allowed to deduct as a taxable expense 200 percent of the worker's first year's wages or salary, 180 percent of the second year's, 150 percent of the third year's, and 125 percent of the fourth year's. There would be a five-year loss carry-forward provision. This would mean, for example, that a qualifying PEC employee in the first year earning $15,000 would create a tax credit for the employer of $6,900 if that employer were in the 46 percent tax bracket.

PECs would be expected to compete with private-sector contractors and to operate, like any other contractor, with the idea of making a profit. PECs would have the complete power to hire and fire employees, including those with PLCs. PECs would be subject to existing minimum wage, health, safety, and equal opportunity regulations.

The chronically unemployed need a ladder of opportunity to climb, not dead-end employment. Since the PEC is a for-profit corporation utilizing skilled labor as well as unskilled, it would provide room for advancement within an existing framework. Workers would be given an opportunity to prove their worth to the company with the help of the four-year sliding subsidy. The work would not be make-work in any sense since the work would be limited to government contracts or to business serving a certified public policy goal, engaged in for a profit. The PECs would also tend to moderate the costs of infrastructure repair for federal, state, and local governments. The PECs have the further advantage that not only blue-collar workers but clerical and managerial personnel as well would qualify for employment. Furthermore, the employer would be actively seeking to find unemployed people who could be hired.

Organized labor will surely oppose the creation of PECs. It will argue that government will tend to substitute PEC labor for private-contract labor and tend to force wage rates down by the Davis-Bacon exemption. Yet if the government's creation of PECs is matched by a rapid expansion of public works project monies on the federal, state, and local levels, union employees need not fear the loss of their jobs. There will be plenty of work for everyone. These lower wage rates will make it possible dramatically to increase the level of employment in America in the public area without full job subsidies, as in many other programs.

We need to make it possible for companies to hire people at lower wage rates in some areas until the overall productivity of the economy is strong enough to bid up the price of labor. The PEC is a way of doing it so that people can expect a future. The alternative is not full employment at high wage rates. It is more unemployment with fewer people earning those wage rates. With the PEC proposal, the existing wage structure can be preserved, while the PECs take up the unemployment slack.

Fourth, although the system of PECs would expand rapidly, many of the chronic unemployed may still not be reached, even with an expanding economy. The legacy of the past is deep. One idea that may have merit is a new form of two-tiered employment. To avoid wholesale layoffs, it may be necessary to spread part-time employment among an existing work force. The part-time workers will need to find second jobs to supplement their reduced earnings. Many part-time public-sector jobs that would perform a useful service can be created. These range from the pothole-filling and bridge-painting category to such activities as day care work, census taking, highway beautification, recreational services for the young, repairing public buildings, energy audits, safety patrols, subway patrols, voter registration, cleaning up rural areas, rehabilitating public housing, retuning oil furnaces on a periodic basis, and conservation activities. Training would be required for many of these, but they could provide supplementary income for part-time workers.

We might need even more. There are tough choices to be made. Do we want to bring back the Civilian Conservation Corps (CCC) and the Works Projects Administration (WPA)? There are many arguments against doing so. The public support will be much less for this than for a PEC. They can easily become crime- and corruption-ridden. It would take a tough cadre of ex-marine sergeants to run them properly. Local communities where they work may often object to their presence, as they did in the 1930s. My preference is clearly to attack the problem through the schools and through an expanding system of PECs. But I would not rule this option out entirely. If it were set up like the World War II army training programs, it might just help some people. It is better than shantytowns and soup kitchens.

With educational training and employment programs such as these, we can begin to improve the employment opportunities of the American people and give them a chance to make a greater contribution to our national well-being. But we need more than mere programs. We must rediscover in America a new spirit of pride in accomplishment and hope for the future. We need a renewed sense of purpose.

Americans used to be proud that we were the best-educated, best-nourished, and healthiest country in the world. This was not a false pride born of satisfaction that others were worse off than we were but a positive belief in our own accomplishments and a hope that others could benefit from our example.

I would like to see a society in which most people leaving the school system can read and write; are computer-literate; are scientifically literate; are culturally aware, well read, fully competent in a second language, able to distinguish style from substance, able to cope with the complexities of society, ethically sensitive to the concerns of others, and street-wise. This means at least four years of college for nearly all our citizens, a scholarship system to sustain this, a vastly improved school and university system, and a menu of practical experience for students. This is a tall order for a society that is slipping backward, but it should not be an impossible goal for a nation that already enrolls half its relevant age-group in postsecondary schools. We must add a qualitative revolution to the quantitative revolution of the 1960s.

To succeed, we need more than plans and commitments. We need leadership. Not just charismatic leadership at the top but responsible leadership throughout American society—in the classroom, in the principal's office, on the school board, in Congress, and in the White House. Not public relations gimmicks and political spectaculars but solid, determined leadership committed to quality in education and job training.

Where will that leadership come from? Largely from the American people themselves if the government will level with them, trust them, and convey to them with honesty what is needed to prepare for the realities of the future. For this to happen, however, we need new political leadership in America.

We must begin by outmaneuvering the radical Right. The Right has mounted a major campaign against the public school system. It has radicalized the debate by stressing such issues as evolution, sex education, and prayers in the schools. This ideological assault has deprived education of support within the Republican party and has neutralized support among many Democrats who fear the wrath of the Right at the polls. Reagan remains solidly committed to undercutting the public schools through his tuition credit and voucher ideas. All his bluster and rhetoric about aiding public education serve only to disguise his policies of cutting back on federal support for it.

There is only one way to break the logjam. That is to bring the business community foursquare into the balance behind the rebuilding of the school system and the creation of training programs. It is in the interest of business that the system be rebuilt. Business needs literate and computer-literate people both as employees and as customers. Business needs skilled people to be part of integrated production systems utilizing the new technology so that these systems cannot be duplicated abroad. Business itself is now spending billions to educate people because the school systems are not functioning properly. Both the stagnant and lively sectors can use a sound education and training system. With business aboard, the Right will be in no position to stop what needs to be done.

Business will not be alone. Professionals also have an interest in rebuilding the school system—as do unions, blacks, Hispanics, working people, parents, and young people. It should be possible to assemble a powerful coalition behind this objective that transcends the issues of Left and Right. It is there for the asking.

But the Republicans can't put it together. They are boxed in by their own right wing. The Democrats would like to, but they can't either. Lacking the confidence of the business community, their coalition is not large enough, and their efforts can easily become branded as partisan by the Right. Such a branding will reduce the possibility that Republicans will join in bipartisan support. The issue of education alone is sufficient to demonstrate the need for a new political coalition in this country.

We need a new political party. A party committed to high levels of academic achievement for all Americans. A party which recognizes that only through such levels of achievement can we compete in the global economy of the future. A party that understands the relationship between a poor education and a poor job. A party willing to acknowledge that the only way we can prevent America from becoming a permanently divided society is through quality education for everyone. A party whose resolution to succeed matches the magnitude of the problem. A party committed, in the words of Jefferson, to an educational system that will bring about an aristocracy of achievement out of a democracy of opportunity.

11

MANAGEMENT, LABOR, AND THE BUILDING OF A NEW INDUSTRIAL RELATIONSHIP

T H E support system of the American economy cannot be rebuilt easily or quickly. It will not be rebuilt at all unless we stop playing politics with the economy. But if it is rebuilt properly, we should begin to see results immediately.

Small business will quickly take advantage of the extension service, the new tax climate, and the expanded market opportunities. It will use the enlarged SBA and the local development banks. It will easily adopt new technologies and methods, and it will make good use of a more skilled work force. Policies to lower interest rates, encourage price flexibility, and enhance free trade will have an immediate and beneficial impact. No arm twisting will be necessary to convince the owners of small firms to take advantage of the improved support system.

Growth industries will also use the system quickly and entrepreneurially. They will benefit from the measures designed to aid small business. They will profit from the ability to finance growth more easily out of retained earnings. They will borrow from the investment banks. They will enjoy a respite from predatory takeovers. They will take advantage of new engineering talent. They will benefit from a flow of well-trained people from the school system, retraining programs, and the Regional Technology Institutes (RTIs). Capital, technology, resource availability, and skilled workers will be easily fitted into the structure of new and growing companies which look to the future.

With stagnant industries, however, the story is different. They will gain from a more rational regulatory environment, lower interest rates, energy price stability, and a better-educated work force, but their bureaucratic structure will make it difficult for many of them to take full advantage of the rebuilt supply system. Create new technology, and they won't absorb it. Produce new capital equipment, and they won't buy it. Enact investment tax breaks, and they will play paper games. Educate scientists and engineers, and they will chew them up in the bureaucracy. Train skilled workers, and they will waste their talents with outmoded personnel procedures and rigid work practices. Management in stagnant industries is conditioned to resist change induced from either inside or outside. This is one reason why Reagan's tax incentives didn't work.

How do we deal with stagnation per se? To begin, we must quarantine the effects of stagnant companies on the livelier sector by giving them the incentives to moderate their pricing policies. Prices in stagnant industries will not easily fall because wage and salary costs are usually locked in either by custom or by union contracts. With employee compensation representing two-thirds of production costs in many industries, it is not surprising that economists have focused on wage settlements as a major source of price inflation.

Why do union contracts lock in rigid or expanding wage rates? One reason is that the structure of collective bargaining in America treats the gains of workers like territory in a war that has been taken in a major battle costly to both winner and loser. This is especially true if there are prolonged strikes because employees give up real income for a period of time in order to win a higher wage rate. They paid for the gain, and they are understandably reluctant to give it up. Furthermore, contract negotiations typically begin where the previous contract left off, and the rules of the bargaining game do not encourage retreat. Finally, the union leadership in many industries has created rising expectations among individual workers: "We've only begun to get our fair share." Expecting gains, they have made commitments, such as mortgages and educational plans for their children, and it is now very difficult to take a wage cut, even if it would protect the jobs of their fellow workers.

With inflation widespread throughout the economy, wage increases are often the means of just staying even. In the 1970s wage settlements actually lagged behind price increases in many cases.

Unions are reluctant to negotiate contracts that would provide for falling wages, even if this would protect jobs, because they are afraid that they will never see the old wage rates again without another fight. They are also hesitant to make wage concessions to enable companies to lower prices because the company may not lower those prices far enough to increase sales or save jobs and instead may just pocket the difference. They are also reluctant because the worker will carry most of the risk if foreign competition lowers its prices and wipes out the advantage.

One solution offered to encourage both wage and price restraint is a Tax-based Incomes Policy (TIP). This proposal would apply only to large corporations, thereby including many of our stagnant industries. TIP would provide a carrot and a stick. The carrot would be a tax break for employees whose wage increases did not exceed a given guideline, usually tied to the projected inflation rate. The stick would be a surtax on corporate profits if the wage increases exceeded those guidelines. The tax break and the surtax could be graduated to reward and penalize greater or lesser deviations from the norm. The purpose of TIP is to encourage employees to accept a lower wage increase and to give companies the incentive to take a more economically responsible position with their employees during contract negotiations. The underlying assumption behind TIP is that with less "cost-push" from escalating wage settlements, prices will not rise as fast. I would favor the adoption of TIP with one further proviso: Companies would be exempt from the surtax if they adopted approved profit-sharing plans.

I would be willing to recommend this exemption because profit-sharing plans can help overcome the pricing problems of stagnant industries. If a significant share of a worker's annual compensation came from a profit-sharing plan, then companies could experience more flexibility in their labor costs in bad years and could lower prices to encourage sales. They could also afford to keep more workers on the job. All would share misfortune in a downturn, just as they would share prosperity in good times. These arrangements would normally be spelled out in profit-sharing plans negotiated through the collective bargaining process. In expansionary times, with profits high, compensation would be higher, even though sometimes deferred until the year's end. Profit-sharing plans might also include an option for employees to take payment in company stock so that the company would have more resources available for expansion.

With a stake in the company, both workers and management would benefit from increases in productivity and plant efficiency. The growth of industrial democracy, which is still absent in many large, stagnant industries, would be advanced, and with it, the goals of a more cooperative labor-management regime.

TIP would be a strong incentive for companies to adopt profit-sharing plans since the base wage rate would be easy to keep in line with the federal guidelines if profit sharing were an important element of compensation. The exemption from the profit surtax would be another incentive. I would also favor tax advantages for companies and employees that adopted significant profit-sharing plans. Government, after all, has a financial stake in any arrangements which will tend to stabilize employment and create downward price flexibility.

Profit-sharing plans, however, will fail unless the larger relationship between management and labor is relatively harmonious. So, too, will attempts at improving productivity and efficiency in the plant. Business often perceives the ability to modernize as the ability to fire, to close plants, to reassign workers, to eliminate jobs, to establish new work rules, and even, in some cases, to cut pay. Labor sees its interest as preserving jobs and pay scales, minimizing dislocations, maintaining seniority, and protecting its membership's life-style.

Something must be done to bring the two more closely together. Many experts agree that the international competitiveness of American firms can be improved most quickly in the short run by making more efficient use of existing plant and equipment. There is slack to be taken up. Like the use of conservation to alleviate the energy crisis, improved plant efficiency is an obvious first step to solve the productivity problems that plague many stagnant industries today.

There is also wide agreement that the best way to achieve such improvements is through close cooperation between management and production workers on the factory floor. This must be genuine. Many companies have instituted "quality circles" as public relations gimmicks, as means of impressing their boards of directors, or even as devices to pursue antiunion activities. This fools nobody. What we need is a true spirit of cooperative problem solving, whatever it may be called, to make the operation run better. Treating people decently, showing them respect, giving them latitude, and encouraging them to show initiative will pay dividends. There are many industrial success stories to prove this, both here and in Japan.

If a plant is not operating efficiently, management and labor should be able to sit down, identify the problems, discuss them, and work together to find solutions in a more rational and open way. If plants must be closed, adequate advance notice should be given so that workers will have the opportunity to seek relocation, retraining, and new jobs. Help should be given them to do so. If new plants are to be constructed, it would certainly be advantageous to workers and communities if they were located in the areas where old ones have been closed. Although Canada has successfully instituted such arrangements, few of these practices are common in America today. The adversarial relationship precludes them. Problems become structured around bargaining interests.

In many stagnant industries there are sharp vertical antagonisms among labor, management, and government. Simultaneously, because labor is usually organized across the whole industry, and management in stagnant industries often follows other management in lock step, we often have horizontal harmony. The Japanese have precisely the opposite system: vertical harmony and horizontal conflict. This description risks oversimplification, but it is still a useful model. More vertical harmony would enable us to solve some problems in ways beneficial to companies, workers, and the public. Profit sharing will make this possible, but more is needed.

The government should create a series of Industrial Development Councils (IDCs) for major stagnant industries to bring together representatives of management, labor, and government in an effort to establish an ongoing cooperative problem-solving atmosphere which will enable these industries to improve production methods, adopt new technologies, and compete in the global marketplace.

The agenda of these councils would include: improving investment patterns; productivity; ways of lowering prices; foreign competition; plans to increase exports; the economic, environmental, and human impact of plant expansion, relocation, and closing; efficient operating units; the impact of legislation and government policies on particular industries; meeting affirmative action objectives; safety in the workplace; and broad strategic concerns for industry survival and prosperity.

The councils would be working groups, not symbolic gestures. They would have permanent staffs and would serve as a central focus and clearing house for coordinating government policies that affect an industry. One major objective would be to build enough trust between business and labor to encourage closer cooperation in the factory. Although industry-wide strategy would be a central concern, they would emphatically not be agencies to set prices, set market shares, or reduce market competition. To emphasize their importance, they would be located in the executive office of the president.

A major responsibility of the IDCs would be to coordinate governmental and industrial response to economic dislocation caused by automation and by plant closings. We need to supplement countercyclical policies with proregional measures which can provide support to areas that are hard hit and can give them a chance to rebuild their economic bases. To accomplish this task effectively, the IDCs would have a central staff, reporting directly to the president, which would be given broad powers to coordinate the federal government's response to local and regional economic upheavals and disasters. This staff would also work with the staffs of other federal, state, and local agencies to help closed plants reopen under the aegis of local managements and employees. The staff would also coordinate a major effort to encourage other industries to expand in areas vacated by the departing firms. An IDC crisis management team would have a significant budget to institute outreach programs and establish job-retraining centers quickly in areas of major plant closings. Government's response to economic upheaval can therefore be more coordinated, rational, timely, and effective.

Profit-sharing plans, cooperation on the factory floor, and higher-level cooperation in Washington all will help alleviate stagnation if they are properly carried out. But by themselves they are not enough. Stagnant industries need large amounts of capital to adopt new technologies, to restructure their production process, and to maintain a long-term edge over the foreign competition.

In normal times these industries can raise capital from the private banking system, which is more than willing to lend money to the seemingly secure companies that constitute an established industry. However, when stagnation finally catches up, the capital problem suddenly becomes acute, especially if that company faces an advanced-stage market penetration strategy from overseas. Banks are put in an exposed position. The company cannot get financing for desperately needed rejuvenation. Whole industries can stagger because their foreign competition is typically in a better debt position.

This pattern of financial crisis will be repeated at an alarming rate during the coming decade throughout a broad spectrum of American industry. Valid solutions, however, are hard to find. For example, ad hoc congressional bailouts are not good economic policy. I voted against the Chrysler loan even though there was a large Chrysler assembly plant in my district. I am certainly not sorry to see Chrysler make a go of it, but I do not regret this vote because the principle it represented was sound.

Another approach is set forth in the industrial policy plans offered by the Democrats as alternatives to Reaganomics. These plans vary, but most envision a central funding source, such as a national investment bank or a Reconstruction Finance Corporation (RFC) to provide direct loans or grants to companies in targeted industries to give them the capital to survive.

This is an understandable aim, but the approach is wrong. Advocates envision an alliance among government, labor, management, and financial interests to serve the objectives of each. The problem is that these interests may be more committed to preserving the status quo than to shaking up that status quo enough to enable American industry to compete again. The unions may be committed to maintaining current job practices and will drag their heels on productivity. Upper-level management, viewing an RFC as an assured means of avoiding bankruptcy, may have little incentive to improve its existing practices. The banks, which are beginning to realize that their vast holdings of stagnant commercial paper will soon be about as valuable as their Brazilian bonds, are anxious to convert that paper into Treasury promises; but once this has happened, they will have little further interest in industrial rejuvenation. The politicians regard the RFC as a vehicle for avoiding tough choices, not for making them.

To the degree that an industry's problems are truly structural, cooperative efforts to throw money at them will not be an answer, any more than throwing money at the defense budget is an answer to problems of national security. Indeed, a new cash flow may simply provide a temporary rescue for an operation that is globally inefficient. If companies did not use money well when they could borrow it on their own, what guarantee is there that they will do so when that money comes from the government? Vague promises to rejuvenate will be effective neither in restructuring corporate bureaucracies nor in eliminating outmoded employment practices. American industry will remain highly susceptible to overseas market penetration strategies like those discussed in Chapter IV.

The Chrysler rescue, which no doubt will serve both as a model and as a justification for such industrial policies, is not a compelling case. Chrysler was unique. It was given a chance which the ethos of a free market system said it did not deserve. This provided a powerful incentive to succeed. It played David to Goliath in the eyes of the American public. That helped sales. Support for a whole industry would produce neither of these results. Moreover. Chrysler, while regaining competitiveness against American automobile manufacturers, still lags far behind the Japanese in productivity.

Furthermore, if the government is to invest large sums of money in an industry, it will have a great stake in making that investment successful. Therefore, market allocation schemes and de facto price-fixing arrangements are almost inevitable by-products of the Democrats' industrial policies, as they were of similar industrial policy plans in the 1930s. So is protectionism of all sorts. If the government invests $50 billion in Big Steel, will it let South Korea drive that industry to the wall? For that matter, will it let the minimills of North Carolina do so?

Finally, industrial planning, with centralized institutions, will create an enormous concentration of political and economic power. The RFC (or a national investment bank) will have the ability to make or break industries, communities, even whole states and regions. It will be able to direct the ebbs and flows of sectional wealth. If the government is to press hard for new industrial practices, tight government controls over the use of federal funds can easily become tight government controls over an entire industry. Many Democrats have urged the creation of an independent Fed-style board to prevent the intense political bargaining over the spoils that would otherwise occur. Yet ironically, many of the same people are calling to make the Fed itself more responsive to the popular will. You just can't have it both ways.

This is all wrong. Creeping corporatism will exalt stagnation, not cure it. The Democrats are selling us an imported retread that has failed in Europe, where the economies are less lively and innovative than ours, where the current employment record is worse, and where the use of new technology lags far behind. We don't need this. The way to rescue jobs, industries, and the financial system is not to lock in bad investments but to make better ones.

I favor a different approach to meeting the capital needs of stagnant industries, an approach that deals directly with their problems.

One of the most successful strategies for rejuvenating companies is to establish new entrepreneurial divisions which are kept free of the older parts of the company so that they are not contaminated by existing bureaucratic concerns and traditional assumptions. If a company in a stagnant industry is willing to be bold and to set up an entirely new division which will develop and use radically new production methods, fully exploiting state-of-the-art technology, and if it can demonstrate that by doing so, the result will be a product manufactured more efficiently than in other countries, then I would be willing to use public funds on a matching basis to help underwrite such a pilot project. If managers are willing to act like entrepreneurs, then let's give them a chance to do so.

I am not talking here about buying new machinery or developing some new process on a small basis, nor am I talking about lending money in the vague expectation that improvements will be made. I am talking about creating a new manufacturing plant or production unit of the company so that new capital equipment, new production processes, and often new management teams can be creatively employed. One major criterion for supporting such a venture would be the degree to which it could demonstrate potential productivity improvements. A second criterion would be whether or not flexibility would be added to the overall production process. A third would be top management's willingness to keep the operation reasonably separate from the existing company, so it would not be sabotaged from within. A fourth would be the company's ability to demonstrate that it was capable of creating a cooperative industrial relationship with its employees.

I would justify the public-sector involvement on several grounds. First, if the industry is in bad financial shape, the private sector will probably be unwilling to undertake the investment not because it is intrinsically unpromising but because the industry's large debt position makes it more risky. Second, there will be unusually high nonrecurring development costs if the techniques are truly innovative, as they should be. There is a public benefit to developing these techniques which ultimately could have a much wider application. Third, if the effort was successful, the potential result would be a rejuvenated industry with all the larger economic benefits that this would bring.

If the experiment should succeed, the parent company would have a powerful instrument for economic recovery. By demonstrating that its new division was globally competitive, it could convince private lending agencies to advance it capital for expanding and duplicating the new facility. Morale would improve as the industry recognized that it had a chance. The company could redirect its resources away from its antiquated and inflexible production lines to a more promising alternative. With such a base to build on, it could begin to escape the problems caused by stagnation. Liquidating old divisions and building new ones, the company might not remain as large as before, but it would be much sounder and more competitive than before. The overall efficiency of the industry would improve. The company, like its Japanese competition, would face the promising economics of expansion instead of the deadening economics of contraction.

If the experiment should fail, then at least all concerned, government and banks alike, would be better able to judge the viability of the industry. This would reduce the likelihood that the government and the banks would commit vast sums of money to large futile rescue programs as they would with an RFC. If the experiment should succeed, but the company was so shaky financially that it could not exploit the possibilities opened to it, then the new division would be available for sale to other American companies. The industry as a whole would still benefit, and with it, the larger economy.

To implement such pilot projects, I propose the creation of an Industrial Development Authority (IDA), staffed by people with financial, technical, and commercial experience. It would be authorized to make loans, grants, and loan guarantees. Most of these would be on a matching basis so that the company and the private lending institution would each have a significant stake in the venture. Market considerations would thereby be present in the decision-making process. The IDA would typically launch a venture with more than one company in an industry so that competition would be preserved. It would not limit itself to companies which had failed to modernize because that would penalize forward-looking firms that were willing to innovate on their own and that might be the best prospects for even further innovative leaps. The IDA would not be restricted to existing companies in the industry. Occasionally a company from outside the industry might wish to enter. In the name of competition, this also should be permitted. The IDA would have additional funds available for underwriting research in industrial processes.

The IDA would be governed by a board appointed by the president and confirmed by Congress. It would be given an adequate professional staff to evaluate proposals presented to it. Built into its charter would be a set of specific criteria for performing such evaluations. Central to these criteria would be the mandate that proposals should be evaluated on their individual merits, not on the basis of a targeting scheme.

The IDA approach is better than the RFC approach in several ways. It is designed to produce new productive units, not to rescue old companies. It will encourage firms to adopt state-of-the-art processes and abandon incrementalism. It will preserve an element of risk to keep companies on their toes. Each project will be a one-time operation. This will mean that government control of entire corporate structures can be largely avoided, in contrast with the RFC schemes. It will encourage, not bar, the entry of new firms to the industry and the growth of small firms already in the industry. It is not a bailout scheme: Companies must commit some of their own funds, and there is nothing to prevent bankruptcy. It is designed to avoid the need for protectionism, price fixing, and market share allocations which the RFC model will lead to.

The IDA would enable us to launch a broad-based attack on the problems of stagnation, an attack leveled directly at the production process where these problems seem to be. Autos, steel, aluminum, shipbuilding, farm and construction machinery, transportation equipment, and especially capital goods come immediately to mind as industries which could take advantage of an IDA if they wished to do so.

This will be an expensive investment for the government and for the taxpayer. People may object that the availability of billions of dollars in IDA support will divert financial resources to stagnant industries which will not be available to growth industries, but I believe that serious efforts to reduce the federal deficit and stimulate savings can ensure the availability of sufficient capital for both.

Despite the efforts of an IDA, many large companies may still face bankruptcy. The 1978 bankruptcy laws are generally sound and should be left intact. There are, however, still many unresolved problem areas associated with large bankruptcies. When a major corporation fails, assets are sold off to repay creditors, and the company may be completely restructured. This can be a very disruptive process not only for the employees but also for some perfectly competitive functioning divisions of the larger company. To make the process of liquidation more economically rational, capital might be made available to those who wished to purchase and operate separate divisions of large bankrupt corporations: the workers in the plants, divisional management teams, or other companies. Capital might also be available for further investment in these plants. The IDA should be given the lending authority and loan guarantee authority to provide the bankruptcy courts with the option of selling off parts of bankrupt corporations to employees or management teams, with federal loans to such prospective buyers. This would have to be done with realistic objectives, but it could ease some of the problems that bankruptcy creates while preserving viable economic units. It might also be a source of venture capital for workers or managers who wish to purchase and operate plants that are being closed by nonbankrupt concerns.

The profit-sharing incentives, the IDCs, and the IDA will encourage stagnant companies to adopt new technology, raise productivity, improve management practices, and rediscover price flexibility. They will establish a necessary climate of cooperation among business, government, and labor. With new growth industries proliferating and stagnant industries rejuvenating, we should see emerging during the next decade an industrial system composed of lively manufacturing enterprises. These enterprises will differ substantially from the dinosaurs of today. What will they look like? How will they take advantage of the new support system?

To begin, they will be decentralized with many separate divisions or manufacturing units so that they can respond quickly to changing market forces. The managers of these units will be given wide latitude to run their division entrepreneurially and to share in its profits. In some cases these "divisions" will be semi-independent ventures, legally separate corporations, with stock held jointly by employees and the central parent company. Most successful managers will have both business training and technological training.

Each successful division will be market- and customer-oriented and will be very sensitive to considerations of quality, variety, and price. In many cases such companies will take advantage of new direct-to-consumer electronic marketing techniques. They will benefit from the government's efforts to ensure that all companies have access to the emerging markets. Automated inventory control, warehousing, and shipping facilities linked to a revitalized national transportation and communications network will enhance corporate flexibility and national market efficiency.

To avoid the negatives of bureaucratic rigidity, the companies will expand more often by spawning new divisions than by enlarging existing ones. Some of these new divisions may be financed through the IDA. New management teams with new sets of incentives will be recruited from inside and outside each company as the new divisions are created. Some of them will come from the RTIs. In this way companies will build up large cadres of experienced and well-trained managers, kept lively by the competitive position they will enjoy within the firm. Often the divisions will be permitted to compete directly with each other in the marketplace.

These independent divisions will, therefore, have managers trained in the making of direct investments. The company as a whole will be able to draw upon the expertise and capital of the investment banking system to fund expansion without fear of predatory takeover.

The existence of many separate divisions and the custom of creating new ones will enable companies to experiment with innovative production methods and new capital systems. Investments will tend to be original, not incremental or piecemeal. The new tax laws will encourage this. Technology development and absorption will become a primary mission of company divisions. In-house research and development, encouraged by the tax laws, will be given a high priority. The successful company will take full advantage of automated equipment, robotics, computer-based manufacturing systems, and other capital systems developed by the Regional Technology Institutes to provide cost advantages and flexibility. Products will be quickly changed in response to changes in demand.

The heart of a company's competitive position will be its personnel, whose ability to use the new capital systems will determine whether the company succeeds or fails in international competition. These will include trained engineers, designers, programmers, and production specialists whose role will be to marry efficiency with flexibility to produce a competitive quality product. Trained people will come from the rejuvenated university system and the RTIs. In many cases they will be given leave to spend time at the RTIs, studying new production methods and participating in joint development projects.

The successful company will be resource-conscious. Energy savings, materials savings, and the ability to substitute different resources for one another in response to changing market conditions will be built into the planning process. The emphasis on design change and the rapid turnover of capital will make substitutions easier. Federal efforts to break the OPEC cartel and create an open energy market will help.

Employees at all levels, from top management to line workers, will participate in profit-sharing plans, taking advantage of government incentives. Bonuses will probably be calculated on the basis of divisional performance. Everyone will have a stake in productivity and plant efficiency. Industrial cooperation, therefore, will become a meaningful part of the productive process. Whether quality circles, quality of work life programs, stock ownership plans, or just traditional profit-sharing concepts are employed, the successful firm will "share the gains" with its workers.

As our school system is rebuilt, companies will draw upon a much larger pool of employable people who can contribute to a company's competitive position. As the retraining system is developed, firms can be assured that they will find qualified workers for just about any job they create. Successful companies will also invest heavily in their own staff. "Lifetime" employees will probably not be common, but wise corporations which have invested heavily in the skills of their workers will have a strong incentive to retain them.

The central management in efficiently run companies of the future will be smaller. It will have its own collection of in-house consultants (it's cheaper to employ them than to retrain them), troubleshooters, and specialists to provide support to the divisions. It will typically run a research and development operation for the whole company. The central division may also allocate resources among the others and provide central accounting, auditing, and oversight functions. The dynamic firm will not turn these merely into control devices to frustrate the activities of the divisional management. The most successful enterprises will probably be not conglomerates but companies operating in related areas, either vertically or horizontally, so that manufacturing expertise and shared experiences can provide management depth to the company. Ideally the board of directors and stockholders should play an expanded role in monitoring the long-range problems and plans of the firm.

Companies will typically have overseas sales forces and overseas divisions to take advantage of an expanding global marketplace. In successful firms these will be attuned to local marketing conditions and will be peopled with employees who are familiar with the local language and culture. They will keep fully on top of changing market conditions and new technologies developed abroad. Like their stateside counterparts, overseas managers will be customer-oriented and responsive to change. Many products will be made in America to meet overseas specifications and local market requirements.

Enterprises such as these should populate the American economy of the future. This is not a utopian vision. Many companies today have adopted such a decentralized approach to company organization. As other companies do, they will be able to take maximum advantage of the tax laws, invest capital wisely, absorb new technology rapidly, deal with resource crises, and use people to the best advantage of everybody. They will also produce a wide variety of quality products at competitive prices. Change will be their central concern. They will be able to compete with any company in the world on equal terms without subsidies. And they will be the means by which goods are produced in American plants by American workers who will be proud of their products, their jobs, and their contribution to American society. Stagnation will be on the run.

If this should be our vision for the future of American companies, what should be our vision for the future of American labor? Will the industries of tomorrow be unionized? Will the professions?

At first glance the future of American unions seems bleak. Automation will decimate their industrial ranks. Capital mobility will alter their bargaining position. Professionalization of factory jobs will change the profile of their membership. Their natural center of gravity will migrate from industrial unions to public employee unions, white-collar unions, service unions, and professional unions.

The loss of a strong industrial core will fragment labor and reduce its power. For example, striking public employee unions are highly vulnerable to enraged retaliation. The Reagan Right would like nothing more than public employee strikes which would undermine public support for labor and create the political climate to make possible the repeal of key New Deal labor provisions. Moreover, white-collar unions themselves are subject to automation, and many service and professional unions, being diverse in nature, lack the kind of interunion solidarity that gave industrial unions much of their power. The remaining blue-collar unions, largely in industries like transportation and construction that are not easily subject to foreign competition, will retain some clout but will suffer from their brethren's decline.

It is not surprising that faced with these prospects, many unions look to government as the means of preserving the industrial component of their power base. This is why domestic-content legislation and an RFC have strong union support. Still, if organized labor is to be a progressive force in the economy of the future, it cannot remain wedded to policies that will lock in stagnation, raise prices, throw other workers out of jobs, and lower the standard of living. Such a strategy is not a solid foundation for maintaining or building economic, social, or political power.

Besides, it is unclear at present whether union members will benefit as much from an RFC as they expect to. It would not be surprising, in view of current political and economic bargaining positions, to see the interests of management met first, those of finance second, and those of workers third. In cooperative ventures to preserve stagnation, wage rollbacks are a far more likely outcome than productivity increases, even with liberal infusions of federal cash.

Organized labor should have a creative future in America, but to do so, it must join the fight against stagnation. Labor has an interest in keeping large numbers of high-paying jobs in America. It has an interest in the health of the industries in which its members work. It has an interest in improving productivity because if plants cannot compete globally, all jobs will be lost to workers overseas. Labor may also take a tangibly direct interest in the future of industry through stock ownership plans for its membership and direct investment of its pension fund monies. Enlightened unions recognize these interests, but they are wary that management will take advantage of this recognition and try to exploit it.

Even more than these, labor has an interest in the transformation of capital goods into capital systems which require highly skilled people to make them work. As a company becomes a more integrated operating unit, as it becomes more dependent upon the skills of its employees, and as it invests more heavily in them, the nature of the collective bargaining relationship will change. Employees will have more leverage with their employers since they will be more indispensable. Unions of the future will have a much greater interest in the training and skills of their membership.

They will also have a greater stake in not harming the interpersonal relationships upon which the success of their company will depend in the highly competitive global market. Strikes will be fewer, cooperative approaches to solving disputes greater, the division between "management" and "employee" less sharp, and the logic of the old bargaining structure less relevant.

That logic will not disappear altogether. Employee compensation, the terms of profit-sharing plans, employee health and safety, job security, affirmative action, and other terms and conditions of employment will still be objects of collective bargaining. The role of unions in creating and preserving decent working conditions and jobs will remain exceedingly important.

But unions, like management, will have to adapt to new conditions if they are to succeed in the economy of the future. As industry becomes more professionalized, the craft or professional union model may replace the industrial model of union organization. Unions, with government support, may also play an enlarged role in training and retraining people, in motivating them to seek new employment when industries decline, and even in helping them to relocate in new jobs. Unions will also have an increasingly important human function to help give their members more social stability, employment support, and personal services. Unions, by helping the productive process and by helping the people they serve, can enhance their position, carve out new roles for themselves, and play an expanded role in the economy of the future. None of this, however, will happen unless management changes many of its attitudes and stops looking upon union efforts to help industry as signs of weakness to be exploited.

We need a new and cooperative industrial relationship in America. It will require honesty and trust on the part of both labor and management. It will take time to build. It will suffer many setbacks. Profit sharing and government efforts at cooperation on the national level will help. But what will *not* help is a political system that institutionalizes the split between business and labor by incorporating their current antagonism into the party system itself.

The proposals I present constitute a plan to alleviate the supply problems of the American economy. It should be abundantly clear that I do not favor a traditional supply-side economics with its narrow focus on one or two factors of supply and its unwillingness to concede the important role that government can and must play.

Nor do I present an economic "plan" in the traditional meaning of the word. Nevertheless, I am making an appeal to abandon the sophistry that the present market mechanisms represent some magical, self-creating, self-equilibrating power that will rebuild the supply base of the American economy. Markets are tools to be used, not gods to be worshiped. We need positive federal action to ensure that our markets do work and that the economy operates effectively once again.

To succeed, the government must enlist the support of the private sector itself. In my proposals for rebuilding the supply base, I have suggested that we take maximum advantage of private initiative, and I have recommended that we create conditions to encourage the development of new private growth industries which would themselves become a central part of the support system. In all cases, we would still rely heavily upon rejuvenated but currently existing marketing, banking, university, and school systems.

In these examples and others I have also shown how American industry and American finance can take advantage of the economics of expansion, as the Japanese are now doing, to restructure by building anew. In suggesting that we exploit the opportunities of growth, however, I have rejected a mindless commitment to unlimited growth that thoughtful people rightfully condemn. We will grow, but our first priority is replacement growth, not simply additional growth. This means that we should grow in quality and variety as well as in size.

Furthermore, my emphasis is upon decentralized systems. These are absolutely essential if we are to regain our economic flexibility. I envision an entrepreneurial structure with businesses and professions of all sizes and descriptions competing in an open and dynamic national marketplace. I propose many different sources of financing for these enterprises, including a banking system with a wide range of specialties. I propose a diversified system of public and private institutions to create and disseminate knowledge and a diversified funding system for basic research. I propose a variegated approach to the creation of new capital equipment, consisting of many research facilities, public and private, working with many different companies, both existing and newly created. I propose measures to encourage the development of new energy sources to open up the market and make substitution possible. I propose a large system of public and private schools and training centers to give people many opportunities to acquire needed skills. I propose attacking chronic unemployment in a decentralized way by use of the private sector to create thousands of Public Enterprise Corporations. I propose that stagnation itself be attacked on several levels: surrounding it with growth industries, giving companies the financial opportunity to spin off new divisions, and encouraging profit sharing and other cooperative efforts to improve the competitive position of existing companies.

Finally, my strongest emphasis is upon people, be they entrepreneurs, managers, investment bankers, scientists, service professionals, engineers, health workers, technicians, clerical workers, production workers, teachers, or students. Their education, training, motivation, individualism, sense of participation, sense of cooperation, and sense of purpose, their willingness to work, to save, to invest, and to take risks—all these are the most important dimensions of an economics of supply.

The government, too, must play a special role in rebuilding the supply base. In some cases this role will be catalytic; in others, regulative; in yet others, supplementary. In all cases, however, the government should ensure that the system is in place, that it works, that it is dynamic and responsive, that it is basically governed by market mechanisms, and that all enterprises of whatever size or description, from individuals or professional partnerships to giant producers, have an open and unfettered access to the sources of supply.

It is also the responsibility of the government to make sure that the systems themselves work creatively with one another, unsubverted by special interests grounded in one or more of them. The parts of the economy cannot be permitted to obtain special advantage at the expense of the whole. The government must mediate and work to harmonize the interests of entrepreneurs and bankers, manufacturers and oil producers, professionals and workers, so that the larger economic marketplace functions effectively.

There is nothing radically new about this approach. It is just an application of simple and classical principles of economics that have been widely agreed upon for centuries. More important, it is common sense.

Principles such as these can indeed be called an industrial policy, but what I am really presenting is an *economic* policy, one which will give the government a set of objectives and standards which it can use to assess its own actions to make sure that they are consistent and purposeful.

But to carry out these proposals, we need a new political party in America. A party representing the national interest and drawing its power directly from the people. A party, unlike the Democrats and Republicans, that recognizes the need to emphasize all elements of supply. A party beholden neither to business nor to labor. A party willing to demand sacrifice from both. A party committed to bringing both together in a cooperative venture to restore health to the economy.

Such a new party must be forthright and honest in its dealings with all interest groups. It must say just exactly what it will do and what it will not. It must be open about the need for sacrifice in the national interest. It must try to be fair. It must always keep its sights upon the larger objective of a true economic recovery.

The American economy is not a basket case. There are splints to be applied and sutures to be used, but the patient can survive and enjoy a robust life again. We can have an exciting economy with flair and panache to replace the stagnant one we have today. We can have industries and professions that are attractive to creative people. We can have an economy that is consistent with a livable and humane society and supportive of our needs and values. We can have an economy that works.

But we cannot just sit back and expect it to happen. We must work at it. We must earn it. And we must begin to do so now. Indeed, as the letter of one exasperated publisher, whose renewal notice I had ignored, put it: "The end is in sight." I don't believe it is for us yet, but time, like my subscription, is running out.

III

The Demand Side: Inflation, Employment, and Income

12

DEMAND AND
INFLATION

BUILDING a strong support system is a good beginning, but "supply" is not enough. Industry will not buy new capital equipment unless there is a market for its products. Investors will not form Public Enterprise Corporations unless there is business for them to do. People will not retrain unless there are jobs. Management will not restructure if there is no prospect of sales. Without sufficient demand, an economy can operate below or even far below its full potential for sustained periods of time. Without adequate demand, we will not have adequate employment.

The problem is, of course, that policies which encourage demand seem also to encourage inflation. Is it possible to control inflation while providing an effective demand stimulus?

Our recent economic woes have made one fact clear: no single instrument of policy is adequate to create both high levels of employment and low levels of inflation. No matter how hard we try to fine-tune the economy, if we use a single economic instrument, the economy will never land in the desired location. It might be otherwise in a world of perfect information, perfect markets, and complete price flexibility, but such a world does not exist today. We must use a wide range of instruments to attempt a simultaneous control of both unemployment and inflation. It also seems clear that no method or combination of methods will produce fully satisfactory results until the supply base is repaired, but even under today's conditions we can attain substantially better results than we have seen for years if we use our national economic instruments wisely.

I believe that the best strategy is to use monetary restraint, augmented by a tax-based incomes policy, to control inflation; and investment-oriented demand stimulus, augmented by a vigorous export strategy, to provide high levels of employment.

Let us begin with inflation. The evidence of the last few years is that monetary restraint is the single most important means of ensuring price restraint. During the Great Recession, for example, tight money reduced inflation even in the teeth of huge budget deficits. But if monetary policy is the central weapon for controlling inflation, we face some difficult choices. Draconian limits on the expansion of the money supply can raise interest rates, dampen investment, discourage consumer borrowing, and contribute to unemployment and bankruptcy. High interest rates, as I have said, can also boost the value of the dollar, encourage imports, discourage exports, and raise unemployment. In short, tight money can create severe and protracted economic recession.

Furthermore, it is not a balanced remedy. High interest rates hit the credit-sensitive sectors of the economy disproportionately hard because consumers understandably postpone the purchase of a new home, a new car, or a new stove: during the Great Recession, the housing industry collapsed; autos and consumer durables fared almost as poorly. The cost of controlling inflation is very high indeed if we sacrifice a large part of our productive capacity in the process.

Moreover, it is no longer clear that economists know what "money" is. The basic money supply, called M1, effectively consists of actual currency, traveller's checks, and the balances in checking accounts. Traditionally it was a safe assumption that a large growth in M1 would be matched by an equivalent inflation of prices, although after a lag in time. (In other words, double M1 over ten years, and prices would roughly double.)

Today, however, the game has changed. Money market mutual funds with checking privileges, "NOW" accounts, and even super "NOW" accounts have revolutionized the financial world and created new forms of readily available resources. For the purpose of affecting prices, no one knows for sure whether these are "investments" or "money." Even the president of one Federal Reserve Bank recently admitted that he no longer knew what "money" was. In addition, there now appears to be less confidence in the explanations of how short-term swings in the money supply affect prices, economic activity, and interest rates. Also, the rate at which money circulates, its "velocity," can speed up or slow down and confound the experts. During the Great Recession, it slowed down substantially and no one knew with confidence how to discount this when formulating policy. It will take us years to sort things out, but we can't wait years to act.

If we are no longer certain what "money" is, we are also unsure about how to control its growth. Monetarists traditionally believed that such control was well within the power of the Federal Reserve Board. But the size of M1 has fluctuated erratically in recent years despite efforts by the FED to smooth out the swings. In 1981, the FED undershot its targeted growth for M1; in 1982, it overshot it by a wide margin.

I do not wish to overstate the case: in large measure, it can be ascertained whether money is loose or tight and, in large measure, the supply of money can be controlled. What cannot be done is to use the money supply by itself as an exact instrument of policy to fine-tune the economy painlessly and with precision.

How, then, do we fight inflation? First, despite its many imperfections, monetary restraint remains a central weapon. It need not be Draconian, especially if a condition of price stability has already been established, but the growth of the money supply must be relatively steady and must approximate the growth of the economy. Better instruments of measurement and control are needed to enable the FED to achieve this goal, but the lack of precise tools cannot be an excuse for massive expansion or contraction.

If we are to mitigate the harmful side effects that tight money brings, however, we need additional tools to fight inflation. One of them is TIP, outlined in the previous chapter, which discourages price increases throughout a large and central sector of the economy. A TIP program will make it possible for the FED to employ less Draconian monetary policies without risking inflation. In this way, we can ease the price and credit pressures on the flexible sectors of the economy, reduce bankruptcies, alleviate the unemployment problem, and encourage interest rates to fall. TIP can smooth out the effects of monetary policy, compensate for some of its imprecision, alleviate inflationary expectations, and add to a climate of stability.

Inflation fighting measures can be even more effective if greater price flexibility is reintroduced to the supply base of the economy. With more growth industries, lower energy costs, extended profit-sharing plans, and a lively industrial sector, our economy will come to resemble a classical marketplace where aggregate policies take effect quickly and evenly. When this happens, monetary restraint will have a much less negative impact on the economy than it now does and the need for TIP will lessen.

Since we must operate within the context of monetary restraint to control inflation, fiscal policy must respect this limiting condition. We must recognize that large deficits will not generate fresh economic activity if the FED pursues a strategy of relatively tight money. Government borrowing to finance either a tax cut or a spending program merely transfers money from one economic use to another and puts pressures on the credit market.

Large deficits under these conditions can have enormously negative side effects. In the short run these include high interest rates, less private-sector borrowing, lower rates of national investment, less consumer spending, an overvalued dollar, and a bigger trade deficit. As in the Great Recession, these can outweigh any stimulative effect of the deficit and contribute to unemployment.

Moreover, big budget deficits pose an enormous long-term threat to the economy. They can spiral out of control, they can become so large that they absorb most of the new money available for credit, they can push interest rates sky high, explode the size of the national debt, raise substantially the percentage of federal revenues needed to finance that debt, and present the policymaker with the deadly alternatives of economy-shattering tax increases or double digit inflation designed to keep one jump ahead of escalating interest rates. Also, in an economy starved for credit and in danger of financial collapse, the need to increase the money supply rapidly to infuse new reserves into the banking system inevitably takes priority over inflation fighting. When this happens, deficits do indeed become inflationary. If the economy should enter another sharp recession in the next few years at a time when the deficit is in the two to three hundred billion dollar range, the country could come uncomfortably close to an uncontrollable deficit spiral.

Reagan's deficit, created to pay for consumption-oriented defense spending and consumption-oriented tax cuts, is especially pernicious because its accompanying high interest rates, low savings rates, and probable inflationary follow-through discourage real investment in economic growth at the same time that the deficit itself is heaping a trillion dollars of new debt on the economy. Thus we are experiencing the worst of both worlds. Generating debt while retarding investment is catastrophic. We are building towards a financial and economic disaster of the first magnitude because we are creating an enormous claim on future savings which, in the absence of growth-stimulating investment, can only be met with inflation or much higher taxes.

Deficits accommodated by monetary expansion have not caused financial catastrophe in the past because the accompanying inflation reduced the significance of the accumulated debt. Inflation helps debtors and the government is a debtor. Inflation, however, has been a form of hidden taxation by which the government reduced its financial obligations and the impact of its borrowings.

It is still possible for the government to use inflation as a form of taxation, but it will be harder for it to do so in the future than it was in the past. The financial markets are well aware of the inflation game. They are no longer willing to pay the inflation tax. Today, serious sustained monetary expansion will generate high interest rates in anticipation of an inflationary follow-through. These higher interest rates, in turn, will severely complicate the government's ability to resolve its financial problems through inflation. Rapid monetary expansion, therefore, is becoming a much less potent remedy for alleviating the financial impact of large deficits. People used to say that the government never had to worry about the debt because we could always "print the money" to pay for it. This is true in a literal sense, but the cost of printing that money is now double-digit inflation, double-digit interest rates, and renewed financial crisis. This is what the "Rational Expectations" school of economics is telling us, and in this respect they are right.

If significant deficits fully accommodated by expanding the money supply are inflationary and if significant deficits accompanied by monetary restraint crowd out private borrowing, discourage investment, and slacken demand, does this mean that we must abandon the deficit altogether as an instrument of demand stimulus? Not necessarily. But it does mean that the government must have a much more sophisticated understanding of the impact its borrowing has on the credit markets and on the economy as a whole.

There are at least two conditions under which government borrowings generally create no long-term problems: first, when the current deficit is due to an economic downturn and is matched by a surplus in prosperous times, and, second, when money is borrowed to make investments which will earn a real return to the Treasury, usually in the form of increased tax receipts, over a period of time.

The private sector provides an illustration of this second principle at work. Many corporations continually add to their indebtedness. Their surroundings are used largely to finance investments. As long as the company makes profitable investments, it can continue to grow and continue to borrow. It can get into trouble if it makes bad investments or if its debt load is too high when the market turns down, but companies can prosper and avoid bankruptcy if they manage their borrowings and investments wisely.

The government can also borrow and invest its borrowings in the economy. If it makes good investments and the economy expands, the government over the years will earn a return on its investment in the form of higher tax revenues. If, however, the government borrows and does not spend its borrowings wisely, and if the economy does not expand, then the government may not earn an adequate return. It will be left with a legacy of debt which it will have to finance through increased taxation or which it will have to "reduce" through inflation. In either case, its own economic effectiveness will be proportionately impaired.

The government, therefore, can use deficit spending to stimulate economic activity. But it cannot do so unconditionally. Its borrowings must either be matched by a later surplus in true anticyclical fashion, or they must be used for genuine investment purposes which will contribute to an overall long-term expansion of economic activity and eventually to increased tax revenues. In this sense, the government, too, must learn how to invest. If it does, we can still run deficits to stimulate demand, just as long as we pay careful attention to the purpose for which the expenditure is made.

For too long we have taken a "green eyeshade" approach to government spending, not recognizing that some expenditures represent an investment in our future, while others do not. To promote long-term growth, the government should borrow with an eye to investment, not consumption. This means that expenditures for consumption as a general rule should be covered by taxes, not borrowings, whenever possible. This is not the case at present with the Reagan deficits; by no stretch of David Stockman's imagination is the government today making real investments at the rate of $200 billion per year.

It is here that I part company with the Keynesians. I fully agree that expenditures under certain conditions can have a stimulative effect on the economy. And it would be utter folly to ignore this fact which has been demonstrated by experience. But I do not believe that we can continue to run deficits designed primarily to stimulate consumption, as the Keynesians and Reaganites would have us do. Deficits should only be run for investment purposes.

Moreover, borrowing to spend for investment purposes in times of economic recession is still a form of demand stimulus, potentially just as potent as borrowing to spend for consumption. In the short term, the effects may be similar, but in the long term they are decidedly different. For example, if the government builds a highway system, the money spent will contribute immediately to stimulating demand in the short run since contractors will be hired, cement and asphalt bought, and workers paid. But the highway system, if well conceived, will also contribute to the growth of national economic activity. As it does, the government will earn a return through increased tax receipts over the long run even if it does not put a toll booth on the highway.

Alternatively, if the government spends that same money to build an aircraft carrier, this expenditure will also contribute to short-term demand. The long-term result, however, will be different. The program may increase our ability to build warships in the future, but this new capacity will not contribute to our overall economic growth the way building a needed highway does. We may have to have the ships to defend ourselves, but from an economic standpoint, they are consumption items. The government earns no return on them.

As another example, if the government borrows money to finance a personal income tax cut, it is pursuing a policy of consumption-oriented, not investment-oriented, demand stimulus, supply-side arguments notwithstanding, as the Great Recession demonstrated when the level of savings and investment fell substantially.

Shifting spending for demand stimulus from a consumption orientation to an investment orientation can be done. The government has many opportunities for investment. There are traditional "infrastructural" areas where new construction or repairs to existing facilities will produce an economic benefit or forestall an economic loss. There is also the larger economic support system itself which should now be treated as an opportunity for this type of investment. Education, incentives to entrepreneurship, the facilities for scientific and technological research, energy savings, health and nutrition, and community projects to build local economies are all potential areas for investment. With imagination, many can be used anticyclically.

Furthermore, the objective of rebuilding the economic support system provides the opportunities for real government investments which will benefit the entire range of low, middle, and high income people. In this way we can creatively combine the principles of both genuine supply-side and intelligent demand-side economics to achieve the objective of long-term growth.

In spending for such projects, however, the government must avoid phony investments. If we build highways that are not needed, if we spend money on education and training programs that don't improve people's skills, or if we just throw away money on community boondoggles, then we are back to spending money for consumption, not investment. Making wise decisions about public expenditures is not an easy task, but it is a necessary one if we are to engage in demand stimulus which is consistent with monetary restraint and long-term fiscal probity.

Changing our approach from consumption-oriented demand stimulus to investment-oriented demand stimulus should be a policy that reflects a larger national investment strategy designed to stimulate long-term economic growth. But partisan politics today bars the adoption of such a strategy.

Republican conservatives are not interested in a national investment strategy. They reject entirely the role of government in this area. In their philosophy, the government consumes; it does not invest. Its only role is to foster a climate that encourages private investment.

The basic problem with this approach is that government policies do have a fearsome impact upon national investment patterns, private as well as public, qualitative as well as quantitative. This impact can be neither eliminated nor ignored. The interest rate, the inflation rate, and the savings rate are all shaped by government policy. Each affects the level and nature of investment.

Moreover, investment must come from savings, and the way savings are used is shaped by government action: are savings turned back into consumption through the intermediation of a government deficit to finance a personal tax cut? Are savings sent overseas to pay for imported oil through complex financial arrangements because the government is unwilling to enact tough energy conservation measures? Are savings used for speculation in land, currency, and commodities because the government has created inflationary expectations? Or are savings used to rebuild the productive capacity of the country? It really does make a difference. Equally important, Republicans are very reluctant to admit that public investments of the "infrastructural" variety can contribute to long-term economic expansion.

The Democrats, alternatively, understand that government plays a major role in national investment. But to them that role is secondary. Following Keynesian theory, they assume that if we stimulate consumption, investment will follow. But stimulating investment indirectly through stimulating consumption can be inflationary and therefore self-defeating when it comes to stimulating investment. This is especially true when there is widespread industrial stagnation. Also, there can be times, such as now, when fiscal policies designed to stimulate consumption can themselves directly retard investment through high interest rates.

We need new approaches. We especially need a new recognition that quality investments play a central role in the American economy, that they contribute to long-term growth, that they can include public-sector investments, and that the making of public-sector investments has a demand-side as well as a supply-side impact on our economy.

A national investment strategy should have several aims. These include price stability, low interest rates, a high savings rate, a rebuilt supply base, and government spending patterns consistent with a sustained high rate of national investment when both private and public sectors are considered. The monetary and fiscal policies set forth above are consistent with these aims. So is the proposed pattern of taxing and spending set forth below.

A national investment policy must also provide guidelines for the policymaker that define the relationship between private-sector and public-sector borrowing. The government must recognize that in times of monetary restraint borrowings must come from new savings and savings are a scarce resource. Government borrowing, therefore, comes at the expense of private-sector investments and credit-based consumption. Borrowing by the government for the purpose of investment only makes sense in the context of a national investment strategy if the government makes better use of the money than the private sector will. Responsible policy makers should recognize that this is certainly not always the case. If, however, private-sector investments fall, as they do in times of recession, then it makes sense for the government to increase its own investment spending so that demand is stimulated and the total level of national investment spending remains relatively high.

A national investment strategy, therefore, must pay close attention to the relationship between public-sector borrowing and private-sector borrowing as both affect the credit markets. The basic economic guideline that government should use is the rate of return on investments, both public and private. When the private rate is high and the public is low, then the government should cut back on or eliminate its borrowing. When the situation is reversed, then it may make sense for the government to borrow, if necessary, to maintain a high level of national real investment and aggregate demand. But the net increase in expenditures should be used for projects designed to enhance long-term prospects for increased economic activity.

I have set forth the conditions under which I believe it is possible to run deficits without ill effects, but my fiscal preference always has been for taxes instead of borrowing, even to cover investment expenditures. This is especially true in times of expansion. If we can reduce our level of borrowing over the next decade and finance government expenditures from taxation, then the country will find itself on a much firmer fiscal foundation.

These policies, if pursued responsibly, prudently, and predictably, will reestablish a climate of confidence in the economic probity of the federal government. We must end the uncertainties associated with the policies of the last decade and a half. Fear, based on uncertainty, has become a major impediment to sustained economic recovery. We must convince both business and consumers that government is committed to stable, non-inflationary growth. Government should become a steady, predictable point of reference for the entire economy.

In more specific terms, how, then, should we proceed? First, we must repeal Reaganomics and bring the deficit under control. Second, as we do so, we must shift the nature of federal spending towards investment outlays to the greatest extent possible. Third, we must put in place new fiscal practices and new instruments of policy to make these changes possible.

There are no easy ways to reduce the deficit, only hard choices. We must raise taxes as well as control spending.

First, we must take swift action to prevent the "indexing" of tax brackets that will take effect in 1985, although we should continue to index the standard deduction. Indexing is intended to stop the inflation-induced "bracket creep" that automatically increases the effective rate of taxation. I was co-sponsor of an indexing proposal in the 95th Congress, but indexing is not a fiscally sound notion when we run huge budget deficits. This action alone can save $40 billion annually by fiscal 1988.

Second, we must raise energy taxes. In addition to the oil import fee discussed in Chapter 9, there should be a windfall profits tax to accompany gas deregulation. Between the two, we can raise another $25 billion annually.

Third, we must close some tax loopholes. Since 1967, "tax expenditures," as loopholes are now called, have risen from $36 billion to well over $300 billion and the tax base has been seriously eroded. For example, there is no reason why we should subsidize the purchase of a second home. Limiting the deduction of mortgage interest payments to $5,000 can save as much as seven or eight billion dollars annually. Terminating, modifying, or phasing out the deductibility of consumer interest payments can save another seven or eight billion. Modifying the tax treatment of foreign oil and gas income and repealing the expensing of intangible oil and gas drilling costs can together save $10 billion annually. A tax on large corporate mergers can net $5 billion. A series of smaller loopholes can be closed to save us another $15 billion. Maintaining some current excise taxes scheduled for reduction in 1986 will net another $5 billion.

Together, these new taxes will raise additional revenues of about $115 billion on an annual basis by fiscal 1988. (See Table I on page 221.) This is a start towards closing a deficit gap of about $267 billion projected by the administration for that year in early 1983.

On the spending side, it is unrealistic to believe that substantially greater cuts can be made in the "discretionary" domestic budget. At the present time discretionary domestic spending accounts for only 14% of the federal budget. While we must seek economies here as well, we must recognize that such economies will have only a small impact on the federal deficit. In many cases, the cuts have already been too severe and should be reversed.

Beyond discretionary domestic spending, we must look at the "entitlement" programs and the defense budget. The largest entitlement expenditure is Social Security, currently approaching $250 billion annually if Medicare payments are included. The Social Security system has been running a large annual deficit. In 1983, Congress, adopting most of the recommendations of the Greenspan Commission, put the system on an improved footing. To do so, they raised payroll taxes, modified the cost of living adjustments, raised the retirement age early in the next century, and made social security income taxable for people above a certain income level. These provisions will save an additional $15 billion annually by 1988.

Medicare is a much more difficult problem. Its costs have been rising by over fourteen percent a year. In 1983, the program will cost more than $53 billion. The financial problems of Medicare go far beyond the program itself; they relate to the still escalating costs of medical care in general.

Congress has enacted a prospective reimbursement program to standardize somewhat the payments for specific medical problems. This may save some money. Proposals to increase deductibles in certain circumstances and to encourage co-insurance can save more money. But there are no easy answers. Those who look for quick savings in this program either fail to understand the problem or are indifferent to the health needs of the millions of elderly Americans who depend on Medicare to help pay their medical bills.

This program should not be impaired. However, I do believe it is inevitable that above a certain income level Medicare payments will have to be means-tested. This principle, which is applied to programs for the poor, should be extended to programs which aid middle-class and upper-income beneficiaries as well.

There is little room for savings in other entitlement areas. Nutrition programs such as school lunches and food stamps have already undergone sharp cutbacks; so, too, have income support programs such as Aid to Families with Dependent Children and Supplemental Security Income for the aged. We should continue efforts to root out the fraudulent abuse of these programs, but let us not deceive ourselves about the potential for large savings. Instead, some of the funds cut by Reagan should be restored.

That leaves us with the defense budget. I am bothered by the inflexibility of an approach that ties us to a percentage increase in this budget year after year. If new thinking can be infused into national defense policy making, then these percentages will become meaningless. As I argue in Chapter XVI, the Reagan buildup is clearly excessive, and many billions can be saved. For example, if we increased our military spending by 3 percent annually in real terms, instead of Reagan's initially projected 9 percent, we would save $47 billion annually by 1988. If we kept military spending constant in real terms, the savings would be close to $60 billion. Actually, I believe we can and must pursue the goal of a substantial reduction in the projected level of outlays.

The tax increases, the savings from entitlements, and a modest control of defense expenditures can close the deficit gap by at least $177 billion annually by fiscal 1988. These reductions will allow us to save another $33 billion in interest annually by fiscal 1988 for a total of $210 billion. Keeping defense costs constant in real terms would save (including interest) at least $225 billion annually by fiscal 1988 and eliminate all but $42 billion of the $267 billion deficit otherwise projected by the Reagan Administration.

I have, however, set forth a program for economic development that itself could cost as much as $42 billion annually to implement. (See Table II.) I believe that the expenditures and additional tax cuts contained in this program are essential if we are to regain our economic competitiveness. Although this program cuts the deficit much more than either the Democratic or the Republican budget proposals do, it still leaves a projected gap of about $85 to $100 billion.

This, however, is a very conservative estimate. It does not include revenue projections that assume improved economic activity generated by the program. These should exceed $25 billion. If it is necessary, and if economic conditions warrant it, I would seek a further combination of new taxes and budget cuts to reduce the deficit by an additional $25 billion to bring it safely below the $50 billion level. I would like to see this even lower, but it is asking too much of the economy to do this in five years. True balance, again if circumstances allowed it, could be achieved two or three years later. The fact that it will take as many as eight years to bring the budget into balance without severe economic shocks is a stark reminder of how far we have strayed from the path of fiscal responsibility under Reagan.

Bringing the deficit under control in this way will release more than $150 billion annually to the credit markets. Of this, about $50 billion would become available to finance infrastructural expenditures (as described in the next chapter); the balance would be available for private-sector borrowing. This will provide the most effective means of generating demand. The large infusion of credit should reduce interest rates, encourage consumer borrowing, stimulate business investment, lower unemployment, and contribute to long-term growth. It should also restore confidence in the fiscal integrity of the government.

Furthermore, this pattern of taxing and spending will reestablish the principle that both the civilian and military sectors must share the burdens of fiscal responsibility. It will lessen the division opening up between the haves and the have-nots. It will ease inflationary pressures and enable the economy to embark on a strong sustained recovery.

As we bring the budget into balance, we must simultaneously shift the spending patterns of government toward investment outlays. Reversing the Reagan emphasis on military spending and enacting the spending program that I have set forth (which is summarized in Table II), will accomplish this objective. Needless to say, the government will still be making large transfer payments for consumption purposes, but investment spending will expand as a percentage of total federal outlays.

To succeed in making these policies work, however, we need to make some major changes in the way the government defines and controls fiscal policy.

First, we need a two-year budget cycle to make public and private investment planning more rational and to eliminate the election-year politics that dominates the budget every other year. The newly-elected Congress should pass a budget resolution by the end of May and a final budget by the end of September, which will go into effect on October 1 and last for two years. Changes in this budget should require a three-fifths vote of both Houses, so there is a strong incentive not to go through the whole process again with supplemental appropriations the following year.

In passing a two-year budget, Congress could also give to the president the authority to raise or lower certain categories of taxes and certain categories of expenditures by a specified percentage under clearly specified conditions (so that predictability and accountability are preserved). These powers would enable the government to respond to new or unforeseen economic conditions over the two-year budget cycle.

We must also redesign the budget itself. For some years, many economists, including Hendrik Houthakker and Albert Sommers, have been urging Congress to adopt a separate current accounts budget and a "capital" budget that would distinguish between those programs or initiatives that merely transfer wealth or consume tax dollars and those that have some form of return to government or society as a whole. I would urge the creation of a budgeting procedure in which the funding sources for consumption and investment each would be kept distinct, with the current accounts budget normally being funded exclusively through taxation. This budget would include all transfer payments and the operating expenses of the government. Tax revenues would first be assigned to the current accounts budget. The surplus would be transferred to the capital account. In normal times, therefore, many or all capital expenditures would also be funded through taxation.

In times of severe economic downturns, when expenditures for transfer payments in the current accounts budget increase, less money would be available for the capital budget from general revenues. Borrowings would therefore be expected to increase. The increase in borrowings, however, under this arrangement would have to be spent for real investments through the capital budget process. This should impose a greater fiscal discipline on the system because the government's deficit would always be matched by a larger level of net real investment. With economic recovery and with fiscal probity, it can even be possible for all capital expenditures to be made out of current revenues. I favor this, although it will take several years to reach that condition. Pay-as-you-go government in times of economic prosperity adds to financial stability.

Capital budgeting, to be effective, however, must be honest. Phony "investments" with no real payback are forms of consumption and should not be counted in a capital budget. This is not, therefore, an easy suggestion to institute or to police. To make it work, I would create a special project evaluation division in the Office of Management and Budget staffed by professional investment analysts to examine each proposed capital expenditure and to evaluate its potential return. OMB should have an expanded auditing capability to provide an ongoing assessment of a project's worth and the way it is being managed.

With this budgeting procedure, the OMB could more easily assess the impact of federal borrowings on the entire investment pattern of the country in a given year. In times of extensive private-sector investments, government ideally would ease back on its own investments to keep interest rates under control. When real investment by the private sector is slack, however, then government can plan to increase its own investments. In this way, national real investments overall would not plummet as they did during the Great Recession.

These measures would enable the government to establish more direct control over taxing and spending and would enable Congress and the White House to formulate fiscal policies which would contribute to a more coherent national investment strategy for the economic redevelopment of America.

Within this larger context of a national investment strategy, we should then proceed to devise those instruments of investment-oriented demand stimulus that can be used in times of economic downturns.

First, I recommend that we create two anticyclical trust funds, one a Community Transportation Trust Fund, the other a Community Capital Trust Fund, to rebuild our "infrastructure" of transportation facilities, roads, bridges, sewers, and water mains, an objective set forth in my 1980 campaign platform. These funds would receive revenues from a dedicated source, such as the energy taxes proposed above, and could therefore obtain a predictable amount of revenue from year to year. The president would have the authority under certain specified conditions (such as an unemployment rate above 8 percent or below 6 percent) to raise or lower the amount spent by the fund in that given year. Depending on the nature of the fund, these monies could be used for leverage, as discussed in Chapter 13. In times of prosperity, some of the money would be banked. In times of downturn, it would be spent. The fund, in conditions of extreme downturn, could borrow against future revenues, but this borrowing would have to be retired.

The OMB should be given the responsibility to evaluate the potential impact of each project on long-term economic growth and development. Congress should authorize programs in advance (such as public works projects) so that they could be let out when the time warranted. A steady backlog of projects would be maintained so that in times of downturn, contracts could be quickly let out under conditions that would ensure their rapid implementation. Accelerated public works programs have not been well handled in the past, but there is no excuse for this. Such programs can be made to work by competent administrators backed up by Congressional authority.

I would also use the government's enormous purchasing capacity to stimulate demand in truly serious recessions. This would not be an investment measure, but a true "countercyclical" stabilizing measure. The government could, for example, stockpile strategic materials in times of sharp downturn and gradually sell them off in times of prosperity. The Strategic and Critical Materials Stockpiling Act provides that materials be stockpiled in the interest of national defense, but it does not permit additional stockpiling for countercyclical purposes. It should. A government policy of buying at a low price and selling again at a somewhat higher price could cover the costs of borrowing, and moderate future prices.

The arguments for stockpiling can also be applied to the timing of government purchases. During slack economic times, it may be appropriate for the Defense Department to accelerate its purchase of trucks and jeeps, of spare parts, small arms, and even uniforms, as long as such purchases are appropriately reduced in more prosperous times. To do this effectively, however, a list of appropriate purchases must be approved in advance, and the standby authority provided.

I would institute a series of anticyclical "buy-down" provisions for reducing the mortgage rate on the purchase of houses and possibly even automobiles. These programs would, in effect, be an interest rate subsidy to stimulate large expenditures by consumers. The Great Recession confirmed that such purchases were interest-sensitive. Buy-down procedures can be expensive and they can leave the government with debt obligations until interest rates fall by as much as the amount of the buy-down, but they can be very powerful tools of demand stimulus since they lever private money into the market. Nineteen eighty-two would have been an excellent year to have put such programs into operation.

We should use the vehicle of sheltered savings to influence private decisions to spend or consume. In Chapter 7, I recommended that individuals be permitted to shelter a greater percentage of their income in accounts (such as an IRA account) which had no restrictions of time.

These funds should be established so that the government could vary the percentage of income that could be sheltered each year.

219

In expansionary times, that ceiling could be set quite high to encourage savings. In periods of recession, it could be lowered to encourage consumption. This would give to the government a tool to encourage a higher or a lower rate of savings as an instrument to fight recessions, dampen booms, or stimulate long-term growth.

These instruments for stimulating demand will work. They are consistent with monetary restraint. They are noninflationary. They are generally investment-oriented. They will provide good remedies for combatting short-term downswings in the business cycle. They can be effectively implemented, often in cooperation with state and local governments. They are not token measures. The two trust funds alone could be used to lever a combined total of $50 billion annually in federal, state, local, and private capital expenditures, as discussed in the following chapter.

By themselves, however, these measures may prove unequal to the enormous task of creating an inflation-free full-employment economy. Employment is a complex issue that requires attention at all levels of government. States and communities must play a supporting role both in enhancing the quality of demand-stimulating investments and in helping to expand actual employment opportunities. "Subnational government," as it is called, must have a larger role in the economy of the future than it has had in the economy of the past.

Furthermore, demand stimulus must be seen in the context of our overseas trade balance. Unless we position ourselves more adroitly in the world economy of the future, domestic attempts to create a full-employment economy will fail. We must become a much more export-oriented country if we wish to maintain high levels of demand and of employment in the decades ahead.

If we are to pursue a comprehensive economic policy, employing all instruments of demand stimulus, we need a party system that will allow us to do so. We need a party system that will emphasize national unity, not disunity. We can no longer oscillate back and forth between policies that stimulate employment and those that control inflation when clearly we need a broad-based attack on both.

We need a new political party. A party of the center that is willing to get tough on the economy. A party willing to emphasize investment over consumption.

Equally, we need a party capable of streamlining government to make it work properly. A party that can create and manage the agencies that government needs to make a coordinated economic policy succeed. A party that can attract the best people to government. Most of all, a party capable of convincing the country that it is willing to put aside the narrow concerns of partisanship and lead.

Table I
Tax Increases:
Revenues Produced by 1988*
(in $ billions)

Repeal of Indexing		$ 40.0
Energy Taxes		25.0
Closing of Tax Loopholes		
Limit Mortgage Deduction	$ 7.5	
Remove Deductibility of		
Consumer Interest Payments	7.5	
Modify Tax Treatment of		
Foreign Oil/Gas Income *and*		
Repeal Expensing of Intangible		
Drilling Costs	10.0	
Other Smaller Reforms	15.0	
	$ 40.0	40.0
Maintenance of Current Excise Taxes		
Scheduled for Repeal		5.0
Tax on Large Corporate Mergers		5.0
		$ 115.0

* On an annual basis.

Table II
Expenditure Increases over Projected FY 1988 Levels
(in $ billions)

Additional Tax Relief	$ 1.5
Local Development Banks (seed money)	1.5*
Higher Education	1.0*
Regional Technology Institutes	2.5*
Space	1.5
National Science Foundation	1.0
Educational System, Health, and Retraining	4.0*
Public Enterprise Corporations	4.5
Profit-sharing Incentives	1.0
IDA	4.0
Transportation Trust Fund	5.5†
Community Capital Fund	8.0†
Welfare Adjustments	1.0
Housing Buy-downs	1.0
Foreign Assistance	3.0
	$ 41.5

* To be matched by states and localities.
† To be used in part to lever state, local, and private capital expenditures.

13

THE CONTRIBUTION
OF CREATIVE
FEDERALISM

O u r problems of economic development and job creation
are so great that the federal government needs state and local
assistance to solve them. But states and communities today are in
no position to give that assistance. To be sure, states and localities
are concerned with economic affairs. Many have industrial or
economic development commissions. But these are designed primarily to attract industry, not to create it. States and localities
"develop" their economies most often by cutting taxes, subsidizing
services, and wheedling businesses away from other areas with
packages of expensive incentives. This beggar-thy-neighbor policy
may help the local economy, but it does little to improve the
national economy. It is negative competition.

Some communities are in a stronger position than others to attract industry. When cities grow and their revenue bases expand,
they can easily finance development, improve services, and attract
business. If growth stops, however, revenues fall, services de-

teriorate, tax rates increase, and business (together with people) departs for greener pastures. The community spirals downward. This well-understood pattern of urban decay is even more difficult to reverse than the analogous decline of stagnant industries when they are under advanced attack by overseas rivals. It puts a community at a competitive disadvantage because growing communities can offer better services per tax dollar.

Community economic stagnation is widespread. Many of our major cities were built more than a century ago, when people left the farms to enter the factories. Expanding tax bases enabled them to construct the roads, bridges, sewers, and water systems which they still use. Public transit was built by the private sector, often with government help. It also relied upon an economics of projected expansion.

Contraction in many urban areas began after the Second World War, when members of the middle class bought automobiles, deserted the cities, and built the suburbs, which could then use *their* expanding tax bases to provide better services than the inner cities did. Contraction continued in northern cities during the 1960s, when cheaper labor and warmer climates began to attract capital, corporate headquarters, and skilled people to the Sun Belt cities of the South and Southwest, which in turn experienced a period of rapid expansion. Also during the 1960s, a steady stream of unskilled labor continued to migrate to the urban centers of the Northeast and Midwest in search of unskilled jobs.

In the absence of a coherent national welfare policy, many northern and midwestern states established a social service network to respond to the needs of the poor and unemployed. With a resulting higher demand for tax revenues, the cities were squeezed. They began to defer upkeep and maintenance on their physical capital plants while they diverted resources to more immediate human needs. By 1980 investment in public works accounted for about 40 percent less of the GNP than it did in 1960. Many cities still suffer from large social service burdens, deteriorating capital plants, and abysmal prospects for revenue growth. Their poor competitive situation means there is little chance to pull themselves out of stagnation without help. And without such help they are in no position to make a major contribution to national economic development.

We need to reverse this condition of negative competition between states and communities and replace it with a condition of positive competition, in which state and local efforts to attract industry contribute to the growth of the overall economy. To succeed, we need some new thinking about federalism.

Politicians, when they wish to sound reflective, enjoy talking about federalism. I have done so myself. Conservative politicians, in pursuit of federalist ideals, continually talk about returning power to the states and localities. What they usually mean by *power* is "responsibility." And this means "burdens."

Ronald Reagan's New Federalism was designed to increase, not to alleviate, negative competition between states. He proposed to return power to the states by throwing burdens at them. Given tax competition between the states, the erosion of their tax bases, and their current fiscal health, many states and communities had to abandon or neglect their new responsibilities. Reagan proposed to transfer revenue sources to the states, but even so, negative local and interstate tax competition would still tend to push support for many vital programs downward. This may make sense if the primary objective is to reduce or liquidate the programs, but it hardly empowers state and local governments in any sense of the word.

We need to try something different. We need a creative approach to federalism. First, the federal government should assume a more direct responsibility for transfer payments, such as health and welfare support, either by eliminating the inequities between the state systems or by eventually taking over the payments completely. This is especially needed for Medicaid. Second, the federal government should assume a larger responsibility for rebuilding the existing community support system of roads, bridges, sewers, and transportation networks. As in the case of health and welfare, this would reduce the condition of negative competition between states and communities. Thirdly, the states should be encouraged by the federal government to play an expanded role in genuine economic development—in rebuilding the marketing facilities of the inner cities, in creating local development banks, in building Regional Technology Institutes, in expanding and redirecting the library systems, in developing energy programs, in rebuilding the school systems, in creating retraining facilities, in working with small but important older industries, and in contributing to the expansion of the national economy.

In all these cases, states and communities should expect to receive the support of the federal government, but the drive and competitive dynamism of state and local governments must play the major role. Local businesses, local labor officials, and local politicians will have a very strong interest in the success of these programs. They will form the basis of a powerful constituency to make them work. Everyone will compete in encouraging business, not just pirating it away.

The first of these proposals, federal responsibility for transfer payments, would constitute a major shift in federal-state relations. Since our first priority at the moment is to regain control of the federal budget, we must move gradually in this area. As a first step, we should set federal standards for state transfer payments, adjusted to match local conditions, that would reduce the negative competition between states and regions. Then, gradually, we should begin to federalize the transfer payment functions of the states, program by program. These would include Medicaid, unemployment compensation, and many existing welfare programs. This would take more than a decade to complete and would eventually create the need for an expanded federal revenue base to fund it. The states might continue to administer many of these programs. They still might pay a fixed percentage of the costs. They could retain the right to experiment with other kinds of programs. But the negative competition should be eliminated. It's a first step toward breaking the cycle of tax-based community stagnation.

The second step toward a more creative federalism should be an expansion of the federal role in rebuilding the deteriorating community capital plant. Doing so would help break community stagnation and eliminate the negative competition between states and localities. While this recommendation has enjoyed wide support in the past, little has been done other than to expand the highway trust fund. Many politicians got their public relations mileage out of infrastructure and passed on to other things.

The problem is still there, and it is growing. The longer we wait, the worse it will be. For example, the Department of Transportation (DOT) estimates that $33 billion will be needed during the 1980s simply to repair the 40,500-mile interstate highway system. An additional $500 billion will be required to maintain the existing level of service on the nation's nonurban highways. The DOT also estimates that 45 percent of the nation's half million bridges are structurally deficient or obsolete. Necessary repairs could cost as much as $48 billion.

The subterranean water and sewer systems of many cities are latent disasters. New York City, for example, depends on two giant water tunnels which were built fifty-five years ago and have never been inspected. Seven hundred fifty-six cities must spend between $75 and $110 billion to maintain their water systems through the year 2000. Water quality may be an even more serious problem than water quantity. Meeting pollution control standards is expected to cost an additional $25 billion over a five-year period. Many public buildings in our nation's cities, including schools, hospitals, police and fire stations, are more than a half century old and in a state of hazardous deterioration. Of the nation's 3,500 prisons, as many as 3,000 may need substantial renovation or expansion.

Even the Sun Belt cities face staggering capital investment expenditures. Dallas, for example, will require $700 million over the next nine years to modernize and expand its sewage and water systems and another $109 million to repair its deteriorating streets.

Of course, we can simply neglect all this—let the potholes grow ("Drive around 'em"); let the bridges crumble ("No trucks over five tons"); let the water purification systems break down ("Boil it"); or let the sewer systems break ("No swimming")—but I doubt that many Americans really want to do so. It is important to our whole outlook—economic, political, and cultural—that we live in a society that works and in a community we can be proud of.

Effective federal leadership can ensure that the substantial capital investment required to rebuild the capital plants of our communities will be utilized as a countercyclical tool to increase demand in times of recession, to foster national economic stabilization, and to assist specific distressed geographic areas and industrial sectors.

Fewer industries respond to economic cycles with greater rapidity than the construction industry, in which almost half a million firms employ well over 4 million workers. For every on-site construction job created by a public works project, two or three additional jobs are created in related services and industries. Thus, capital investment in the cities can be a highly effective way to stimulate employment in depressed areas and to encourage economic development.

The passage of the Federal Public Transportation Act of 1982—adding to the federal gas tax five cents, one cent of which is dedicated to mass transit—represents a small step in the direction of a unified Transportation Trust Fund that would provide a dedicated source of funding for community transportation improvements.

This concept requires substantial expansion. An oil import fee can provide the revenue base for a comprehensive Transportation Trust Fund of greater magnitude. As the pressure on the credit markets eases with better budgetary control, these monies could be made available to lever more funds into transportation capital projects through interest subsidies to states, localities, and private transportation companies. In this way, capital approaching $30 billion a year could be made available over the next twenty to twenty-five years. This level of funding will begin to equal the magnitude of the task, when supplemented by state and local direct expenditures.

Money from the Transportation Trust Fund would be utilized for road, street, and bridge construction; rehabilitation and maintenance; capital assistance to local public mass transit systems; rehabilitation and expansion of port facilities; maintenance, restoration, and expansion of commuter rail services; and the development of intermodal community transportation networks.

State and city governments should be provided flexibility in determining how transportation funds would be used to meet overall community and regional planning objectives, energy conservation goals, environmental protection requirements, and obligations to provide access to the transportation system for all citizens of the community. The rate of federal funding should be designed to overcome a bias in favor of any particular form of transportation.

Furthermore, the matching grant formula for roads should be adjusted so that maintenance in most cases is supported at the same level as new construction. With good maintenance, the rebuilt state and community capital plant will not deteriorate as fast as before and the investment will be protected. In fact, maintenance in many cases can itself be one of the wisest forms of investment.

To get the most for the taxpayer's dollar and to fight recessionary downturns, this trust fund should be set up as an anticyclical fund, described in the previous chapter, with accelerated activity in hard times and money banked in good times.

A similar countercyclical trust fund with dedicated financing from energy taxes should be established to provide for the maintenance, reconstruction, and improvement of sewers, water systems, police and fire stations, municipal recreational and park facilities, libraries, museums, and other public facilities. As much as $8 billion in revenues should be raised annually for distribution to metropolitan areas and rural communities. Such an amount could be used to lever $20 or $30 billion annually from the credit markets to meet the very large needs in this area over the next two decades.

Distribution of this trust fund should be on the basis of a three-factor formula: forty-year-old housing stock (weighted 50 percent); population and poverty (weighted 30 percent); population loss (weighted 20 percent). This formula reflects the two most relevant dimensions of community need: the degree of decay of capital stock and the ability to raise and use tax revenues for maintenance. With a forty-year requirement for housing starts, the fund's allocations would change over the years, reflecting current needs. Today the needs are principally in older urban centers; twenty years from now the needs will be more in suburban areas; thirty years from now, the Sun Belt; and so forth.

State and local matching fund requirements should be established, and user charges encouraged. Local communities should have substantial flexibility in determining how to spend the funds made available to them from this trust fund, although there should also be federal requirements relating to job creation, equal employment opportunity, and benefits to distressed neighborhoods.

Both the trust funds should be governed by a board of trustees who would include members of the legislative and executive branches of the federal government as well as representatives of state and local governments. These trustees would have the authority to prioritize projects approved for support by Congress. Authorization of expenditures from the trust fund would be for three- to five-year periods, thereby enabling local governments to plan for the most efficient allocation of resources and for long-term construction projects. Monies from the trust fund could be used to pay principal and interest on bond issues, enabling local communities to generate up front financing based on the future commitment of federal assistance.

If states and localities are freed from the restraints of negative competition, they can play a much more dynamic role in the economic process by engaging in a positive competition to rebuild their own local economic support systems.

The states, for example, can play a major part in building the Regional Technology Institutes and in rejuvenating the existing university systems. The experiences of Massachusetts, North Carolina, and California show that university research facilities are of critical importance to high-tech industries. Using a matching grant program, the federal government can encourage the states to participate in the building of retraining centers that would become part of the national job bank network.

The federal government must also take the lead in encouraging more regional cooperation between the states. The mid-Atlantic states, the central Deep South, and the Midwest were especially hard hit during the Great Recession. The economies of these regions are highly dependent on many stagnant industries. Regional economic development may require the introduction of new technologies to existing industries and create new ones. Specific regional concerns, therefore, should be addressed in the creation of technology institutes, training facilities, and investment banks.

The cities and towns of America must also make a contribution to our economic restructuring. Positive competition will work here, too. For example, consider the enterprise zone. This was the linchpin of the Reagan administration's urban renewal "program," typically a one-factor solution to a multifactor problem. This concept is a fundamentally sound idea. It seeks to attract business to run-down urban areas by lowering existing federal, state, and local taxes. It can be shaped by local governments to fulfill many different entrepreneurial objectives, from encouraging small business and light industry to creating new "Quincy Markets" and "Baltimore Harbors." It is not, however, a panacea for all urban ills, nor is it a substitute for federal leadership. Other institutions are needed.

Another initiative is the local development bank discussed in Chapter VII that can be used as a catalyst to bring together the public and private sectors to provide capital for projects designed to revitalize the community economic base. Development banks could enhance the necessary functions performed by metropolitan planning committees and provide the financing for projects that conformed to good planning and development concepts.

These banks would be a major source of funding for the Public Enterprise Corporations. They would provide low-interest loans for the development of small businesses in distressed neighborhoods. They would lend to private individuals for energy-conservation home improvement projects or for housing rehabilitation and restoration projects in distressed neighborhoods. Loans to communities for investment in transportation centers, recreational areas, and other public facilities would be designed to support commercial and residential development as well as family home improvement activities.

Although these banks would be subject to federal or state audit, decision making at the local level would be substituted for the federal bureaucratic review which accompanies direct federal aid. However, state and federal government elected officials as well as representatives of the private financial and business sectors would serve on the boards of directors and be active participants in the locally based decision-making process.

The federal government and the local communities could also cooperate in rebuilding local libraries and in expanding their role in local economic development. As repositories of knowledge, libraries should continue to emphasize inspiration, learning, reflection, and culture. But local libraries, like local schools, can be brought into the electronic age. They can be centers for the retrieval of information in the public domain. Within a few years they will be able to hook into national information systems and provide their clientele with sophisticated technical information, scientific journals, commercial publications, and federal marketing and international trade analyses. Eventually the entire collection of the Library of Congress could be made accessible on the local level. These developments will not only vastly extend the cultural opportunities available to all citizens but will also enable small entrepreneurial high-tech industries to locate conveniently in almost any neighborhood or community.

Libraries should also be encouraged to establish their own outreach and training programs to instruct people how to access information. With their educational, recreational, and commercial functions clearly established, libraries should be able to obtain the local funding necessary to resume their proper place in every community. If private enterprise does not do it, the federal government should set up a public national information network and let communities develop their own uses for it.

Communities using the local development banks can also become active in the energy resource area. They can encourage conservation measures, waste recycling, the construction of solar houses and solar public buildings. They can sponsor the energy-saving rehabilitation of old factories and buildings. They can finance cogeneration systems not only where electricity is pumped into the utility grid by private producers but also where excess industrial steam in urban areas is used for heating homes and businesses. When solar energy becomes more economical, the local development banks can help fund its wide adoption.

The most important community contribution to rebuilding the American economy will be the revitalization of America's schools, bringing them into the electronic age, creating new vocational training facilities for the jobs of the future (especially in those industries of local and regional relevance), and developing outreach programs in areas of high youth unemployment. Since a highly trained work force emerging from the schools, community colleges, and universities will be what employers of the future need most, the historic competition between localities to improve their facilities and thereby attract industry should be redirected at educational development.

Thus, local communities, too, can play a creative role in fostering entrepreneurship, capital, knowledge, resources, and human skills.

To make community development work well, however, we also need neighborhood development. For too long, many federal policies have discouraged and neglected neighborhoods. Urban renewal programs too often have obliterated existing neighborhoods and replaced them with public housing projects, highways, and office buildings. Greater attention must be focused on neighborhoods and their role as community builders.

Some changes have already been made. The administrators of the Urban Development Action Grant (UDAG) programs are today much more sensitive to neighborhood problems than many of their predecessors were. But more is needed than UDAG. For example, we should have a neighborhood improvement tax credit, which would provide an 80 percent credit on the first $50 of each taxpayer's contribution to a qualifying neighborhood development group. Federal matching funds should be made available to local neighborhood improvement groups in designated distressed areas. Small Business Administration loan programs should be directed toward neighborhood revitalization activities. Finally, neighborhoods should be allowed to levy special taxes on themselves for specified neighborhood improvement projects, such as creating parks, providing more police protection, or beautifying the neighborhood.

The largest neighborhood problem is housing. Indeed, there probably is no greater physical indicator of the quality of a person's life than the circumstances under which he or she makes a home. Yet the condition of the nation's housing markets, which have been in a deep recession for four years and are only now showing some signs of recovery, reveals a quality of life in the process of deterioration The 1.1 million housing starts in 1981 were the fewest since 1957. Yet the underlying demand for housing is very strong and will grow substantially. During the 1980s, 41 million Americans will reach the prime home-buying age, compared with 31 million in the previous decade.

Escalating operating costs and high interest rates have also nearly shut down the private construction of rental housing. In the three years from 1980 to 1982 there was an annual net loss of nearly 2 percent in rental units. As a result, the nationwide multifamily vacancy rate fell to the lowest level ever recorded.

An increasing number of young Americans find it impossible to finance their own living accommodations, and we face a serious threat to the nation's traditional assumptions about our quality of life. It is extraordinary hypocrisy for an administration that claims to be profamily to pursue policies that make it financially difficult for many people to form a family and to provide that family with decent living conditions. In the household-forming age-group of twenty to twenty-four years of age, unemployment rose from 1.4 million in 1977 to over 2.5 million in 1982. The result, no doubt, is fewer families and more stress on those that are formed. The elderly, too, have housing problems. Characteristically the Reagan administration's budget request for housing assistance to elderly and handicapped people was just about half the 1980 level.

The first line of attack, obviously, must be the stabilization of the nation's economy and the lowering of interest rates. With mortgage rates in the mid-teens, fewer than three out of ten families can afford to buy a home. Federal leadership is also required to create a countercyclical capacity in the housing industry. To work, a countercyclical stimulus must be initiated, implemented, and terminated with precision. It must have an immediate impact on the economy and then must be withdrawn before the recovery is well under way. Direct interest subsidies, such as discounts on government-purchased loans or self-implementing tax subsidies, meet these criteria for quick implementation. A countercyclical mortgage subsidy program, such as that sponsored by former Senator Edward Brooke and Senator Alan Cranston, would provide an effective, low-cost, temporary, recoverable government investment in housing which would be triggered automatically whenever housing starts fell below a designated level for a significant length of time.

The federal government also must step into the vacuum by providing leadership in the review of federal, state, and local regulations affecting housing construction and renovation. Since compliance with regulations is estimated to add 20 percent to the cost of each new unit, simplification of the regulations, elimination of duplication and conflicting regulatory requirements, and adaptation of regulatory objectives to new concepts in housing, both traditional and manufactured, would significantly reduce costs.

Yet another area for immediate action is the deteriorating condition of public housing. Many large urban public housing projects are deteriorating rapidly because maintenance has been inadequate. Generally speaking, the government has underwritten the construction costs and left maintenance to the localities. In many cases the localities have failed. After the 1980 election I spent some time in Chicago doing television commentary. I did one report in front of such a housing project where several murders had been committed and where people lived in wretched conditions. Shortly afterward Mayor Jane Byrne, in a highly visible political action, moved into the complex amid much publicity. The deteriorated conditions, however, remain.

The problems of these new high-rise slums go far beyond the

physical conditions of the buildings, but those conditions are important. We face a choice: Dynamite them, as happened in St. Louis, or rehabilitate them. We should rehabilitate. Where necessary, we should use federal monies to prevent further deterioration from lack of maintenance.

A final thrust of federal policy should be the encouragement of individual initiative and self-improvement in housing. Programs and tax incentives should be designed to enable individuals at all income levels to contribute to the renovation and rehabilitation of deteriorated housing and to accumulate an equity interest in their own residences. Urban homesteading programs, such as those successfully introduced in Baltimore, should be initiated by the local communities and encouraged by federal support, technical assistance, demonstration funding, and tax incentives. Urban homesteading, however, to make an impact, must be instituted on a much larger scale.

Taken together, these proposals represent a restructuring of the relationships between the public and private sectors and the federal, state, and local governments in responding to the needs of the nation's urban, suburban, and rural communities. If implemented, these measures will significantly increase the role of state and local governments in the rebuilding of our national economy. Gradually freed of the crushing burdens imposed on them by transfer payments (and freed of the negative economic competition resulting from the transfer payment system), communities can become dynamic agents of economic and industrial change. Furthermore, they can play a significant role in keeping the economy decentralized. Through their creation of local funding sources, their establishment of Regional Technology Institutes, and their enhanced role in education and training, states and communities will serve as a check on the strong tendency to centralize the development and dissemination of information in the economy of the future.

Equally important, the trust funds provide a mechanism for generating demand stimulus in recessionary periods. That is consistent with the idea that federal monies be invested in useful projects to bring about enhanced economic activity and real long-range returns. The community programs, while not necessarily adding to national aggregate demand, will play a major role in converting demand directly to useful jobs. Local initiatives, therefore, can be important components of a larger demand-side strategy.

Creative federalism on the governmental level will require creative approaches to party politics. We need a national party devoted to the national interest, but we also need a party willing to play an active role in local politics. A party committed to taking local initiatives and to mobilizing people to achieve local objectives.

14

EXPORTING TO THE
GLOBAL ECONOMY

FEDERAL fiscal and monetary policies, even augmented by local initiatives, may not by themselves stimulate enough demand to produce a full-employment inflation-free economy. We must do more. The obvious supplement to domestically created demand is demand from overseas. Creating that demand, however, will not be a trivial undertaking. We must increase our exports, but to do so, we must surmount enormous barriers.

Protectionism is on the rise in the world. Countries abroad have unemployment, too. No amount of American jawboning will enable us to export our own joblessness. Others will just slam the door. Protectionism aside, the world is still recovering from recession. It cannot yet afford to buy our products today in the quantities needed to cut unemployment substantially in America. In fact, the world is looking to us to be its engine of growth.

Nor can we solve all our problems by realigning the value of the dollar to make our products cheaper, although this will help. There are simply limits beyond which we cannot go, given our current high interest rates and our international responsibilities.

There is no magic. The answers are clearly understood but hard to effectuate: We must indeed have a more competitive dollar; we must increase the efficiency of the American productive process and the quality of our products; we must launch an ambitious effort to encourage growth in the world economy by financing and exporting to others the capital goods and economic support systems that we develop here to rebuild our own supply base; and we must work closely with other countries to expand world trade generally.

The first step is to do something about the dollar, the high value of which against other currencies is discouraging American exports. The rise in the dollar came at a time when we were already experiencing record trade deficits. In former years the value of the dollar might have fallen against other currencies as the American trade balance worsened, but it rose instead because currency, attracted by our high interest rates, flowed into America. Because American exports are more expensive and foreign imports are cheaper, hundreds of thousands, possibly millions of jobs are being lost. A major first step toward improving the American export position, then, is to lower interest rates.

Equal emphasis must be placed on restoring the global competitiveness of American products and on devising the means of turning that competitiveness into a strong export position. To succeed, we must understand what we can do and what we cannot do.

Where can we compete? Where do our advantages lie? What are our strengths and weaknesses?

First, we can compete in several major commodities. In agriculture, our capital-intensive and land-intensive system will remain globally competitive if we preserve its decentralized structure, upgrade the quality of our crops, conserve our topsoil, and maintain our research facilities. Genetic engineering will help us develop strains of nitrogen-fixing corn and wheat crops which will cut fertilizer usage, help replenish the soil, and reduce American dependence on fossil fuels.

Our ability to expand agricultural exports, however, has limits. Countries most dependent on our products are often those least able to pay. Countries that can pay often have strong protectionist policies. For example, the centrist, generally pro-Western parties of both Japan and France, which depend on the farm vote for electoral success, are unlikely to abandon their political bases. Finally, limits are set because we must not push our own land to the point of serious soil depletion.

There is also the conundrum of exports to the Soviet bloc. I supported the grain embargo imposed in response to the Russian invasion of Afghanistan. Carter was right in using it to express America's outrage. It was an important statement. Those who used the embargo as a political football to score points with wheat farmers during the presidential primary season did the nation a disservice. President Reagan lifted the embargo, and grain sales have resumed. I see no reason now to alter this circumstance in the absence of another major shift in Soviet policy. Grain sales to the East should be included in our strategy for expanding American agricultural exports, but they can never be fully counted on. Despite all these difficulties, America can make significant gains in agricultural exports by the end of the decade.

Timber exports can also be expanded. They are much less subject to protectionist impulses. They can continue to make a significant contribution to our trade balance. Science can eventually provide the means of improving forest yields even more than it has in the past. But here, too, there are limits. I do not favor increasing the acreage of public lands used for logging, nor do most Americans. Our domestic needs will continue to command a large percentage of our timber resources, especially with the construction program I have outlined. Doubling our timber exports over the next decade may be more than we can achieve.

Coal exports can play a major role in our balance of trade, as I argued in Chapter 9. If we can export pollution control devices along with the coal, we will have an added export industry. With the better transportation and port facilities that are now coming on line, with further improvements in the future, and with due attention to environmental safeguards, we should be able to double our coal exports during the decade if the global economy recovers.

If commodities hold out promise for expanding our exports, do manufactured goods? I believe they do.

To begin, there is no inherent reason why, with the new technology, we cannot create factory systems of the future that are just as fully automated as those of our competitors. There is no reason why our professional staff running these enterprises and working in them cannot be fully as competent. As the human component becomes a professional component, cheap overseas labor will cease to be a decisive advantage.

Traditional manufactured products (autos, appliances, farm equipment, transportation equipment, furniture, machinery, hardware, electrical equipment, and other established products) can be produced in flexible and fully automated environments. Success in overseas markets will come from better use of the equipment, better marketing skills, a better understanding of foreign cultures, and the ability to respond more quickly and effectively than the competition can to changes in overseas demand patterns. Nonstagnant American corporations can succeed in highly competitive conditions if they commit themselves to a rapid improvement of capital systems, including human skills. There may be fewer employees per unit of output in these industries, but there will still be employees. Exports will add significantly to their numbers.

We can also maintain our competitive edge in aircraft and computers if manufacturing techniques are continually improved and if our engineering and design skills remain the world's best. In all these areas, the development and application of advanced computer technology will be a major factor in determining the competitiveness of the industry.

In other industries we can pursue an aggressive market penetration strategy. I have already mentioned shipbuilding. Consumer electronics may soon present new opportunities. Digital televisions offer a revolutionary chance to enter the market from below and defeat the Japanese dominance. In a nontraditional way, manufactured housing can compete with local construction industries overseas that would normally be immune to outside competition, a fact we should remember with respect to some of our own construction industry's vulnerability to outside attack.

Most of all, we should be able to export new products and specialty goods which rely heavily upon technology. Specialty steels, state-of-the-art glass products, plastics, new materials, chemicals, drugs, the products of genetic engineering, communications equipment and systems, space-manufactured products, new consumer items, and a vast range of other manufactured goods made possible by the microchip—all are strong possibilities. In these areas our national scientific, engineering, organizational, and marketing skills will be the key to success.

With a rebuilt supply base and with a renewed national awareness of the vast potential the overseas market affords, we can look to export possibilities with some optimism. Let us not concede manufacturing to Japan and the newly industrializing countries of Asia. There are times when I believe that the biggest obstacle to besting Japan is the subconscious and fully erroneous belief that Japan is unbeatable.

During the 1970s services such as banking, insurance, communications, and transportation were our fastest-growing export industries. These exports still hold great promise in the short run, but our ability to increase them will depend upon several factors in the future: the expansion of the world economy, the political stability of the recipient countries, the degree to which we can discourage informal barriers to service importation, and the continuing international competitiveness of the services we are, in fact, providing.

The provision of services, moreover, is about to undergo a profound transformation as we move into a more "knowledge-based" global economy. America, if it is at the forefront of this development, will be able to expand its export of services in currently untapped fields. The computer and communications revolutions can make it possible for many American domestic service providers to enter overseas markets hitherto inaccessible. Skills developed here can be exported through artificial intelligence programming. For example, educational services can now be

offered globally through broadcasts, tapes, and interactive programs. Health and hygiene services can be exported by development of the hardware and software electronically to train overseas
people who in turn can provide the services to other people in
their own countries. Virtually any professional service will have an
export potential either directly through improved communications or indirectly through the development of simulated training
facilities. With the advent of the fifth-generation computer, personal services will be revolutionized and also made exportable in
many cases. The better our language skills and the greater our
familiarity with other cultures, the faster these exports of services
will grow. All this will mean jobs in America, especially in
programming and software fields, if we have people who are
trained to fill those jobs.

We have it within our power to bring about steady increases
in our exports of commodities, manufactured goods, and services.
But if exports are to make a truly fundamental contribution to the
American employment picture, we must do even more. As long as
the global economy is in a shambles, there are severe limits placed
on our ability to export, no matter how competitive we are and no
matter how hard we try.

Faced with this situation, America must make a major effort to
rebuild the global economy. One way is to use our own exports as
a means of doing so. This was what we did with the Marshall Plan.
We lent money to Europe after the Second World War so that
Europe could import capital goods from America, thereby rebuild
its own capital plant, and recover economically from the war's
devastation. The Marshall Plan encouraged the forces of stability
in Europe. It created a large export market for American manufactured products and capital goods. It created a pattern of world
commerce upon which we built a sound international financial
system. With the Marshall Plan, we exported investment opportunities. The Europeans borrowed from us because they could not
pay for our capital exports at first, but because they used them
well and rebuilt their own economies, the world economy pros-
pered, and we recovered our investment.

I have emphasized throughout this book the need to rebuild the American supply base to pave the way for our entry into the high-technology era. As we rebuild this base in America, we will develop new processes, techniques, real capital, and software that will be eminently exportable to other countries so that the rest of the world, too, can build or rebuild its economic support system. The current obsolescence of European capital provides us with the opportunity to repeat the experience of the Marshall Plan if we are the first country to develop the new capital systems and the larger economic support systems of which they will be a part. Countries in other parts of the world can use them, too. By producing and exporting these systems, we can make a major contribution to developing the global economy and at the same time provide a demand for American goods and services that will create jobs here.

For example, as we develop electronic marketing systems, we can export them to Europe and to the newly industrializing countries of Asia. We can also extend their reach so that the global marketplace is more unified, and small American producers can sell abroad more easily.

As we develop robotics, computer-aided design and manufacturing systems, and other forms of new capital systems, we can export them globally. Equally important, we can develop the simulation equipment and software to train people how to make the systems work and can export these as well. We can export information retrieval, educational, and other knowledge-based systems to back up the export of the capital systems.

Our ability to succeed, needless to say, will depend on our ability to develop these systems in the first place and to do so with more proficiency than our competitors have. The market, however, is there for the asking. The European economy is as large as ours. For every capital system we produce for domestic use, there is potentially a market for one in Europe, not to mention other parts of the globe.

The export of capital goods always brings forth concerns about foreign competition, but these concerns are largely unfounded or misdirected. Global prosperity requires strong global competition.

Furthermore, America itself should be able to use the capital systems which we produce just as expertly as others can use them.

The export of capital goods is also subject to charges of economic imperialism, as indeed, it should be if it is used to create instruments of control. But if we export to others what they want and need—namely, the ability to compete, to create new jobs, and to build or rebuild their economies—then they will gain as well as we. Conducted responsibly, trade need not fetter either party.

Having this large export market will also spread development costs over a wide number of items and reduce the expense of new capital equipment in America. Developing these new systems should enable us to keep on top of world manufacturing processes and help us preserve a broad-based manufacturing industry at home. Moreover, we also will be able to take strong advantage of the economics of market expansion.

This strategy will help other American exports. As the world economy grows, spurred by a high level of investment, it will increase its demand for American commodities, manufactured goods, and services. Financial services, insurance, communications, and transportation all will have a growing economy to serve.

Exporting real capital and economic support systems to other countries will also circumvent protectionist barriers because the other countries, hoping to develop their own economies, will understand why importing these systems will be more to their advantage than waiting to develop the systems themselves. We will be in a position of working with, not against, strong economic forces in other countries. Finally, the export of real capital can be financed. Lending for this purpose, if done wisely, certainly makes more sense than lending for consumption.

American economic expansion and that of other countries should feed back positively upon each other. Furthermore, a major American export surplus, if tied to the export of real capital, will help stabilize the world economy. It will reverse the oil import game which has been such a source of instability. It will enable us to *earn* back some of those famous Eurodollars that are piling up, a much sounder arrangement than attracting them back with high interest rates. The dollar could be stable, as it was in the 1950s, without high interest rates. Interest rates, in turn, could be allowed to fall and help fuel long-term capital investments both here and overseas.

Equally important, we can rebuild the American-based international financial system on a much sounder footing. It will have an expanded menu of opportunities for investment in productive enterprises. It can then gradually cut itself loose from the oil and commodities game. As its portfolio of manufacturing and service-providing companies grows, it can experience more stable lending patterns. The international debt and credit crisis then can ease.

I am presenting no panacea for our ills. The new technology which will make all this possible is a chicken not fully hatched and not entirely to be counted on. Unless we rebuild our supply base, others will move in ahead of us. Still, it is possible to see how preparing the way in America for the development of the new technology holds out real promise for the development of the global economy as well. This is another reason why it is so important for us to do so.

If America is to make dramatic export gains, we must work to improve the international climate for trade, and we must streamline our own government institutions that are concerned with export promotion. At a minimum we must avoid the trade war that is hanging like a Damoclean sword over the world economy. Beyond this, America should use its still-formidable economic power to persuade other countries to reduce their barriers to trade. The General Agreement on Tariffs and Trade (GATT) exists for this purpose, and we must take the diplomatic lead in revitalizing the GATT process.

Working through GATT or through a more powerful successor to GATT, we must reduce informal barriers to trade. We must seek international agreement to control the spread of counter-trade, a form of barter in which companies are forced to buy a product from a country in order to sell their products to that country. We must seek to liberalize world trade in services. To do so, we must seek international agreements to reduce the many informal barriers to services which exist today. We must devise an international means of defining, regulating, and eventually eliminating unfair export subsidies. Throughout this process, frequent and sustained informal consultations within the Organization for Economic Cooperation and Development (OECD) framework would be particularly helpful. Many of these suggestions are obvious, but our activities have been sluggish.

We should also take some practical administrative steps to encourage exports. To emphasize the importance of this objective and to give visibility to the goal of trade expansion, we should create a new Department of Trade and Investment Expansion. This department could work closely with trade and industry associations to assist in the development of export strategies. It would have three primary missions: gathering and disseminating information about world economic developments, negotiating a reduction in trade barriers, and arranging finance for exports. All these functions are now performed to varying degrees by separate agencies inside and outside the Commerce Department.

We can start by upgrading the information collection and dissemination functions now found within the Trade Development Division of Commerce. We need a truly first-class overseas information-gathering service to monitor market developments, new manufacturing processes, and general economic trends. The staff that now performs these functions is very small and needs to be augmented. I would envision a major research and analytic operation here to provide American industry with quality information on a very current basis. Such information could be provided directly to large exporters and indirectly to small exporters through the commercial extension services described in Chapter VI.

In the new cabinet department I would include the Office of Special Trade Negotiations, the first task of which would be to launch an aggressive program of trade expansion, beginning with sustained consultation among the OECD members. I would create special negotiating strike forces to set specific targets and then give them the full backing of the White House in achieving their objectives. One obvious focus would be to reduce barriers to the export of services, especially in the telecommunications area. This division would be given additional broad powers to police international trade laws and to provide quick responses to their violation when we are directly affected.

Another division is needed with the special function of encouraging trade with the less developed countries (LDCs).

Finally, I would place the Export-Import (Ex-Im) Bank in this department and expand its role. The Ex-Im Bank has focused primarily on loans for the purchase of aircraft and certain other high-technology products and has been criticized for this focus. Without upsetting these programs, which seem to be working, I would like to see an enlarged bank expand into a wider range of activity.

These modest administrative changes, when combined with the rebuilding of the American supply base, can bring about significant increases in American exports, but to have trade expansion really work requires tough political support. The nation will gain through trade expansion, but some people will lose in the short run. This is why political courage in Washington is needed to represent the national interest. Both major parties are dragging their heels on trade expansion, but the Democrats are especially remiss. Soon the Republicans may be, too. This is all wrong. Trade expansion is ultimately in the interests of all Americans. But to make it possible, we need a new patriotism in America. A new commitment to long-range objectives. To building a viable strategy for the future.

We need a new political party. A party which will not succumb to protectionist tendencies. A party of free trade which recognizes that to export, we must also import. Put simply, a party of the future willing to represent the national interest.

15

ACCESS TO
EMPLOYMENT
AND INCOME

THE plan presented in the previous chapters, if adopted, should lay the foundations of a full-employment economy. The inflation-fighting measures I have set forth are robust: monetary restraint, deficit control, TIP, profit-sharing incentives, freer markets, industrial restructuring, and a climate to encourage growth industries with their typically falling prices. With these policies, inflation will be attacked at both macro- and microeconomic levels.

The employment-generating measures I have outlined are equally robust: extensive new federal countercyclical instruments, including two large construction trust funds, stand-by government purchasing programs, a rejuvenated supply base that can compete with overseas producers, local incentives to encourage employment, help for small businesses, Public Enterprise Corporations, and especially a major export strategy. These, too, contain micro- and macroeconomic initiatives.

Together the inflation-fighting and employment-generating measures should enable us to conquer the stagflation we have experienced for nearly twenty years. Still, it is necessary to demonstrate how these programs will produce an economy that provides Americans with a high standard of living and also guarantees widespread access to prosperity.

Can we hold out hope that America will not, in fact, become a dual society? Can we hold out hope for the unemployed workers in stagnant industries? For people in depressed regions of the country? For minorities? For women?

These questions are not trivial. It is theoretically easy to provide employment to everyone at some level of compensation. We can always set up make-work programs to keep people on the job. We can lower wages and salaries. We can protect or subsidize stagnant industries to maintain employment in them. We can artificially stimulate demand with programs that are bound to be inflationary. But such measures will fight unemployment only in a context of static or a falling standard of living for everyone. They will prove a drain on the whole economy. There are times when we must have programs like these to help people in need. And it would be preferable to have people working at lower wages than not working at all. But we can, in fact, do better than this.

To begin, we must create more real wealth in America to lay the basis for a rising standard of living and to escape the fate of the zero-sum society. Today, with increased life expectancy and chronic unemployment, fewer people are supporting more people. By the end of the century the squeeze on wage earners will be even greater as the baby boom generation reaches retirement age. If we are to keep ahead of the demographics and are to raise the living standards of poorer people as well, the economy will have to undergo dramatic growth during the next two decades. This, in turn, means dramatic increases in productivity. That is why I emphasize investments so strongly. It is through wise investments in capital goods, in knowledge, in resources, and especially in people that we will extend our capabilities both quantitatively and qualitatively.

To achieve these ends, I offer a new national investment strategy. At the macroeconomic level this strategy includes deficit control to release billions to the private credit markets; fiscal stability to create a climate of predictability and confidence; price stability to encourage both savings and investment; low interest rates (another result of deficit control) to make possible a wider range of real investments; income sheltering to accelerate savings accumulation; tax incentives to encourage the rapid turnover of real capital; budgetary procedures to encourage public investments (both in physical infrastructure and the larger economic support systems), and countercyclical devices to keep the total level of national investment high. These proposals, which stand in sharp contrast with Reagan's policies of budget deficits, consumption-oriented tax cuts, and wasteful defense spending, will lay the foundations of a new investment era for America.

But merely creating a climate for investments is not enough. People still need something to invest in, and they need the expertise to make and manage those investments wisely. I have therefore called for programs at the microeconomic level both to improve investment practices and to increase investment opportunities. These include the fashioning of entrepreneurial incentives to encourage new ventures and new growth industries; a restructured banking system with new banks designed to encourage expertise in the making of real investments; the development and the distribution of new technologies; the training of people to use them, especially in the area of new capital goods and systems; government investment in science, energy research, space, and other promising areas which will open new private investment opportunities in the future; investments in education and training to improve the skills of the American people; an Industrial Development Authority to spur new real investment in the stagnant sector; a creative federalism to encourage state and local governments to stimulate productive investments on the community level; and a major overseas investment program from which both the American economy and the American financial community will greatly benefit.

One result of this investment strategy will be to reinforce financial stability. Another result will be dramatic productivity gains. The most important result will be the creation of new economic resources to enable America to sustain and improve its standard of living.

Where will this new wealth come from? First, from the automation of the manufacturing sector. We will see sustainable labor productivity gains, price competitiveness, and quality products.

Second, from the new industries of the future. These will also create vast economic resources for America.

Third, from the growth of the capital goods and systems sector, with its large domestic and foreign market possibilities and its own wealth-generating potential.

Fourth, through productivity gains and improvements in quality, as the new technology spreads to the service sector.

Fifth, from reversing the trade deficit.

These five areas should give America an expanding base of national wealth to increase its income and provide full employment opportunities.

I present here a strategy of growth. Emphasis on the new technology and rapid capital turnover should help make that growth environmentally sound. So should strong EPA enforcement procedures and the rapid resolution of regulatory disputes. But growth alone will not solve our problems. Indeed, uncontrolled growth merely for the sake of growth will add to these problems. If middle- and upper-class Americans temporarily benefit from growth while the rest of America is left behind, our social and economic difficulties will remain. It is not possible to secure durable economic prosperity unless every socioeconomic group participates. We must therefore ask: If new wealth is to be created, how is it to be distributed?

Trickle-down economics are no answer. In the context of an emerging new technology, trickle-down economics will create a dual society in which that technology is tightly held for the benefit of a few. Great but closely controlled wealth will give us a country like that of Kuwait or Saudi Arabia. No right-thinking American wants that.

If the new technology is not adopted and we continue to stagnate, trickle-down economics will lead to a "Latin Americanization" of our economy with increasing distance between rich and poor, a declining middle class, and a lower average standard of living for all Americans.

Real wealth does not trickle down. It percolates up from broad-based economic activity. It is more than just a cliché to suggest that the policies of the past few years have served only to help the rich get richer and the poor get poorer.

The principal Democratic alternative to Republican trickle-down economics is redistributionism, which means taxing and spending to spread the wealth. Certain kinds of redistribution are widely accepted and necessary practices in a fully integrated society such as ours. Only the most mean-spirited among us would deny that we have a social obligation to care for the elderly, the young, the poor, and the destitute when they themselves or their families cannot do so. Even the Reagan administration talks about safety nets. There is room for dispute over how much support to give and how to pay for it, but the welfare state is a widely endorsed means of achieving these objectives.

Still, there are limits beyond which the welfare state cannot expand without creating enormous burdens on the economy and without producing side effects that will be harmful in the future even to its own objectives. We can extend the principles of redistribution to the point where it imposes crushing tax burdens on the wage earner and positively harms our ability to produce needed new wealth. Borrowing to redistribute creates additional problems of its own.

This the majority of the Democratic party has never fully understood. Democrats have not only failed to give adequate attention to policies that improve our ability to create new wealth but also failed to find any coherent alternative to an economic policy of redistributionism. Their principal initiatives for half a century have been to extend the welfare state model of redistribution to ever-widening categories of recipients. Even programs designed to achieve other objectives, such as CETA, have effectively become redistributionist schemes. The recent failures of the Democratic party, both electorally and administratively, reflect the fact that we are today reaching the practical limits of such approaches. Not all Democrats are committed to redistribution, just as not all Republicans are committed to trickle-down economics, but the majority seems to be so in both cases.

Redistributionism is not a viable philosophy for a broad-based allocation of wealth throughout our larger society. It has never worked in America because political and economic forces are too strong to let it work. Our distribution of wealth today is roughly the same as it was before the New Deal. The tax burden has tended to fall on the middle class more than on the rich. If this is changed and wealth is taxed substantially more, it might simply leave the country and not be reinvested here. Creating wealth centrally and then distributing it broadly will simply not happen.

Furthermore, broad-based srategies for redistributing wealth will not be desirable in the knowledge-based economy of the future because they will lock in a condition of economic dependence that will lead to political dependence. On the surface, redistributionism may create a more humane society than trickle-down economics will, but that society will still be divided. Any way you look at it, a community with large numbers of supplicants, however well supported, is not a healthy and viable social order. Paternalism, however well intentioned, cuts against the grain of the American spirit.

Direct access by people to the fruits of economic expansion is a far better alternative. Stated differently: We need broad-based opportunities to earn real wealth. Our need to provide this access will grow in the future, as the new technology takes hold. But the problem is stark enough today. Millions of Americans right now lack access to jobs of any kind. Millions more lack access to jobs that provide adequate and equitable compensation.

For example, we face a persistent unemployment problem in the stagnant industries of the mid-Atlantic, southern, and midwestern regions of the country. Even at the end of summer 1983, with recovery under way for two-thirds of a year, double-digit unemployment persisted in the megastates of Pennsylvania, Ohio, Michigan, and Illinois. In many communities it was nearly 20 percent. In the construction industry it exceeded 18 percent. Worse figures were available for autos, machinery, and farm equipment. Some of these workers will never have access to their familiar jobs again.

Black unemployment also remains exceptionally high. It rose to 20 percent during the Great Recession. Black teen-age unemployment broke 50 percent. Black median family income is about three-fifths that of white family income. Any way you measure it, and for whatever reason, blacks lack the access to jobs that whites enjoy.

Women suffer, too. On the average they receive about sixty cents for every dollar that men do in wages and salaries. Only 2 percent of higher level business managers are women. Women's median earnings are $12,000, compared to men's earnings of $20,260. Even more startling, at every level of educational achievement women earn less than men. Median earnings today for men with four or more years of college, for example, is $28,174; for women with the same education it is $17,800. In fact, a male high school graduate will earn more than a woman with a college degree. Millions of women are also in the economically stressful role of being a single parent. Again we have an extraordinary problem of access.

To give all Americans access to the newly created wealth of the future, three requirements must be met. First, we need a vast range of well-paying jobs spread across all sectors of the economy and appropriately distributed throughout the country. Second, people must have the motivation and skills to perform these jobs. Third, there must be no artificial barriers to access, such as race and sex discrimination.

The reconstruction of our supply base and the implementation of an intelligent investment strategy, taken together with adequate demand stimulus, domestic and foreign, should generate enough well-paying jobs to create a full-employment economy, but the job profile across America will be quite different from the profile today. Where will the jobs of the future be located, and what will those jobs be?

First, the future will be bright for steady agricultural employment with export promotion.

Second, traditional manufacturing will join agriculture as an equally automated, entrepreneurial, and capital-intensive industry. Although nearly two-thirds of its present jobs will be lost during the balance of the century, those employees that remain (such as managers, engineers, designers, programmers, specialized technicians, specialized clerical workers, and marketing experts) will have high value-added jobs, and they will be very well paid.

Third, many new manufacturing jobs will be created in growth industries such as electronics, computers, communications, and new appliances. Innovative "low-tech" industries will also make a significant contribution. It is not clear that these industries will produce steady jobs. Some new products, like the home computer, will become fixtures in the economy. Companies that make them will grow to provide stable employment. But other products will come and go. Initially new industries will provide many assembly-line jobs. Firms that survive the global competition, however, will quickly become automated and professionalized, just as the traditional manufacturing industries must. Although these new industries will contribute to a full-employment economy and many of their jobs will be well paid, the chance to build video games will not solve all the problems of auto workers who five years from now will really never again have jobs in that industry.

Fourth, the capital goods industry, broadly defined, which today employs about 3 million people, can be transferred into a capital systems industry and can undergo a dramatic expansion as it builds the systems to retool American, European, and other overseas economies. Initially, expanded employment would include many blue-collar workers from the stagnant sector. Someone, after all, has to build the robots, the control systems, the sensing devices, the automated warehouses, and so forth.

The capital systems industry, however, will also begin to automate. Software skills will become prevalent as the knowledge component continually increases in importance and the new capital equipment becomes sufficiently sophisticated to build itself. Jobs will therefore become increasingly specialized over the next two decades. They should, however, command high levels of pay.

Fifth, rebuilding the economic support system of the supply base itself will also produce new jobs. Employment in marketing should remain steady because the economy of the future, with its emphasis on quality and variety, will need a large number of individuals with professional marketing skills. Overseas marketing will require many new people well acquainted with other languages and cultures. The level of pay in marketing should increase, even as the number of jobs stabilizes.

The finance capital sector (banking, investment, and related services), despite computerization and automation of many clerical jobs, should be able to enjoy steady employment, especially, if the proposed new banking systems are created and if banking as a whole remains decentralized. Compensation levels should keep pace with increases in the economy as a whole.

The knowledge-generating sector (science, technology, energy research, space, and related areas), if we give it the emphasis needed over the next decade and a half, should see a substantial increase in well-compensated employment. Information storage and retrieval itself should also become a growth industry with high-paying job prospects.

The resource area should provide increased employment. Solar energy equipment and other alternative energy sources should more than offset a probable decline in oil-related employment. Sophisticated and effective waste disposal systems will also create new jobs. The jobs will enjoy wage levels competitive with other industries.

Teaching jobs will become even more specialized and professionalized than they are now. The decade-long decline in employment will be reversed if we make the commitments to creating the new age of knowledge that we need to remain globally competitive. Compensation will increase with specialization. In addition, the electronic revolution will create many high-paying jobs in software industries that support the educational and training professions of the future.

Sixth, the service sector, such as health services, personal services, repair services, transportation, and many other services not already listed above, will continue to be a rapidly growing employer. The aging of our population will create large demands for health services and geriatric social services. The tastes of our consumers will probably demand a wider range of personal services. Electronics will tend to improve quality more than to reduce jobs.

Seventh, small and medium-sized businesses have been a major source of new employment in America over the last decade. With programs to encourage their proliferation, they will continue to be.

Finally, a massive, publicly financed construction program for the next two decades, together with lower interest rates, should create literally millions of new construction jobs. This will provide a major employment alternative, with well-paying jobs for those who do not become highly trained workers. Even in construction, however, automation and productivity improvements can be expected if costs are to be kept in line.

I envision a decentralized and uncontrolled economy in which the work force will become increasingly specialized and professionalized. Yet this economy will also retain millions of blue-collar jobs in industries not readily subject to automation or to foreign competition. It will contain millions of needed white-collar clerical jobs made more productive by the new technology.

Will this job profile of the future provide adequate employment for those people from the stagnant sector who have lost the jobs they now hold or who will do so over the next decade? I believe it will. First, a significant number of working people will remain in the automated factories of the future as mechanics, robot repairers, technicians, clerical workers, and salespeople. The industries themselves will retrain them. Second, others, especially those who are young, will retrain and enter the new manufacturing fields as jobs are created. Third, millions of new construction jobs—good jobs—will be available to yet another group of traditional working people whether in the PECs or in traditional firms. They will also have access to on-the-job training. Fourth, my emphasis on capital goods and capital systems will create a major growth industry, probably in the very states where stagnant industries are now concentrated. This will provide substantial numbers of jobs, many in areas related to the skills of those now employed by the stagnant firms. Fifth, jobs in the stagnant sector will not disappear overnight, and many people will retire over the next decade or two as these events transpire. Finally, with management, government, and labor working together through the Industrial Development Councils, as described in Chapter XI, it should be possible to convince industry to relocate in areas of high unemployment caused by the automation or failure of currently stagnant companies.

The opportunity for America to create high-paying jobs is there. But will all Americans have the skills to take advantage of these opportunities so that they can obtain access to the newly created wealth? So that they can contribute to demand? So that they can contribute to savings and further investment?

The creation of new job opportunities will produce powerful incentives for people to train and retrain. But this incentive by itself will not be enough for many people with deficient educational backgrounds or who lack sufficient economic socialization or motivation. They will assume that the new jobs are not for them or that someone else will get them anyway. They will give up easily or just not try at all. This is why outreach programs are so important, not only for the black teen-ager in Bedford-Stuyvesant and the disadvantaged white in Appalachia but also for unemployed workers in their fifties and sixties in Flint. This is why I have emphasized increased attention to vocational opportunity programs in the school curriculum. This is why I would enlist the support of unions in developing outreach programs to encourage people to train, retrain, and seek new jobs.

One of the most vigorous efforts we must make in educational reform is to motivate young blacks, other minorities, and disadvantaged whites to seek the skills of the future while they are in school so that they will have access to the same standard of living enjoyed by the rest of society. We simply must increase the level of professional training of those leaving the school systems now so that they do not in the future add to our already substantial problem of retraining large numbers of people currently in the work force. Again, there is no magic. It is a case of improving the school system, of building the outreach programs, and of bringing the technology of the future, together with the people who know how to use it, to the classrooms of today. It is a case of stubborn commitment to decent objectives.

We must also make a commitment to provide women with better training. The jobs of the future, as outlined above, should create many opportunities to reduce the job segregation that today sees women and men typically performing very different jobs in our economy. This segregation is partly responsible for pay differentials between the sexes. Science, technology, engineering, programming, marketing, software development, investment banking, and capital systems development are today male-dominated professions. They need not be in the economy of the future. Furthermore, as traditional manufacturing jobs become more automated, women should have new opportunities to work in the production areas of traditionally male-dominated industries. Primary and secondary education, where women now have good employment prospects, should see compensation levels rise as they become even more specialized. With the expansion of these areas and with proper training and motivation, women should have the opportunity for major material advancement. This will not be an instant process, but it should be a steady one.

Furthermore, we must create and fund special training programs for young women who have left school, displaced homemakers, single parents, and adults receiving Aid to Families with Dependent Children. To give such programs a chance to succeed, we also need to provide trainees with stipends, transportation, child care, and other support services.

Women, however, will not gain access to new high-paying jobs if they do not seek them. Sex stereotyping in the school system, which encourages women to enter traditional "women's jobs," must be overcome as the result of conscious policy decisions by the local, state, and federal governments. In addition, the Department of Education's Office of Civil Rights must be given adequate staff support to investigate the practice of discrimination in schools and universities.

Education and training in their broadest sense are the keys to success. If people are fully employable in an expanding economy of the future, many of them will be able to find good jobs because market forces will be on their side. Despite the persistence of discrimination in America, there are large numbers of employers who *don't* discriminate on the grounds of race and sex. The more the barriers break down, the easier it will be to break other barriers down.

Still, access to jobs is also denied by outright discrimination in America, and we might as well admit it. Discrimination exists in many forms. Some are quite overt; some are quite subtle. Many people, because of their backgrounds and training, have discriminatory attitudes of which they are not even aware. Sex-role typing is an especially widespread source of bias. Discrimination is not a problem of one region or of one ethnic background or of a given set of professions. Discrimination against women professionals on the campus is notorious. Nor will discrimination disappear overnight or even in a decade. It will never disappear unless we keep working at it. My own commitment to ending discrimination is deep. I supported every major piece of civil rights legislation that came before Congress during my twenty years' tenure.

The law is clear, powerful, and important. The Equal Pay Act of 1963 (prohibiting sex discrimination in wages and fringe benefits between jobs of equal skill), Title VII of the Civil Rights Act of 1964 (which prohibits employment discrimination on the basis of sex, race, religion, color, and national origin), Executive Order No. 11246 of 1965 (which requires federal contractors to comply with all federal legislation regarding employment and wage discrimination), and Title IX of the Education Amendments of 1972 (which prohibits discrimination on the basis of sex in educational programs or activities receiving federal financial assistance) represent an excellent legal framework to correct discrimination.

We also should enact and ratify the Equal Rights Amendment (ERA). It will prohibit sex discrimination by public employers, encourage state legislatures to rescind discriminatory laws, tighten the standards by which sex discrimination suits are reviewed, guide the courts when adjudicating laws, and close the loopholes that have plagued existing legislation for years.

But a law is only as effective as its enforcement. The Reagan administration has not worked to enforce civil rights laws and regulations adequately. Indeed, it has attempted to sabotage them. Its principal ploy has been to cut the budgets and staffs of enforcement agencies.

As a result, litigation to enforce equal employment opportunity laws has been curtailed. For example, the Equal Employment Opportunity Commission (EEOC), the office in charge of enforcing the Equal Pay Act and Title VII, had a backlog of 12,500 cases in 1983. Cases filed in 1982 were 73.9 percent fewer than in 1981. Fewer charges are being settled. The length of time for processing individual charges in 1983 was nearly double that of 1980.

The Office of Federal Contracts Compliance Programs (OFCCP) of the Department of Labor, which enforces Executive Order No 11246, has suffered the same fate. Back pay claims and other monetary benefits obtained by the OFCCP as a remedy for discrimination decreased from $9.2 million in fiscal 1980 to $2.1 million in 1982.

In addition to funding and staffing problems, equal employment opportunity policies depend on an aggressive commitment by the personnel of the enforcement agencies. "Voluntary compliance" under the guise of reducing government intrusion or ineffective negotiated settlements instead of mandated remedies have been used to make a mockery of civil rights statutes.

It is my reading of the Constitution that the president is mandated to ensure that the laws are faithfully executed. The president is not given discretion to pick and choose among the laws to be enforced. It follows from this that the president must ask Congress for sufficient resources to hire the staff to enforce the law.

Nor is the attorney general's discretion to choose which cases he thinks he can win a license to litigate only those cases he personally wants to win. By its appointment of special counsel in the *Bob Jones* case, the Burger Court quite properly signaled its displeasure at the growing Justice Department practice of not litigating violations of federal statutes that conflict with its ideological preferences.

A denial of access to employment derives not only from discrimination but also from circumstance. For example, women heading single-parent families have the double burden of caring for themselves and for their children. Without adequate child support payments and outlets for good-paying jobs, they cannot afford quality child care. They often cannot afford the day care service that could free them to look for employment. In many instances, women will opt for welfare, lacking both the opportunity and the incentive to become productive members of the community. Inadequate child care support continues to be a barrier denying women access to employment, training, and educational opportunities.

The government can play a leading role in assisting female heads of household obtain access to jobs in the economy of the future. We should have a national policy on child care embodied in legislation that supports increased day care services, including local after-school programs; that provides for child care in federally funded job-training programs; and that encourages the private sector to include provisions for child care in benefit plans. Finally, we need a mechanism for collecting, monitoring, and disbursing child support payments by fathers living apart from their children.

The benefits to the economy of creating opportunities for many single-parent women to leave welfare rolls and become productive members of the economy far outweigh the costs to the economy of the needed assistance programs. Here is an opportunity for investment in the future we all should support.

I cannot emphasize too strongly how important it is to all Americans that all other Americans have direct access to the wealth of the future through their direct contribution to creating that wealth. Not only will we escape the political dangers that come from a divided society or a paternalistic community, not only will we create a greater demand for the products of our factories, not only will we serve legitimate humanitarian objectives, but all of us stand to gain. A market economy is not a zero-sum game. It is a positive-sum game when it is fettered and controlled neither from within nor from without.

If a large percentage of the working-age population of the United States consisted of skilled and trained professionals performing their millions of jobs with a high degree of excellence, then the quality of life in America would be far better for everyone. Skilled people, be they on the factory floor, in the operating room, on the farm, at the computer terminal, in the classroom, in the executive boardroom, or in the cab of a new locomotive, do not work just for themselves. They work for all of us. Denying people access to work, however it may be done and for whatever reason, reduces our national wealth, our international power, our universal respect, and our own personal circumstances. For better or for worse we are all here together in one country, and we had better make the most of it. It is this message, more than any other, that a new party of national unity must convey.

I believe that we can solve the long-term unemployment problem in America. We can work to create direct access to well-paying jobs for all Americans. We can do so in the face of rapid productivity increases in the manufacturing industries. We can do so and still maintain a high standard of living. We can do so without exporting our unemployment overseas.

But there are no guarantees. I do not predict; I only demonstrate what is possible. We cannot manipulate our way to prosperity; we can only *earn* it. But there is a future to be won. We must aim at nothing short of the nearly universal professionalization of the entire American workforce.

I see America as a nation of highly skilled achievers, a country where the vast majority of its population in the coming generation has the skills and training that only a small percentage has today. I see an America where the excitement of the new, tempered by the values of the old, produces a revolutionary economy, much less regimented and concentrated than the economy of today. I see a lively and humane society, using new techniques and new opportunities to further the aspirations of individuals and the values of groups. I see dynamism, variety, and change. Most of all, I see an America that not only can compete successfully with any other economy but can also take the lead in cooperating with other countries to bring about a global economic revolution that will fulfill the hopes of humankind.

These are noble objectives. With work, we can achieve them. But there is a dark shadow under which we labor. This is the shadow of war and the preparations for war. If we cannot lift this shadow, we can never fully realize our vision of a new economy. Military expenditures dominate the economic debate of today; as they are currently planned, they will dominate the economy of tomorrow. Neither can be isolated from the other. We must work to solve the problems of global security in ways compatible with our vision of a brighter economic future, or we will never see that future; perhaps we will see no future at all.

IV

The American Economy and Global Security

16

ARMS AND THE
AMERICAN ECONOMY

WE can create a vigorous, full-employment economy. But to do so, we must make substantial cuts in the projected military budgets, both to bring down the deficit and to release funds for rebuilding the supply base. Can we afford to do this from the standpoint of American and world security? I believe we can. What is more, I believe we can no longer afford *not* to.

The magnitude of the projected defense build-up is awesome. The Reagan administration expects to *increase* military spending by more than $1 trillion (that is, 1 *million* million) during this decade. And it proposes to *borrow* every penny of it. Just by 1984 the administration aims to double the amount of dollars spent in 1980 for the purchase of weapons. This is unprecedented, unparalleled, unconscionable waste, unequaled in American history.

It is waste made even more unconscionable by political leaders in both parties who have failed to act on their own reservations about the size of the build-up. Defense spending has ridden a political bow wave that has washed over every other concern. The degree to which the Democrats in Congress have acquiesced in administration defense plans is, in fact, remarkable. They effectively rubber-stamped the 1981 requests. In 1982 the Democratic alternative to Reagan's proposal on defense spending was only one-half of 1 percent lower. Even in 1983 the concept of a major defense build-up had become so rooted in Washington's thinking that the Democrats were proposing a 5 percent increase for the Defense Department in real terms, while the Republicans were proposing 7½ percent. This blank-check defense policy was not only an abdication of party responsibility, but also a sharp departure from the watchdog role of Congress.

When I first came to Washington, Carl Vinson, the crusty chairman of the House Armed Services Committee, reigned supreme in defense matters, holding a near veto power over administration policy. In the committee room he wielded a mean gavel and rapped his critics into silent oblivion. On the floor he controlled debate time, only grudgingly yielding the floor to the opposition. It took a celebrated walk with John Kennedy in the Rose Garden to change Carl's mind on the B-70. Carl shaped the defense budget and usually got what he wanted. Presidents just came and went.

In the past few years, however, the opposite has occurred. Congressional defense critics now sit at hearings in dumb silence, unwilling to challenge administration witnesses for fear of being labeled soft on defense. A veritable "wish list" is compiled at the Pentagon and rushed uncritically through Congress. The doors of the Treasury are wide-open.

The costs of this politically and ideologically inspired defense build-up go far beyond $1 trillion of new debt. Shifting federal spending from the civilian sector to the military sector has contributed to unemployment. The Congressional Research Service estimates that 8.4 percent more jobs are lost when nondefense spending is cut than when defense spending is cut.

Furthermore, throwing money at a defense industry which cannot easily absorb it lures engineers and other professionals out of the nondefense sector, creates bottlenecks, and thereby drives up costs. Goldman, Sachs estimates that over the period from 1980 to 1986 defense spending as a percentage of the goods-producing sector of the economy will nearly double. Inflationary pressures in the production of capital goods will be especially acute. This will seriously hamper our ability to launch a strategy to become the world's leading exporter of new capital systems. These tendencies will accelerate if we manage to have a sustainable recovery.

Reagan's shift of economic resources from civilian to military expenditures has also led to the militarization of hitherto civilian-dominated sectors of the economy, such as the space program. Here we are sacrificing future commercial opportunities of unlimited economic potential for the sake of military programs of marginal benefit. High-technology research and development is also being brought under defense-related direction and control. If this process continues, it will further guarantee the diversion of new technologies to military and intelligence purposes under the close supervision of the government. The result will be de facto centralized economic planning of the worst sort. Many giant corporations are coming to depend more and more on defense contracts and government financing. The country as a whole is becoming dependent on the export of arms to Middle East and Third World nations to reduce its trade deficit.

Although the military sector of the American economy does not yet dominate the entire economy, it is very influential in many sectors in which the economy is expected to grow: communications, computers, electronics, and a wide range of research-based areas. This influence may easily lead to centralized direction which will guarantee economic stagnation in industries that would otherwise have a bright future.

It is easy to overstate the case. I seriously doubt if the military itself is engaged in some nefarious plot to control the economy. But when an institution or a large organization comes to dominate an economic sector, it is not surprising that it will distort the growth of that sector for its own purposes. The standard operating procedures of military and intelligence bureaucracies are not conducive to the kind of flexible and rapid change that we must have if we are to compete successfully in the global economy of tomorrow. It is absolutely fundamental, not only to the growth of the American economy but also to the long-range security of America, that we not let military dominance be established over the emerging high-technology research areas upon which our future vitally depends.

Let us not forget the example of the Soviet Union. Russia has sacrificed all else to arms. And to what end? It cannot feed itself. It cannot manufacture goods which will meet a market anywhere outside its own satellite system. Its health care network is deteriorating. Its life expectancy is falling. Its technology remains woefully primitive by Western standards. All it can really do well is produce weapons. But even its military technology is decidedly inferior to that of the Western powers, as Middle East wars consistently demonstrate. The Russian economy has many problems, but it is very clear that its extraordinary emphasis on arms is one major source of its economic stagnation.

This is not the way to go. America is not a warrior nation, nor should we become one. We must defend ourselves, and when provoked, we must respond vigorously and effectively. But fighting wars is not what America should be redesigned to do.

I do not believe that America needs the military build-up imposed upon us by the Reagan Right and ratified by the Democrats in Congress. Money is being wasted. The economy is being needlessly hurt. Furthermore, arms are not the single route to security. Is not rebuilding the global economy just as crucial? Does not the viability of NATO depend in the long run upon Europe's economic recovery? Does not our alliance with Japan depend as much upon stable economic relations as upon our military umbrella? Does not the world economy need a strong center to prevent global depression and the wars that can arise from depression? Does not our ability to play a creative role in the developing countries depend more upon our capacity to help them grow and prosper than upon our capacity to sell them weapons? With the world spending $30 on arms for every $1 spent on education, health, and other basic amenities to sustain life, does it not make sense to ask if global political instability is rooted in the soil of social and economic unrest and upheaval?

I believe that making good investments in the world economy is simply more sensible than investing in an arms race. The lurking threats to peace that economic collapse will nurture are a far greater window of vulnerability than any that exists today in the strictly military area.

America must also begin to ask itself serious questions about the efficacy of arms in the world of today. At the strategic or nuclear level, vast expenditures of money have brought us to a condition of stalemate. How much more security will perpetuating the nuclear arms race bring us?

And what about proliferation of conventional arms in the Third World? At times arms do achieve political objectives there. Still, if we look at the Third World as a whole, what do we see? We see an escalating flow of ever more sophisticated weapons poured in by Russia and the major powers of the West. We see governments like Libya's maintained by soldiers of fortune. We see states beginning to fall into chaos, where war is the daily routine of life, where people are born, live, and die, never knowing the meaning of a peaceful society, where the causes of war are so remote that people can no longer recall the origins of their misery. We see this chaos spreading throughout Asia, the Middle East, Africa, and Latin America.

And in that chaos, arms themselves may no longer achieve the purposes for which they are wielded. We see guerrilla movements structured to overthrow incumbents and the new incumbents, in turn, subject to new insurgencies. We see economies ruined; we see politics in utter chaos. And we witness the logic of war taking on a life of its own in which political and diplomatic objectives alike become meaningless, subject to the imperatives of continual and often purposeless combat.

International wars can end. Former enemies can become reconciled across international borders. But civil wars and revolutions take generations to end, unless the losers are utterly liquidated, as in Russia. A settlement by arms rarely builds consent, and without consent, a settlement is just a truce.

By pouring arms into the nations of the South, by using the territories of the South as battlegrounds for their own proxy wars, are not the nations of the North creating a condition which will escalate into ever more vicious cycles of violence as the century continues? This must not be. I speak not only to humanity here; a world of chaos is secure for none of its inhabitants.

We must rethink our approach to security. We must recognize that a true assessment of a nation's security depends upon many factors. Arms are one of them. But so is the ability to produce arms—and that depends on the condition of a country's economy and the state of its technology. In addition to these, there is the alignment of powers in the world and the strength and reliability of allies. There is also the degree of tranquillity in the surrounding international environment. These factors in turn may depend not only on military and economic matters but also on questions of values. Even a superpower armed to the teeth can be very insecure if its economy is faltering, its allies are deserting, and its message to the world is unattractive.

Is it possible to escape the deadly logic of the global arms race? Can we really think about security in new and different ways? Can we reduce our reliance on military spending? Can we bring the defense budget under control without major economic dislocation? I believe that we can do all of these, but not unless we are willing to move in new directions and take some risks for peace.

We must begin with a serious, persistent, and widespread commitment to arms control and enter into negotiations with the Soviet Union and our allies on a wide range of issues.

Arms agreements in the past have generally served to redirect the arms race rather than to halt it. They have not led to reductions in arms. Indeed, support for arms control treaties is all too often bought with the promise of some new weapons system outside the ambit of the agreement. We need genuine control, not just a redirection of efforts.

I would attempt to negotiate a mutual and verifiable nuclear freeze at the highest level. This would include a freeze on the deployment of the MX and Pershing missiles and the development of the Midgetman missile. We must not put the world on a hair trigger with both America and Russia committed to launching their missiles merely upon the warning of an attack. The MX and Pershing would move us much closer to that dangerous condition, while the Midgetman's deployment would work against national means of verifying compliance with arms control agreements.

We also must forestall the testing and deployment of cruise missiles in a nuclear mode. The cruise missile, even more than the Midgetman, can be easily concealed. It is very tempting for us to proceed with it because we have a significant lead over the Soviets. The short-run advantages are great. But as with MIRV, the Soviets will themselves get the cruise someday and complicate mightily our own security position as a result. Back in 1969 I was a prime cosponsor of a resolution in the House to halt the testing of MIRV. Had there been a mutual freeze on MIRV testing, we would today be spared the vulnerability of our Minuteman system which is the principal source of nuclear instability. Remembering this lost opportunity, we must work harder to prevent the same type of arms race disaster from occurring with Midgetman and with the cruise missile.

I realize these proposals will be anathema to those who see arms control negotiations as a game of high-stakes international poker in which plans for sophisticated new weapons systems are piled high on the table like chips so players can bluff their adversaries. But I believe the bargaining chip theory is an all too convenient refuge for those who don't really have much faith in arms control anyway. As more and more technological breakthroughs give us more and more weapons of mass destruction, the bargaining chip myth becomes an exceedingly dangerous concept that deserves to be discarded in favor of genuine arms reduction talks.

Unless we first succeed in halting the upward spiral in both design and scope of new nuclear weapons systems, it is futile to talk about a reduction in the level of these arms. As soon as a freeze is in place, however, we should proceed to negotiate a reduction in both strategic launch vehicles and warheads. We should also work hard for a successful treaty limiting theater nuclear weapons in Europe. Serious negotiations should replace theatrical

275

gestures cynically advanced with the full knowledge that they are unrealistic.

The United States should seek to negotiate a treaty renouncing the first use of nuclear weapons. The primary mission of our nuclear weapons system should be to deter the Soviets from using theirs. We should proceed to implement a comprehensive test ban treaty. We should work to negotiate a treaty that would limit the militarization of outer space. In all these matters we should proceed only in close consultation with our allies.

One related area where we should *increase* spending is in the monitoring of the international traffic and use of nuclear materials. The International Atomic Energy Agency needs to be overhauled, and its performance substantially upgraded. Indeed, its activities may have to be supplemented by increased national surveillance.

We should also initiate new proceedings to try to limit the international production, stockpiling, and use of chemical and biological weapons. Current arrangements are grossly inadequate.

We should also place conventional arms limitation negotiations high on the international agenda. A conventional war between West and East fought in Europe could become a deadly war of attrition on a scale unmatched by either world war. We should therefore intensify the effort to negotiate a mutual balanced force reduction in Europe.

We should also revive the effort to reach an international agreement to limit the flow of arms to the developing world. This will be a very difficult negotiating task because agreement must be reached not only with the Soviets but with our European allies (who are also major exporters of arms) and with industrial states such as Israel, Japan, and South Korea, which could become large arms exporters if others agreed to quit the trade.

I have no illusions about the practical difficulties of reaching, monitoring, and then enforcing conventional arms transfer limitations. The task will be very hard. The process will take time. The results will be small at first. But it is a process we should set in train. If we are successful in rebuilding the global economy, the dangers of insurgency will recede and make genuine arms control of this variety more strategically and politically feasible. Gun control is not simply a domestic concern.

These are ambitious objectives. They will take years of tough negotiations to achieve. None may be achieved fully. We should have no illusions about our adversaries, their special agendas, and their desire to seek advantage at our expense. But it still makes no sense for the world to keep piling up arms. It makes no sense for war to become a way of life in so many places. It makes no sense at all for countries to bankrupt themselves to maintain large and expanding military establishments. In the summer of 1983 *U.S. News & World Report* catalogued forty separate wars in the world taking place at that time. Surely the human race can do better than this.

Genuine arms control will save billions of dollars. It will ease international tensions and reduce the strains on our economy. But it will not occur overnight. Furthermore, even if the arms race is brought under control and then reversed, America will still need a defense establishment. Realistically, total world disarmament remains a distant objective in view of the deep divisions in the global community. Regrettably, we will continue to need arms to defend ourselves, even though we try to reduce their numbers and their impact upon our lives. And we will still spend billions on them. But some of these billions can be saved. To do so, we should make major changes in the way the government and the defense industry operate. This would be true even if we were not successful in achieving the arms control objectives we wished to.

The problems of the defense industry are enormous. The government shares responsibility for many of them. The industry is stagnant in terms of competition. It is characterized by rising prices, by reduced efficiency, by a decline in the variety of its products, by increased concentration in fewer firms, by a growing management bureaucracy, and, generally, by a lack of competitiveness—all this despite its use of advanced technology. We are pricing ourselves out of the defense market just the same way that we are pricing ourselves out of other markets. Because we are less efficient, a greater portion of our economy must be committed to achieve a given level of defense capability. More time is needed to achieve peak production levels.

The defense sector, therefore, cries out for fundamental reform. There are several areas that need immediate attention.

We can start by cutting back or eliminating programs that we simply do not need, such as the MX, the B-1 bomber, and the Midgetman.

A second area for savings lies in the whole approach we use to develop weapons. Many observers, such as James Fallows, Richard Garwin, Frank Spinney, Thomas Aimlee, and Senator Gary Hart, have argued that less expensive, more reliable weapons systems can be purchased in greater numbers. Although this claim cannot be made in all cases, it can in many. There are some very basic strategic questions at work here. The more sophisticated a weapon is, the more expensive and the less reliable it tends to be. Emphasis upon technological sophistication can therefore reduce our overall capability while increasing our costs. The F-16 is cheaper than the F-15. It was built to be inexpensive and reliable. It is not weighted down with excessive sophistication. Even so, it can nearly match the performance characteristics of the F-15 at a fraction of the cost.

The navy could also purchase smaller ships at greatly reduced costs. Additional American ships would complicate Soviet military calculations. They would also provide the opportunity for more people to experience the responsibilities of command. Two conventional aircraft carriers can be bought and maintained at a price roughly equal to that of one nuclear carrier. In this same vein, advances in mine technology may be cheaper than attack submarines; deploying more antitank weapons may be cheaper than fielding more tanks.

Another area for reform is in the organizational structure of the armed forces themselves. Commentators have shown that the American armed forces are inefficient because the number of people who stand "behind" each combat person is much greater than in the armed forces of any other country. For example, it appears that America requires three times as many people to field a division as does the Soviet Union and four times as many people to put a combat aircraft into the sky as does Sweden or Israel. While some of the extra support may be needed to improve the readiness and safety of the combat person and some, no doubt, results from longer supply lines, it is difficult to believe that major improvements cannot be made in such ratios.

Armed forces stagnate just like industries. They become bureaucratized. They become inefficient. Their costs rise. Their personnel can play career games unrelated to the larger mission. Managers and employees replace commanders and soldiers. The routine supersedes the innovative. Strategic flexibility is replaced by managerial rigidity. And wars can be lost.

We must stop managing our armed forces as if they were a dying steel company and begin to think about building organizational and operational flexibility into the military structure. Just as predictable corporate management behavior and established markets make stagnant industries ripe for predatory destruction, so do rigid command positions and routine bureaucratic organizational behavior make armies ripe for defeat. Critics of the command structure include former Chairman of the Joint Chiefs of Staff David Jones, who has written extensively on the subject, and many other ranking officers.

Yet another area for major improvement is in purchasing practices. Here the problems are extensive, occasionally spectacular, and often well publicized. Cost overruns are so common that companies which deliver weapons on time and under budget now advertise this fact by taking full-page ads in national publications. In most industries the costs of new products tend to fall dramatically over time as the technology is perfected, but not in the defense industry.

It is good publicity for a politician to take the floor and hold up a light bulb which the army purchased for $10 but which can be bought in a supermarket for $1, and Senator William Proxmire has commendably focused attention on such problems. Several billion dollars could probably be saved each year by purchasing products directly off the commercial shelf or by instituting more competitive purchasing practices.

Far larger savings are possible in the procurement of major

weapons systems and in the structure of the defense industry which produces those systems. Despite recent attempts at reform, contract bidding arrangements still allow companies to under-estimate costs and then raise prices after the contract has been signed. The system is also designed to encourage major research and development efforts to create very sophisticated state-of-the-art weapons, but much less effort is made to improve the efficiency of the process by which weapons are manufactured. The design competition is fierce, but the production competition hardly exists.

Furthermore, there are major inefficiencies in a system in which one party (the government) is the sole purchaser, the regulator of the industry, and the appraiser of the product. Finally, there is strong evidence that the overall quality of the defense industry is declining as it becomes concentrated in fewer companies.

Reform is needed. Design competition and production competition should be separated so that after a design has been fully developed by a successful bidder, other companies can then bid on the production runs. This will discourage companies from bidding low at the design stage and then making up the difference during the production stage. It would also create a greater incentive for companies to devise less expensive means of producing the equipment. Second sourcing must be encouraged. In 1983 an attempt was made to allow second sourcing for the M-1 tank. Although proponents made a good case that this would save the taxpayer millions, the effort was foiled by intensive lobbying by the prime contractor.

More research and development money should be set aside to improve the efficiency of the production process. Improved means of production could also have valuable spin-offs for the private sector generally. This is one area in which an increase of funds in the short run would lead to great returns on the investment in the long run.

At the production stage, better incentives for "on time and under budget" should be built into the contract process. Once a design has been completed, the uncertainties of production costs would fall and more realistic bidding procedures would be possible. Also, once the design is complete, the government should make heroic efforts to halt the process of making changes. The government should set up an entirely independent agency to test and evaluate weapons to ensure that they meet design and performance specifications. These changes will make the production runs of large weapons systems more subject to market forces than they are and will create greater incentives for the prime contractors to improve the efficiency of the production process.

The situation at the subcontractor level is even more serious. Subcontractors and suppliers account for roughly half the cost of a weapons system. Jacques Ganzler has strikingly portrayed this area as the weak link in the whole system, which is now designed primarily to favor the prime contractor and to discourage the subcontractor.

As the system now operates, after the contract has been let, the prime contractor is in a powerful bargaining position and can pass cost increases along rather easily to the government. Profits of prime contractors are, therefore, typically large. The prime contractor, however, deals with the subcontractor in a market situation. Therefore, profits at this level are typically quite low as long as there is meaningful competition. Furthermore, when there are recessions in the industry, the prime contractor tends to produce more components in house, even though it may be expensive to do so. Therefore, spending reductions fall especially heavily on the subcontractors. The threat by the prime contractor to produce in house also can keep the subcontractors' profits down. As a result, the number of subcontractors is decreasing, single-source procurement is rising, prices are escalating, and production bottlenecks are proliferating.

The best solution to these problems is a more flexible and lively economy, but other steps will help. In some instances the government can let contracts which require a greater percentage of the work to be done by subcontractors. In others the government should seek bids directly for some components, instead of relying on the prime contractor. When a sole supplier is all that remains, the government can award research and development contracts to other firms to encourage their market entry.

The government can also improve its defense posture through

better planning. Contract problems are exacerbated by the vagaries of the budget process. A two-year budget cycle would be an immense help. With longer planning horizons, the Defense Department can pay more attention to the crucial problems of preparedness and potential bottlenecks in the supply line. Stockpiling, anticyclical purchasing, and long-range purchasing strategies can also be used to save money, while helping stabilize the larger economy. Actually, with better planning the length of time needed to procure a weapons system can also be reduced. Planning reform should include our NATO allies as well; programs for allied purchasing of standardized parts should be accelerated.

Finally, we come to people. Better training programs are needed to improve the skills of those who are handling, operating, maintaining, and repairing sophisticated military equipment. We can make better use of trained civilian personnel. More command opportunities and more hands-on experience are needed for our officers to ensure a higher retention rate and higher morale. The "up-or-out" system should be revised.

Our armed forces personnel are, after all, our most important military resource. Their training, their morale, and their judgment are at least as important as the equipment they use. Technology at virtually any level can be mastered by an adversary and then overcome or neutralized. It is people who count in conflict situations. Without their contribution, no level of technology or quantity of weapons can guarantee security.

Saving defense dollars makes good economic sense. Military spending is a drag on the economy. On balance, it is not investment-oriented. Among the advanced countries of the world, those that spend less on defense do better on growth. The defense orientation of Reagan's spending program is one reason why the Great Recession was so severe.

But if we cut back on defense spending, what will happen to employment in the defense industries themselves? It will fall, but not by as much as it increases elsewhere. Furthermore, defense contractors can easily compete in many areas of commercial development. The commercialization of space is one. Bringing new technology to shipbuilding is another. Civilian aircraft is a third. Moreover, civilian industries, such as electronics, communications, computers, and related technology fields, will provide expanding opportunities for current defense contractors to exploit should they wish to. There will be many opportunities in the new economy for lively enterprise. If the defense industry shapes up, it will have no lack of business in the commercial sector.

These proposals can save the American taxpayer enormous sums of money over the next decade, but I am not making wild claims. There is no way we can cut the military budget in half and thereby double our defense preparedness. I will leave that kind of spurious rhetoric to the public relations specialists who gave us supply-side economics. What I do claim, however, is that if we work at it, we can save money, repair our armed forces, and help build a more peaceful world.

These are achievable objectives, but today politics stands in the way. The Republicans are hopeless. But the Democrats are also showing no leadership. They may proclaim their allegiance to a nuclear freeze with both piety and gusto, but when it came to a vote, they finally gave Reagan his MX. They backed his defense build-up. They didn't seriously question his military program. We will still have *Star Wars,* an expanding arms race, and a more militarized economy. Putting the Democrats back in office will not make basic changes in the way we formulate strategy or in the way we buy arms. To be sure, there are in both parties voices of sanity that are serious about reform. But their views are not about to command a majority in either party. Not as long as special-interest money commands the attention it does in Washington.

This situation need not be. There is a large national constituency for arms control. The nation wants the freeze. The nation wants an end to the "winning nuclear wars" nonsense. The nation will also support conventional arms control as long as it is part of reciprocal agreements that can be adequately verified. A good case can be made to the country that pouring arms willy-nilly into the Third World is the road to nowhere. As long as Americans are convinced that agreements can be monitored and enforced, they will support them.

To mobilize that support, we need a new political movement in America. Not just a freeze movement or an arms control movement or a peace movement but a movement that is part of a new national political party committed to other objectives as well. A party of the center that can deliver on serious and rational arms control agreements. A party willing to take risks for peace that is also willing to assess those risks carefully and wisely. A party willing to redefine our current concept of national security. A party committed to basic reform in military affairs. A party willing to shake up the Pentagon. A party willing to take on the defense lobby. A party committed to a sane and sober world, which is proud to affirm as its credo:

We believe America needs a party determined to negotiate an end to the arms race, unafraid to affirm the imperative that war in the nuclear age is unthinkable and must be declared obsolete. The party must be overwhelmingly committed to the rule of law in international affairs and to the development of institutions for the settlement of international disputes above the claims of unfettered sovereignty.

17

BUILDING A MORE
PROSPEROUS AND
SECURE WORLD

HELPING nations realize their economic potential is a
more fitting recipe for peace than pouring arms into a tense and
troubled world. Unfortunately American politicians find it far easier to spend money building foreign armies than foreign economies.

Common sense suggests that if the United States wants a more
prosperous and secure global environment, it must work to encourage the preservation and extension of democracy overseas and
to create conditions of economic stability and growth. To do so,
we must help rebuild the existing economies of those democratic
countries that are fully developed and promote the creation of a
large, pluralistic, and dominant middle class in those countries
that are not.

Achieve these objectives, and we will have a more secure world,
relatively free from leftist insurrection, rightist repression, and
xenophobic nationalism.

To begin, we must act to ensure that Europe becomes once again a source of economic, diplomatic, cultural, and, yes, military, strength rather than a burden that someday will contribute to our weakness. We must help Europe escape its own economic stagnation. This we are in a position to do. Lower interest rates in America will reduce interest rates in Europe and quicken European investment. American exports of new capital systems will give Europe the opportunity to rebuild its economy and regain its global competitiveness. International financial stability will help Europe as well as us. Lower trade barriers will hasten the movement of Europe into the age of high technology.

In addition to taking these steps, America must foster greater European economic and political integration. We should not abandon our historic goal of seeing a democratic and unified Western Europe standing as a full partner with America. We should urge the Europeans to strengthen their international political and economic decision-making institutions. We should encourage them to take further steps toward currency integration. We should applaud the efforts of the Common Market to assume economic functions best achieved on a community-wide basis. And we should work with Europe to forestall trade wars, regulate countertrade, modify its Common Agricultural Policy, and remove barriers to service imports. We can also look to Europe for a greater contribution to its own defense.

I believe that economic recovery can give Europe a new sense of pride and purpose, a spirit of accomplishment matching that of the 1950s. If Europe retools and enters a new industrial age, unemployment will fall and large overseas markets will develop. Its enlivened economy will discourage the rise of extremist forces. Democracy will be reaffirmed. Most Europeans today are committed to democracy and to human rights. As the European Community expands, it can strengthen democratic forces and civil liberties throughout all Western Europe and prevent the reemergence of military dictatorships in Spain, Portugal, and Greece. America, backed by resurgent European democracy, would find its own voice immeasurably strengthened in world affairs.

We must work hard, together with those Europeans who share this vision of a united democratic Europe, to make it happen. It is a far better image of the future than that of a stagnant Europe, losing its ability to compete, selling its inferior products only to the Soviet bloc, falling into factional strife, giving rise to extreme political groups, and becoming a vexing concern to America once again.

It is also time to rethink our policies toward Japan. America must make certain that Japan remains firmly in the Western economic and political camp. There is nothing inevitable about this being the case. If the protectionist sentiments sweeping America and Europe today seriously reduce Japanese export opportunities, Japan will look increasingly to China and the Soviet Union. They have the resources that Japan needs. Japan has the technology that they need. The match is possible.

Our military umbrella is no guarantee that Japan will remain a Western power. By the end of the century Japan could well have the capability of defending itself alone against conventional attack. Today it has a GNP nearly half that of the United States. The gap is closing. With its ability to build vehicles, ships, and equipment more efficiently today than America can and with its emerging defense industry, Japan by the end of this century will have an economic base capable of creating and maintaining a substantial navy and air force equipped with reliable weapons of high quality. This force could be large enough to outweigh U.S. strength in the Pacific.

It is, however, in neither Japan's diplomatic interests nor ours for it to build such a large defense establishment. Improvements in Japan's defense posture should take place within the context of a clearly defined U.S.-Japanese defense plan. For that reason, we should not use our military umbrella as a bargaining counter to extract economic concessions from Japan or to keep Japan in its economic "place."

If America rebuilds its own productive base, it has nothing to fear from Japanese competition. On the contrary, it has much to gain from close economic ties to Japan. We must work to increase, not to decrease, commerce between us. We must work to increase reciprocal investment opportunities. Above all, we must avoid isolating ourselves from Japan by engaging in political grandstanding that may play well with American audiences but does little to improve our ability to achieve American economic and diplomatic objectives.

Relations with Japan have reached a critical stage. The Great Recession gave rise to strong protectionist sentiments within America. The response to competitive pressures and to legitimate grievances against Japanese discriminatory practices has taken on a jingoistic tone that serves only to foster trade tensions. Ad hoc wrist slaps generate contempt, not respect. Japan deserves to be treated as a full ally and partner in the task of rebuilding the global supply base. Our trade complaints should be pursued through normal diplomatic channels, not through public recrimination and the constant drumbeat of protectionist threats.

The United States, Western Europe, and Japan have an economic and technological base unchallenged by all other powers combined. Together we have a population three times that of Russia and nearly three-quarters that of China. We have a democratically based cultural entente that no set of potential antagonists will ever have. United, our alliance is stronger than any power or combination of powers that can be erected to challenge us in the foreseeable future. We must place the preservation of this alliance of democracies at the center of all our calculations. It makes equal sense to ensure that all parts of this alliance are prospering economically.

Building on this base, we must also seek to establish a more creative set of relationships with the newly industrializing countries (NICs) on the rim of Asia: South Korea, Taiwan, Hong Kong, and Singapore. These economies are expanding rapidly, adopting new manufacturing technology, and competing effectively with American producers in many industries.

The NICs will continue to create investment opportunities. As they develop further, they will become markets for American products, including newly developed capital systems. They can become large purchasers of American services, which can play a significant role in the expansion of their economic support systems.

We must ensure that American protectionist sentiments do not shut off their markets and create widespread economic dislocation. In return for this assurance, however, countries in the region must cooperate with us more fully in controlling industrial piracy, which to many American manufacturers has become a legitimate source of grievance.

These countries are now in a position to assist their neighbors. They are already a model. During the next decade the Philippines, Indonesia, Thailand, Malaysia, and the island states of Oceania can become NICs with the help of America, Japan, and their rapidly growing Asian neighbors. It is very much in our interest that this take place.

The Association of Southeast Asian Nations (ASEAN) has already demonstrated strong leadership in cooperative, multinational economic development. I propose that the United States, together with Canada, Japan, South Korea, Taiwan, the Philippines, Malaysia, Thailand, Singapore, Indonesia, Australia, New Zealand, and the island states of the Pacific build on the solid accomplishments of ASEAN and create a Pacific Development Association to encourage democracy and economic development in the region. Such an organization could take the form of an expanded ASEAN or an independent organization closely modeled after ASEAN.

This international group could become a vehicle for channeling foreign development assistance and direct grants from the more developed to the less developed countries of the region. The majority of this aid would come from America and Japan, with significant contributions from South Korea, Canada, Australia, and New Zealand. This organization would be designed to supplement, not to replace, current American and Japanese bilateral assistance programs. By providing direct grants and a flow of expertise, it could also supplement the excellent work of the World Bank and the Asian Development Bank as well as many existing bilateral programs.

The organization should set development goals, which would

include the continued rapid growth of countries like South Korea and Taiwan, together with major efforts to bring the rest of the region into a pattern of sustained economic growth. Such an agency could work to help build economic support systems, strengthen democratic institutions, assist small and medium-sized business enterprises, develop markets, and encourage the creative use of new technologies for education, training, and health purposes.

The United States, in full partnership with Japan and the NICs, should also establish closer economic relationships with China. Ever since the opening to China in the early 1970s the big power triangle of America, China, and Russia has been at the center of most Asian and many global diplomatic calculations. When China and Russia were in severe dispute during the 1970s, America was in a position to bargain with both. The Reagan administration's hostility toward the Soviet Union and its affinity for Taiwan has changed all that. It is no longer impossible for Russia to seek rapprochement with China or for China to turn away from its new relationship with America.

We must convince China that its opportunities for future development lie entirely with the West. It is not likely that China will soon become a "Western" power like Japan. It is, however, possible to foresee substantial investment markets in China develop over the next two decades. Western science, technology, real capital, and finance capital all are needed by China. We have already seen major advancements in trade. We must work together with our allies and regional trading partners to encourage a rapid expansion of this trade and of real investments as well.

The other great Asian power is India. It is a democracy. English, its language of unity, is spoken by nearly all educated people. It has long-standing ties to the Western diplomatic and cultural tradition. It should receive far more attention from America than it has in the past.

We should help India enter the circle of rapidly growing economies. Trade expansion is one means of doing so. Our trade with India has already grown significantly between 1970 and 1980, and we showed a surplus.

India can become an even better market for American products over the next two decades. We can help bring to it the communications revolution. We can sell it solar technology. We can sell it the hardware and software to build a more modern educational system. We can sell it flexible capital equipment to build farm machinery and consumer products uniquely tailored to its domestic markets. We can sell it the fruits of genetic engineering research to improve its agriculture. We can develop and export the hardware and software needed by India to expand its community of scientists and engineers. In short, through our exports, we can help India build an economic support system that will enable it to enter the new knowledge-based economic era. Many of these exports, because they will make direct contributions to economic growth, could be financed through long-term loans.

The industrialized countries, the newly industrializing countries, China, and India present America with extraordinary opportunities for exports. They are the starting point of our calculations. But these countries represent only two-thirds of the non-Soviet world. The other third is composed of underdeveloped countries in Asia, the Middle East, Africa, and Latin America. Here, too, it is in our self-interest to promote economic development.

Most of these countries face severe problems, some of them as old as the nation-state itself. Most have small middle classes, usually consisting of government employees. Agricultural production still operates with centuries-old practices. In many cases, housing, clothing, food, education, and information are in short supply. Many lack fuel, not simply oil but even the wood families need for preparing their meals and boiling their water.

Some of these countries are dangerously dependent on one or two basic resources, such as cocoa, copper, phosphates, or even anchovies, for their hard currency. Most depend on the health of the industrial economies which purchase their goods. In many respects the less developed countries (LDCs) experience our recessions and depressions in much the same way as many workers do in the United States. They are the first to be "laid off" and the last to be "rehired."

In addition to all these problems, there is the ever-growing debt burden. Today about 24 percent of export earnings in the LDCs must be set aside for interest payments.

For years we spoke of rising expectations in the developing world. We feared that people would expect too much too quickly. Now we must face the political, economic, and social chaos that can result from falling expectations, as growth rates plummet and people in developing nations lose any realistic hope of improving their lives and those of their children. Chaos can be followed by repression. The dangers are great.

Still, if the world can realize the vast potential that can come from true economic and social programs in these regions, there will be extraordinary rewards for success. Released from the crushing burdens of underdevelopment and given the opportunity to concentrate on matters other than basic survival, millions of fellow humans can provide themselves and us with the results of their intelligence, creativity, and productivity. We can only guess at how this might unfold, but if such a potential is freed, surely it will provide an opportunity for an unimaginable expansion of global cultural, social, and economic benefits. It will also produce a far more secure world.

These countries need help. But help is not always easy to extend. In many instances economic development assistance is of little use unless it is accompanied by political reform within the recipient nation. Unfortunately many developing nations have serious problems of corruption, elitism, overregulation for the benefit of the few, and consistent violations of basic human rights. All too often the political elites in these nations are willing to sacrifice genuine economic development and internal reform to perpetuate their own power. We can no longer afford to waste money on support for governments which refuse to permit political and social reform and thereby destroy the effectiveness of our development assistance.

To be successful, our policy must reflect fundamental values: democracy, socioeconomic equality of opportunity, and basic human rights. Our foreign assistance must be directed toward those developing nations which support this philosophy with actions, not mere words, and which are willing to use our money for its intended purpose. We can't change attitudes by simple fiat. Flexibility and realism are required, but they must not act as excuses for political expediency.

Moreover, we must recognize that we cannot export prosperity to these countries; we can only aid the natural forces of economic development. Our hope is to shape development in ways that will bring benefits to the greatest number of people in the shortest period of time. We are not and cannot be the arbiters of international development. We can only do our fair share.

Today we do not. The 0.27 percent of the gross national product that we contribute as official development assistance is the lowest of the major industrial countries, less than half that of France, for example. This level of support is inadequate; it should be raised steadily throughout this decade.

Each developing nation will provide unique problems and resources that require an individualized approach. Nonetheless, there are some needs that are almost universal in scope. For example:

—A lack of adequate water facilities in many countries creates serious health hazards, impedes agricultural expansion, and retards industrial growth. We have decades of hands-on experience in the development of water resources in our own arid regions. Efforts to transfer this experience and expertise need to be expanded.

—Developing countries need energy. One of the greatest contributions we can make to global economic growth would be to develop cost-effective solar technology.

—Computer technology can help train professionals, increase the productivity of those who are already trained, and alleviate many problems associated with a shortage of skills. During this decade we can help build the computer revolution into the economic system of the developing world in many ingenious ways, both to create new industries and to improve the quality of life.

—Developing countries need better educational systems. We can assist these countries in creating or improving them. We can thereby help reduce the brain drain that occurs when foreign students come to American universities and then stay here, denying the benefits of their education to their own countries.

—Developing countries have persistent health problems which create misery and reduce productivity. Immunization, family planning programs, and the provision of potable water are high-priority areas in which Americans can provide greater assistance.

If we combine an emphasis upon such development programs as these with a commitment to create other economic support systems, we will help the LDCs reach a stage where they can then absorb the real capital needed to begin a genuine and broad-based economic expansion.

To implement a comprehensive program for global economic development, we need to employ many different approaches.

Some will be multilateral. These include the better-known agencies such as the World Bank and the International Monetary Fund, but they also include regional development banks, regional institutions such as the Pan American Health Organization, and global international agencies, such as UNICEF. New multilateral agencies are proposed in this chapter.

The United States should make a firm commitment to expand its support for these multilateral agencies. Their support should take the form of both increased financial assistance *and* timely payment of our assessed contribution, an area in which the United States recently has been particularly remiss.

Other sources of aid will be private. Important work is being done throughout the developing world by nonprofit American organizations, both secular and religious. These private groups often employ people with a deep sense of personal commitment to development who can provide a unique perspective on individual nations. Their efforts may be considerably less colored by political expediency than those of government agencies. The United States Agency for International Development (AID) provides some assistance to these groups today, but further support is needed in the form of matching grants that encourage private organizations to develop their own funding constituencies.

Despite an increased emphasis on multilateral and private programs—which I favor—our most important efforts will continue to be bilateral. These are principally handled by AID. Unfortunately AID has become an overly bureaucratized, frustrated, understaffed, underfinanced, uninspired symbol of all that is wrong with our current development efforts. Such has not always been the case. There were moments of creativity, idealism, and constructive action in the early sixties. But idealism faded, and AID's sense of importance and purpose faded as well. AID should be reorganized, reenergized, and retargeted.

In recent years AID has become a mere conduit for funding. Effective implementation of its development projects has been consciously placed in the hands of consulting firms and other private institutions. The original idea was to save money since it seemed less expensive to retain people from the outside than to hire government employees with all their attendant benefits, pension plans, and other add-ons.

The pendulum, however, has swung too far. AID employees have been reduced to paper pushing. Since they don't implement programs, they gain none of the experience necessary for competent evaluation and future planning. AID-assisted projects should have at least one or two AID employees attached to each. This practice would develop agency expertise and benefit agency morale.

We should also return to earlier agency staffing patterns in which a greater proportion of its employees were located directly within the developing nations close to the programs and projects they were meant to oversee. This is not a call for the expansion of American "ghettos" in foreign capitals. Since much of AID's efforts are directed toward rural development, it seems only logical that many of its staff be located in rural areas.

Individual AID missions located in developing nations should be given greater latitude in the selection and support of projects. The project identification and design process should be significantly shortened. Today agency employees can expect to wait at least two years before a proposed project has moved far enough through the bureaucracy to begin actual implementation.

Large-scale AID projects, as a rule, should be referred to multilateral agencies or be undertaken jointly with such agencies and with other bilateral programs. In this way greater resources can be brought to bear on the problems at the local level, where they are needed.

To coordinate these activities, I would recommend the appointment of an undersecretary of state for international development. Currently the highest ranking official with clear responsibility for international development is the administrator of AID, a comparatively low-level, peripheral position reflecting America's ambivalent attitude toward development.

In the Western Hemisphere we must do more than underwrite traditional development activities. In Central America today we are seeing upheavals resulting from long-standing conditions of political repression and economic deprivation. The most visible of these upheavals is in El Salvador, where an insurgency is far advanced, but El Salvador is just a small part of a much larger regional problem that embraces Mexico and virtually all other countries in the area.

We face some difficult long-range choices in Central America and perhaps in all Latin America. If genuine economic development and political reform are not forthcoming, we will soon see a hemisphere in chaos, torn by guerrilla and international wars, a patchwork quilt of unstable right- and left-wing dictatorships beset by internal upheaval and foreign hostilities. Violence will be a way of life, as it has become for many parts of the Middle East, and arms poured into the area will lead only to a degenerating fabric of social existence. Personal freedoms will disappear. Economic opportunities will be lost. This scenario need not be played out, but time is short.

In El Salvador itself the choices are not easy. There may be glib talk about "political solutions" and "negotiated settlements," but working coalition governments are not easily formed in countries where people have been murdering each other for years. We must seek an internationally supervised settlement in El Salvador, supported by the other nations in the region, but we should have few illusions about our ability to succeed in the short run.

The problems we currently face in El Salvador and its neighbors are likely to pale in comparison to those we may soon face in Mexico. In 1930 there were only 16.5 million Mexican citizens. Today there are 75 million, and their numbers are growing rapidly.

For more than fifty years Mexico has been led by the Partido Revolucionario Institucional (PRI). Although Mexico is a fully functioning democracy with opposition parties, the PRI is the only party that has governed at the federal level. It is the single most influential institution in the nation.

The PRI is dependent, as it should be, on the good will and solid support of the Mexican people. That good will and support, however, are seriously endangered by Mexico's current financial crisis. Oil revenues have fallen sharply; the country cannot simultaneously meet payments on its $85 billion external debt and still finance its health care, educational, and economic development programs, especially those needed for agricultural growth in an arid land. The PRI also has been shaken by repeated allegations of corruption despite current government attempts to correct the situation.

Should there be an economic disaster in Mexico, popular support for the PRI will further erode. If the PRI falls, there is no other national political institution that could confidently take its place. The government of Mexico would likely disintegrate, leading to a fractious battle involving the army, labor groups, and leftist movements.

It would be unfair to ignore the truly impressive efforts being made by the Mexican government, with the support of the PRI, in response to this dangerous situation. The government has moved to eliminate many of its expensive and economically unjustified programs. In the space of a single year Mexico has tried to reduce its public-sector deficit from 16 percent to 8.5 percent of its gross domestic product, a truly incredible effort. Mexico's current political leadership is sophisticated, competent, and aware of the dangers it faces. But that leadership could soon be overwhelmed by events.

If this situation existed in another part of the world, the United States might ignore it, but Mexico is our neighbor. We share a 1,933-mile border with this proud and ambitious nation. Millions of our citizens enjoy a Mexican heritage, and millions of Mexican citizens reside in America.

A socioeconomic and political disaster in Mexico would quickly be felt on this side of the Rio Grande. Mexico is our third largest trading partner and one of the few with which we have had a positive balance of trade in recent years, although exports to Mexico fell sharply after the devaluation of the peso. Unrest in Mexico could unleash a flood of refugees, a situation for which we are completely unprepared. Economic and political disaster in Mexico would leave that nation dependent on massive external assistance for years.

In view of these dangers, it is in our best interests to work with the Mexican government to create a long-term rescue package for Mexico, including provisions for direct aid, debt repayment assistance, expanded trade, and technical assistance. As part of this effort, we might negotiate long-term oil purchase agreements.

For the rest of Central America we should launch a long-term program of significantly expanded bilateral assistance to achieve the following objectives:

—Land reform, facilitated by land banks the function of which would be to purchase land from large absentee landowners and resell it on reasonably generous terms to those who work that land
—Agricultural research and extension to bring a "green" revolution to this region of expanding population
—A stronger economic support system, including both traditional public work projects and the growth of a new

knowledge sector, which would include better schools, training facilities, and an improved higher educational system

—Primary resource development, with the proceeds reinvested within each country

—Industrialization, through investment loans, technology transfer, and trade expansion

—Direct person-to-person assistance, especially through the use of volunteers from all parts of the community

—Increased trade, both with us and throughout the region.

These proposals are not by any means exhaustive. They illustrate, however, what can be done to bring some hope to a region that is suffering from economic and political despair. We must create a sense of future growth and prosperity while taking concrete steps to make it a reality.

Foreign aid is not a popular expenditure with American taxpayers. Both Democratic and Republican politicians are fond of declaiming that we should spend the money here. But this is a perspective of the past. If the American economy is to grow, the world economy must also grow. If we are to become a major exporting economy, others must have the means to import. If we want peace and prosperity, then we must have an alternative to war and upheaval.

We need new leadership to convince the American people that this is the case. We need a new political party in America. A party committed to an international system of sovereign states growing in prosperity. A party willing to recognize the realities of nationalism and cultural diversity. A party mature enough to know that if we insist on having our way everywhere in the world, we will soon have our way nowhere. A party representing the American national interest that understands how closely our fortunes are tied to those of other peoples.

In the early days of this Republic, it was often difficult to obtain genuine cooperation among the many states. Jealousies and differing socioeconomic interests separated Americans, leading often to violent verbal exchanges and sometimes to violence itself. If we had not shared a vision that a better future could flow from national unity, if we had not found leadership that brought people together, the United States would have been a failed experiment. Today's world would be a different and a worse place in which to live. Through our many difficulties, including civil war, depression, and world war, we often had the excuse to turn away from the original dreams described so clearly in our Declaration of Independence, Constitution, and Bill of Rights. We did not turn away. We carried on despite our difficulties. As a result, we gained a global reputation for being both highly pragmatic and highly idealistic, a combination not yet surpassed or improved upon by any other people.

Today those who speak of development for *all* the world's people are often castigated as idealists, do-gooders, and impractical dreamers. This is nonsense. To demand that concrete steps be undertaken to bring about global peace is not simply idealistic but a matter of cold, hard, practical necessity. To require that we face up to the real needs of the developing world is not simply a question of doing good but a logical step that will bring benefits to us as well as others. To advocate the creation of a just, open, and dynamic global economy is not to dream impractically but to plan realistically for a goal which is unavoidable if our own future is to be other than one of misery, stagnation, and hopelessness.

As Americans we did not reject our dreams; we lived them. As human beings we can afford to do no less.

V

Conclusion

18

AN ECONOMY
OF VALUES

To solve our problems, we must first understand them. And understanding begins with truth. We can no longer afford to fool ourselves since we certainly no longer fool anyone else. Common sense and plain dealing are still good watchwords for both public and private conduct. Effective government is honest government.

But honesty is not simply a matter of telling the truth and avoiding lies. It is also a matter of understanding what the truth is. It is the ability to cut through all the pretense and sham, the false hopes and illusions which accompany the trappings of office. Honesty is reality. It is the ability to perceive reality with clarity and balance. It is the ability to know right from wrong and sense from nonsense. It is substance, not style. It is logic, not rhetoric. It is the willingness to admit error and to understand that errors in public life almost always hurt someone—often very badly.

When the margins for error are great, a nation can indulge its fancy, seek refuge in delusion, and ignore its mistakes. This we did in the 1930s, when depression gave birth to world war and America for a long time looked the other way. Today the margins for error are much smaller, and they are narrowing. A protracted economic crisis could in time destroy the Western alliance, generate a hostile Southern Hemisphere, undermine both the economic and diplomatic basis of our security, and eventually threaten our survival as a free nation. The games we are playing are serious and deadly. The price of illusion is very high.

The most tempting illusion of all is that of simplicity: the single answer, the sure cure, the quick fix. Supply. Demand. Tax cut. High tech. Break OPEC. Get the government off our backs. Rearm. The bottom line. In short, "Keep it simple, stupid."

This approach of reducing everything to a single solution or to a fancy abstract model simply will not work. It repudiates all we know about human beings. It also tends to erode values. It divorces the way we think about economics from the larger culture of which an economic system is but a part. The reductionist assumption that everything can be viewed in terms of self-interest is foolish. Greed is not enough to run an economic system or to understand how one works. Humans are complex. They are economic, spiritual, and cultural beings. Their motivations and values far transcend the narrow calculations of gain and loss. They are full of surprises. Free people, like Americans, are full of many surprises.

That is why it is important for us as a society to treat our individual members decently and to invest in them. But if we look upon people as just a training problem, then we miss the point entirely. Skills are important, but they are not everything. People are economic actors, but not exclusively so. Motivation and inspiration are also important. There is no formula by which these can be produced, nor can there ever be.

That is why we must emphasize individuality, pluralism, and uniqueness. Variety is the opposite of reductionism, the antidote to stagnation. It is what America has always stood for. Freedom, cultural richness, and creativity are needed to make an economy such as ours come alive once again. These values are not to be found in narrow economic game plans. They come from a basic sense of decency, from treating people right, from encouraging them, and from inspiring them to further accomplishment.

People have a sense of purpose again, a sense of accomplishment, a sense of pride. And reality must justify these. Quality. Doing things right. Living in a society that works. Living in decent surroundings. Living in a healthful environment. Seeing other people performing skillfully and purposefully. Knowing that the contributions we make are important. These are the attitudes that make an economy work. They are as fundamental as tax deductions and depreciation allowances. They give "soul" to the machine, flexibility to the industry, and worth to the product.

People, however, will not take pride in what they are doing if they are living just for today. They must have faith in the future. They must believe that there will be a future, that we will not be blasted into atoms. They must have a sense that they are building something that will be useful and that will last.

To restore this faith is not an easy task. It requires patience and commitment and a long-range perspective. It requires a sense of knowing who you are, what you can do and cannot do. It requires both pride and humility. And it requires a very strong sense of the past and the future, the old and the young, and why all are important to society and culture in the greater scheme of things.

It we look to the long term, if we succeed in acquiring a sense of history and continuity, then we can understand the meaning of trust since trust is a relationship based on solid expectations of the future. But trust is an important economic value, too. If people cannot trust the government, if fiscal and monetary policies become games to suit the expediencies of the moment, then the economy will suffer real damage. Moreover, it is not only government that needs to operate in a climate of trust. Markets where transactions worth millions are made on the basis of a person's word work much better than markets where every act must be sealed in a contract. More important, trust is the basis of investment. Banks, after all, are *entrusted* with their depositors' money. Their first responsibility is to protect the security of their deposits and not to play wild games which threaten the integrity of the system. Banks cannot operate for long without a climate of trust.

America will not work as a society without a measure of trust. If the government does not trust the people, then it will try to manipulate them. After a spell it may even come to believe its own lies. But the government can't manipulate the people for too long because those who manipulate are usually no smarter than those they are trying to fool. The latter, once burned, will never trust the government again.

This is why there is a difference between management and leadership. Good management is vitally necessary in government to make the government itself work. We know this because good management has been lacking in Washington for quite a while. But management, however good, is manipulative and coercive. Americans want their public business to be managed well. But they themselves don't want to be managed. Government as mere management is the Soviet system, not ours.

It is leadership that gives direction to management and provides it with a greater sense of purpose. Grounded in the authority given to it by the people, leadership must be the trustee of values in a society, the exemplifier, the legitimizer of action. Leadership sets the tone and defines the style of government. In doing so, it must exemplify the values of the American people, or it soon will lose the basis of its authority.

We need leadership in America, and here I am thinking not of a given political office or set of offices but across a broad spectrum of government and society. I mean leadership that will give us again some old-fashioned honesty and integrity, that will not fool the people, fool the stockholder, or fool itself. This integrity should be born of a new sense of pride: pride in workmanship; pride in being part of a country that is a going concern; pride in rebuilding a decent and just society; pride in America. Dishonesty is the refuge of the weak, the ashamed, and the fearful. Honesty is born of confidence and pride in one's own values.

This deeper integrity, this sense of purpose are necessary if we are to transcend the narrow limits of the "me" philosophy, which is one result of the growing belief in our society that nobody cares. That nobody cares if the machine works properly, or if the job is done right, or if the government is run responsibly, or if the person next door needs help, or if employees have decent working

for their lives and aspirations. We will also discourage people today from making those investments in their lives and in our economy that look to a long-term future. That is why we must make an end to the arms race a central objective and why we must repeat the call for an approach to international comity based not on force but on satisfying the most basic needs of people.

When Gabriel García Márquez accepted the Nobel Prize in literature in 1982, his acceptance speech included this moving passage:

> On a day like today, my master William Faulkner said, "I decline to accept the end of man." I would feel unworthy of standing in this place that was his if I were not fully aware of the colossal tragedy he refused to recognize thirty-two years ago is now, for the first time since the beginning of humanity, nothing more than a simple, scientific possibility. Faced with this awesome reality that must have seemed a mere utopia through all of human time, we, the inventors of tales, who will believe anything, feel entitled to believe that it is not too late to engage in the creation of the opposite utopia, a new and sweeping utopia of life, where no one will be able to decide for others how they die; where love will prove true and happiness be possible; and where the races condemned to one hundred years of solitude will have, at last and forever, a second opportunity on earth.

Some, of course, will deride "the inventors of tales, who will believe anything." They will disdain such advice as coming only from those who live in a fantasy world of their own. That cynicism might perhaps suffice if it were not for the fact that few would dispute the claim that the "simple, scientific possibility" that the world will end now does exist and that if we continue on our course, we may see the ultimate destruction of our planet. That moral, political, and economic reality must be placed alongside the plea for the vision of a new utopia, one in which the values of love, autonomy, and regard for human happiness replace the fear, hatred, and reliance on the machines of war that seem today to be the arbiters of our destiny.

EPILOGUE

W<small>E</small> all are aware that a new politics exists in America. It has been with us for a couple of decades, and its distinguishing features are well known: an expensive electoral process financed increasingly by special-interest Political Action Committees (PACs), an impersonalized form of communication between politicians and their constituents relying upon television and other remote media, a severely weakened party structure rapidly being replaced by a system of candidate politics, and an electorate whose traditional commitments to either of the two old parties are steadily eroding.

We have been aware of these tendencies for years. But we have been less aware of how these changes have affected the moral basis of representative democracy in America. Our traditional parties were created around the concept of loyalty. They delivered to their constituencies. They were built on assumptions of mutual trust. At times such loyalties became the source of abuses when politicians delivered spoils to their own cronies, but personal loyalties were nevertheless the cement that held politics together. The parties went to great length to establish and maintain those loyalties. They were "people-oriented." Party officials were close to the citizenry. They knew and represented their views.

Today this has changed. Public officials are no longer dependent on party organizations for election or necessarily on any given set of constituents. To the new politician, loyalties have assumed a merely strategic significance. Many politicians build their electoral strategy around the practice of taking their own supporters for granted while reaching out to larger and more fluid constituencies. The use of the media has also tended to undermine loyalties. Communications have become typically one-way—from the top down, not from the bottom up. With party structures disintegrating, an important communications link from the people to the politicians has gone. Random sample polls are not a fully satisfactory substitute.

This one-way communication has created a politics that is highly manipulative, again in one direction. Whether it is a case of manipulating appearances to disguise reality, or a case of diverting attention away from reality, or some other stimulus-response technique that is used, the result is a much higher degree of sophisticated manipulation than we have ever seen.

There was certainly manipulation in the old party system, but it was two-way manipulation—that is, bargaining. It was direct and personal. It produced results. And it meant that the party became the mediator between interests. Parties had an important economic and social function to perform—namely, to solve disputes. Today disputes are largely settled outside the party system in the courts, in the intense clash of special interests in the legislature, or by the pressure of special interests on administrators.

As the loyalty of the politician to his or her constituents has begun to break down, so has the loyalty of those constituents to the party. People do not want to be taken for granted. For example, as 1984 approached, organized blacks and organized women began to calculate their strategic relationship to the Democratic party. They were torn between two conflicting approaches: Should they work loyally as Democrats on the basis that they must elect "anyone but Reagan," or should they recognize that if they did, the party would simply continue to take them for granted? Should they therefore threaten to withhold their support and increase their bargaining power in the future? The very existence of such calculations is a striking commentary on the breakdown of the party system as we have known it.

Furthermore, as communications have become more one-sided and manipulative, it is not at all surprising that people have organized and tried to make their voices heard outside the party system. The decline of parties has produced not only candidate politics as a by-product but special-interest politics as well. Organized special interests have become the mediators between the citizen and the government, the object in many cases of intense citizen loyalty that three generations ago would have been vested in the parties themselves. Special-interest groups, however, are an inadequate substitute for political parties. Operating outside the disintegrating party structure, these groups can form temporary alliances of convenience, but they can seldom coalesce around broad principles reflecting the national interest for long periods of time. They have replaced the parties to a large degree, but neither are they themselves parties nor can they act as parties. Loyalty within such groups is standard. Loyalty between them, however, is less frequent. The result is political fragmentation of a degree unimaginable under the old party system.

As loyalty to causes has become a more potent force in American politics than loyalty to parties, the two old parties have come under the sway of causes to an unprecedented degree. The Republicans, who used to be a broad-based party with at least the pretense of being a party with an "open door" and a fiscally responsible outlook on the national budget, have been captured by a well-financed band of right-wing ideologues who have forged an alliance which they claim to be holy with the oil, gas, and defense interests. Money and fanaticism of varying degrees of intensity have combined with a relatively narrow band of powerful interests to produce a shameful alliance that has an enormous stake in such diverse policies as $1 trillion of new debt, high interest rates, an overvalued dollar on international exchanges, the reduction of conservation efforts and research into alternative forms of energy, and a defense build-up that can ruin the economy and bankrupt the country.

But the Democrats are also a party of special interests, often linked to causes, which, in the absence of a strong party structure and strong elected officials, now renegotiate their loyalties every two or four years.

We simply no longer have a political system composed of parties in the traditional sense of the word: parties that mediate between special interests (instead of being captured by them); parties that provide a personalized form of communication between citizen and elected official; parties that serve as ombudsmen for the citizens they represent; parties that produce candidates on the national level who tend to appeal to the center of the political spectrum.

The two-party system as it existed for more than half our national history is dying. It once served us well, but it is almost gone. "The party is over," as one noted commentator has put it. I doubt if it will ever return in the form with which we are familiar. We must therefore look for a replacement.

Can that replacement be found Phoenix-like in the ashes of the old structure? I do not believe that it can. At least not unless those ashes are stirred up from outside. The competition today between the two old parties is not producing an improvement in either one. Lacking an up-and-coming competitor, neither party tries harder. Both just wait for the revolving door of voter frustration to turn them in and the other out. Moreover, the expected failure of one old presidential party can easily lead to the radicalization of the other. The Republican Right had no incentive to moderate its views in the 1970s while it strengthened its position in the Republican party and waited for the Democrats to fail. Today its strategy has seemingly been vindicated because it now controls one-half of the two-party system.

This present-day control of the Republican nominating process by right-wing interests is the most important fact of contemporary American politics. It is the logical starting point in any calculation about the future of the American two-party system. It is the principal reason why the present two-party system cannot reform itself from within. The Republican Right will not let this happen. It knows that if it can maintain its control and nothing other than the two-party system exists, then America in the future must undergo recurrent periods of right-wing rule, perhaps far more extreme than anything we have seen to date, unless the Democratic party can continually and perpetually win presidential elections. The Democrats' ability to do so should be viewed in light of the fact that since Franklin Roosevelt their candidate for president has received more than half the popular vote cast for president in only two elections.

I believe that the Republican party will remain in the control of the right wing and that this right wing will become ever more radicalized in the decades ahead as it continues to exploit its strategic position in the two-party system.

The numbers are compelling. The Republican presidential nominating convention numerically has a strong built-in bias that makes it nearly impossible for any moderate to receive the nomination. The apportionment of delegates among the states is heavily weighted by a bonus system that favors the small and medium-sized states, most of which are conservative. The South, the rest of the Sun Belt, and the mountain states, with their growing populations and always solid conservative delegations, have a permanent working majority in a Republican convention, even though they today contain a minority of Republicans nationally.

This situation is not about to change. Court challenges to the bonus system have been dismissed by the U.S. Supreme Court. Internal attempts at reform have been brushed aside by the conservative-controlled party machinery with only minimal concessions to politeness.

Equally important, the ideological basis of conservative power gives right-wing candidates an enormous advantage over Republican moderates during the primary season. "Cause" candidates can raise money and weather setbacks much more easily than "image" candidates (which the moderates have now become). The latter can attract followings and raise opportunity money early on, but any setback, however small, sets things rapidly in reverse. Momentum will not do it for the moderates.

Howard Baker's 1980 campaign, despite money and talent, collapsed when he failed to win a straw poll in Maine that he had counted on winning, a truly ludicrous circumstance. George Bush although he continued to run, collapsed as a truly viable candidate capable of defeating Reagan when I came within a few votes of beating him in the Massachusetts primary. Candidacies that live by the media also die by the media, unless they establish strong constituency bases that transcend personality.

The conservatives have such a base. Ronald Reagan, who lost badly in Iowa in 1980, bounced back in New Hampshire because he had constituency support, just as he bounced back in 1976 after being beaten in a string of primaries by President Gerald Ford. Indeed, he bounced back so well that he nearly took the nomination away from a sitting president, widely admired by his former colleagues in Congress and by traditional Republican party officials throughout the country who were giving him their unqualified support in most cases. The conservative candidacies of the future will be built on the rock of ideological support, while the moderate candidacies rest upon the sand of personality, media manipulation, and opportunity money.

The conservative takeover of the Republican party is not a temporary swing of the pendulum which will reverse itself in due time. At work are fundamental social and demographic forces that are changing the nature of the rank-and-file party voter. Most important of these changes is that the "moderate-conservative" midwestern center of the party is slowly dying. Its Republicans, among other people, are migrating to different parts of the country, especially to the Sun Belt, where their conservative instincts are encouraged and their moderate instincts are discouraged by the political culture into which they are being assimilated. As the traditional center of the party loses its importance, Republicans will be left unassailably in the control of the doctrinaire conservatives and of large selected interest groups. Furthermore, the party is aging, and it is my clear impression that any enthusiastic young people who are joining it today tend to be ideological conservatives.

The one great hope of Republican moderates is that the conservatives will bolt the party and form one of their own. But I do not believe that this will happen. The right wing may be impatient with the "left-wing" Bush partisans in the White House, but the conservatives have a twenty-year investment in the Republican party that they are not about to forgo just when it is beginning to pay dividends. Their ability to control one of the traditional parties gives them enormous advantages under federal election law which they would lose by starting a new party. These include full federal funding of presidential campaigns, guaranteed ballot access, and the residual loyalty of many people to the party name. For these assets, the right wing can afford to tolerate in their party a few moderate White House aides and a few mavericks from the Northeast and Northwest who sit in the Senate. It would be utmost folly for them to surrender the enormous advantages given to them by the two-party system.

But what of the Democrats? Can they consistently deliver the kind of leadership that will be able to defeat right-wing Republican candidates in perpetuity? Can they deliver convincingly on the economy which remains their one great area of broad-based electoral support? Let's not fool ourselves.

Can the Democrats deliver on inflation? Nobody believes that. Can they balance the budget? Nobody believes that either. What about productivity? The record is uninspiring.

Can the Democratic party deliver on structural unemployment? Ask the black community about the Democrats' record in this area. Better than the Republicans', of course. But how good? CETA, after all, was a program of make-work jobs with no future.

Can the Democrats lead the country into the high-technology era? Ask Gary Hart how well he has been received by Democratic constituencies in his bid for the presidency. And ask the consumer what he or she thinks about protectionism as a solution to industrial inefficiency.

It is always difficult to predict the future, but from the perspective of today it appears that the Republican party will become an increasingly unpalatable alternative to the Democrats, and the Democratic party will become an increasingly ineffective alternative to the Republican Right. This seems to be the most likely future of the existing two-party system.

We need a new political party in America. One that actually *is* a party. And we must build it from scratch. I believe that it should be solidly grounded in popular support, funded exclusively by individuals, and designed to do more than just nominate and elect candidates.

Such a party should be different from the two old parties, not only in doctrine but also in form and purpose. A new party can serve many important political functions in America that the old parties have abandoned.

A new party should be close to the people in fact as well as in name. It should grow to have strong local organizations in every American community. These organizations should serve as a means of improving personal communications between citizen and elected officials. They should be a means by which the views of the electorate are recorded and expressed in far more sophisticated ways than the current arrangement of counting mail and taking polls permits.

A new party should work to help people who have problems with government at any level. The ombudsman function today is performed primarily by congressional staffs, newspapers, television and radio stations, private organizations, and even individuals. The candidate orientation of political parties makes it impossible for them to fulfill this historic function. A well-organized political party, however, could. For this to be done effectively, the party would need to recruit professionals and well-trained volunteers. It would have to serve everyone, irrespective of party affiliation, and it would have to develop its capacity to serve over time. Nevertheless, a party that asks individuals if they *need* help instead of just asking people *for* help would be a refreshing change in American politics today. Strict accountability to a code of ethics by people performing these tasks would serve to prevent abuses traditionally associated with the word *patronage.*

A new party can become an active vehicle for mobilizing popular support behind policies it favors. This can be done between elections as well as during elections. It would not have to wait until it elected people to the White House, Congress, or state offices before its voice would be heard. It could organize large numbers of citizens to communicate their views to state and federal officials and could establish itself as a significant political force for progress early in its organizational existence. High on its agenda might well be election law reform to curb the power of special-interest money.

A new party can establish special liaisons to as many organized groups throughout America as possible. In this way, communication can also take place on a more personalized and continuing basis than is generally the case today between parties and interest groups. The first objective of such liaisons would be frank discussions of issues and a defining of relationships. The new party should position itself to support groups whose views coincide with those of the party itself, oppose groups whose views do not, and attempt to persuade groups to change their views when they do not conform to the national interest. In all cases the only way to proceed is on the basis of frank and open discussions. The communications between the party and organized groups should in all cases be a matter of public record. The first priority would be to establish a reputation for integrity. As the party grew in strength and as its popular support became well established, it could begin to play a more active role in mediating disputes between interest groups and in mobilizing groups in support of the political objectives it wants to achieve. To avoid capture by groups, however, a new party should bar the acceptance of PAC money by itself and by all candidates running under its banner.

A new party would have many substantive objectives. Among them would be to build a new economic consensus in America.

Such a consensus can be built today around some very basic and quite traditional principles that have always been valid and that will always be so: that real investment in America is the true source of growth; that people are good investments; that both supply and demand are central regulating forces in a market economy and that each must be considered when making policy; that the onrush of technology is basically a positive force, the effects of which nevertheless must be carefully monitored; that resource shocks must be avoided; that exports are a key component of demand-side policies; that stagnation at the micro level will foil any macroeconomic policy which assumes a classical pattern of market behavior; that affirmative government action must be taken to help give people direct access to the wealth of the future; and that both market expansion and global development are necessary for America's economic well-being.

With such a set of principles, there is much we can do without going too far astray. As a country we can begin once more to make sensible public and private investments. We can fight recessions by purchasing things that we need. We can employ honest and accepted principles of budgeting. We can behave responsibly with our currency. We can treat people decently and invest in them. We can work to restore the ability of our companies to compete effectively, increase their productivity, and keep abreast of the development of new technologies. We can look to conserve our resources and develop alternatives. If we do these things, if we recognize our role in the world economy with its attendant responsibilities, if we are willing to behave humanely toward those who are suffering or in need, if we return to basic principles, and if we are honest with ourselves, then can we be too far away from behaving in an economically sound and just fashion?

It will take a new political party to elevate our political discourse to a new unity of purpose. That purpose must be to listen to new ideas and to abandon old economic structures if they fail to advance the goal of a society in which everyone is entitled to make a contribution to the creation of a more just, equitable, and humane America. This is not a call for a new egalitarianism but a summons to a new kind of patriotism. It will require discipline, imposed not by the state but by the willingness of a majority in our democracy to equate rights with responsibilities. It means that we will strive neither for scientific socialism nor for a government-planned economy but for a new American economic system that is based on something more substantial than present administration beliefs in the magic of the marketplace.

Furthermore, we can no longer rely, as both Democrats and Republicans are willing to do, on an annual battle of the budget to formulate policy. A new party should adopt by democratic procedures a rational plan and statement of our national goals and objectives with a time horizon of at least five or ten years.

If we know now, as we most certainly do, what the profile of the unemployed is today and what it is likely to be in the future, why do we refuse to act on that knowledge? To cite a single specific: In the 1970s, blacks, who constituted 10 percent of the population, averaged 20 percent of the unemployed. In the 1970s they contributed about one out of ten new entrants into the labor force. By the end of the 1980s, however, they will account for more than one out of five new entrants because of higher birth rates. Do we fail to see how ignoring this one fact alone compromises the message of social and economic equality which we should be sending to the world? Yet there is no evidence whatever that we are currently engaged in planning for this development or that we intend to remedy it. The same could be said of youth unemployment and the prospect of massive layoffs of semiskilled people in many basic industries as foreign competition takes its toll and as technology advances.

All we are treated to on both sides of the political aisle are expressions of belief that economic growth by itself will solve all our problems. Make the pie larger, and everyone will share a larger piece. The economic history of the past two decades does not justify that conclusion. We are not all growing. We are dividing in half.

I do not believe in economic planning in the traditional sense of the word or in economic targeting of one industry over another. Planning to produce 100 million tons of steel or 1 million tons of computer chips is simply nonsense. But there are objectives

America can set which will have a widely beneficial impact upon society. We can work to have 90 percent of our high school graduates computer-literate by the end of the 1980s. We can work to repair by then half of those bridges that are deteriorating. We can work to reduce the teen-age unemployment rate by half during the next five years. We can work to regain our lead in high-energy physics by the end of the decade. We can aim to have a budget under control by 1988. We can achieve health and environmental goals. We can rebuild our system of training engineers. We can plan to reduce adult illiteracy by a significant percentage during the decade. We can plan to have a fully operating job bank and job-training system in place within three or four years. We can plan to have an appropriate square footage of manufacturing room available in space by 1990 and an appropriate annual increase thereafter. We can plan to increase our rate of savings. We can aim to reduce the cost of solar energy by a factor of ten over the next decade and have fusion plants on line a decade after that. We can plan to fill our strategic oil reserve over the next few years. We can plan to make our cities livable again.

If, however, we adopt these and similar goals, they should be part of a larger integrated strategy for economic recovery, one that recognizes our resources and our abilities. This is what party platforms are supposed to do. Unfortunately they have become propaganda pieces instead.

Good economic plans will not by themselves draw us ineluctably closer to achieving the goal of a more just and humane society. Their implementation will involve sacrifice, even higher taxes. But until some goals are clearly and rationally established and adopted, we cannot engage in that national debate we should have every four years on what kind of country we should try to be.

How should America proceed? Can a new party of the center be created? Where would its support come from? Could it attract a growing constituency? Yes, if it was thoroughly honest in its communications with people.

It might begin with those sectors of the economy that are

economically alive today. For example, with entrepreneurial business people (no strangers to new ventures), whether they be one person running a small business, managers of growth companies, or executives in lively giants. The party would say to them: You need further tax reform; you need a better climate of entrepreneurship. You also need federal fiscal and monetary restraint, together with lower interest rates that budget sanity will bring. You need free trade. You also need a banking system that understands your special requirements. You need access to markets at home and abroad. You need an educational system that works, one that produces skilled people, trained engineers, scientists, and new investment opportunities for your investment dollar. Neither Democrats nor Republicans can give you this package. We will. But we will also hold you accountable to the laws of the land: to the environmental protection laws, to laws regulating safety in the workplace, and to affirmative action laws. These laws embody valid national principles, and we will, under the Constitution, enforce them.

A new party might say to the farmer: You are the most lively entrepreneur in America, but you are suffering from the high costs and price repression imposed upon you by the stagnant sector. You need all that other entrepeneurs need, especially free trade. But you also need a set of policies designed to hit stagnation hard so you are rewarded, not penalized, for your efficiency. We will enact these policies. Neither Democrats nor Republicans can because they both have a vested interest in stagnation. But we must in all honesty make one other point clear: We will continue to provide price supports for your products to smooth out the fluctuations in the market. But as believers in a market economy we will *not* support artificially high price supports that build up huge and unneeded surpluses.

A new party might say to the professional: You, too, have an interest in free trade. You, too, will benefit from fiscal integrity and budgetary honesty. You, too, will benefit from lower interest rates and from holding the line on marginal tax rates. Furthermore, you know the value of a strong and dynamic educational and training sector. It is not in your interests or those of your children that the Republicans dismantle education or that the Democrats drive up your consumer prices through policies of protectionism. But we will be frank with you about the costs of our programs. We cannot rebuild the educational system of America without spending money. And we will tax you, among others, to raise that money.

A new party might say to young people: You should be the most lively sector of all. But if you are going to hold a job (and afford a car, a house, and a family), you must be trained—more highly trained than your parents were, more highly trained than your older brothers and sisters are. If you cannot handle the new skills, your future is grim. You have a stake in a better school system, in technology institutes, in retraining facilities. You also have a stake in policies that will produce jobs for coming generations of workers, not just make-work jobs but interesting and exciting jobs that will fire your imagination, consume your energies, and stretch your talents to their limits. But we can only work to build a system that makes access possible to those jobs. You yourself must work to earn that access.

A new party might also say to young people: This is your country, your future. We will work to ensure that you will not be killed in a nuclear war or that you will not have to die in any war if it can be helped.

A new party might then say to the workingmen and women of America: What kind of future do the Republicans and the Democrats offer you? The Republicans, whom many of you supported in 1980 because you rightfully wanted a change, led you down the path of unemployment, worry, and often despair. They sold you out. You got nothing while others got much. And what of the Democrats? Do you think that they have changed? Do you really have confidence in their economic judgment, in their consumption-oriented policies? They do offer you protection—but that is a short-term remedy. Unless the companies you work for improve their equipment, make better investments, and increase their productivity, they will fail, and your jobs will disappear. You have an interest in the new technology, too, but you will not be able to take advantage of it unless you retrain. Training and re-training are at the top of our agenda.

But a new party should also say to working people: Unlike the others, we will be fully honest with you. We can put in place some sensible economic policies that will put you back to work (or keep you working) in your old jobs for a few years. But what we cannot do is guarantee that those jobs will be there in a decade. Many just will not. And we are not going to promise you that they will be. But we are going to build a new economy in this country so that manufacturing stays in America. There will be new jobs, many in fields related to those you are working in now. We are pushing for profit sharing so that you will share in the gains when you retrain and when productivity improves at your current plant. And with profit sharing, fewer of you will be laid off in times of downturns. We cannot guarantee that you will always find work at your current wages in your current jobs (and if anyone says he or she can, that person is fooling you), but we can guarantee that there will be good jobs available at good wages. Most of all, we will do everything in our power to make sure that your children will not have to experience what you are going through. They will be trained and educated in a school system built to meet the economic challenges of the future. And if you want it, you yourself will have the opportunity to go back to school and start afresh.

And what will a new party say to the managers of stagnant companies? If you want support for quotas, tariffs, and your merger mania, you will have to look elsewhere. Let's be frank about that. But if you really want a chance to compete again, we will give you that chance—though not with bailouts. A new party might also say to the management of stagnant companies: We know that your instincts are to stick with the Republicans—but what have they given you? Federal deficits, high interest rates, recession, low consumer confidence, falling profits, and debt. Perhaps you want to stay in the party of right-wing ideologues who are devastating the economy of which you are so large a part and who are abandoning education, science, and technology, upon which you depend. But just maybe it would be better for you and your stockholders to have some responsible and sensible people in

Washington for a change, people committed to monetary and fiscal restraint and to your own rejuvenation and new-found liveliness.

And to Big Labor: If you insist on protectionist policies, then we disagree. Let's lay that right on the table. But our aim is to rebuild the industrial base of America, and you should have an interest in that. Our strategy is to bring you and management together to find the means of making existing industry more competitive. You should also have an interest in that. We will help management teams and workers acquire plants abandoned by companies. We will do our best to alleviate the problems caused by plant closings. We support OSHA fully, and we will not back off on that. We will work to keep jobs in America. Productivity improvements are high on our list—as they are on many of your lists. We also have an employment strategy. But we are going in for Davis-Bacon modification, and let's lay that on the table, too. We recognize that you are committed to the Democrats because you control them. But we are not out to destroy labor the way the Reaganites are. We are willing to talk and willing to listen.

And to the financial interests: Some of you have made a mess of things, but we recognize that the integrity of the banking system is the foundation of the economy. We will not let the banks go under, nor will we rescue them without penalty if the difficulty is of their own making (as today it seems to be). We believe that the long-range integrity of the system will be secured not by regulation but by restructuring, so that quality real investments in the growth of the American economy can once again become the foundation of the banking system. We also favor an investment-oriented national policy that cannot fail to put you on the road to recovery, especially when those investments will lead to a rebirth of American real capital exports.

And to the oil and gas interests: You will find us tough but fair. Cartels, oligopolistic pricing, and nonsense like the current natural gas contretemps just will not do. And we will tax both to encourage conservation and to discourage windfalls. But deregulation—total and complete—is also our maxim. A true free market in energy is in America's interest, and in yours.

326

And to all Americans, of every age, gender, and origin: If we work at it, we can put this country back together again, make it lively, give it a future, and go about our business with pride, honesty, and decency.

I believe that a new party can be created in America, dedicated to the proposition that we are one country, indivisible. If current policies persist, this will not remain the case. The great middle class, which has been the bulwark of our Republic, will divide, and with it, our politics and our nation. The Republicans will represent the rich, while using ideological demagoguery to maintain a tenuous hold on the electorate. The Democrats will increasingly come to represent the poor. We need a middle force in America devoted to holding the center together and to bringing into it all who wish to be there. We must not let tax policies be used to divide us. We must not let technology divide us. We must not let stagnation divide us. We must not let race or gender or age divide us. We must not let geography or region divide us. We must not let religion or ideology divide us. We must not let politics divide us. We are truly all in it together.

NOTES

Chapter 1:   The Great Recession

4   Interest rates . . . : See Congressional Research Service, Craig Elwell, *Are Interest Rates a Threat to Sustained Economic Recovery?*, Mini Brief, MB 83229, updated (Washington, D.C.: July 13, 1983), p. 4.

5   the Great Recession: After using this phrase in speeches and incorporating it into early drafts of the manuscript, I came across it in Michael Harrington and Bob Adelman, "Americans in Limbo," *Harper's* (April 1983), p. 53.

6   the deficit jumped . . . : Congressional Budget Office, *The Economic and Budget Outlook: An Update* (Washington, D.C.: August 1983), p. 84.

7   Federal borrowing, as a percentage of the nation's credit . . . : For example, *ibid.*

7   the crowding out . . . : For figures, see Committee on the Budget, U.S. House of Representatives, *President Reagan's Fiscal Year 1984 Budget*, Serial No. CP-1 (Washington, D.C.: February 1983), Table 10, p. 25.

7   Because of the dollar's climb . . . : Christopher Madison, "Dollar Dilemma—an Economic Malady Searching in Vain for a Miracle Cure," *National Journal* (August 20, 1983), pp. 1734–37.

7   More than $250 billion . . . : Committee on the Budget, *op. cit.*, Table 4, p. 15.

8   rose to $80 billion in 1982 and exceeded $150 billion . . . : *Ibid.*

8   Gone was Reagan's campaign promise . . . : For these new projections, see the president's proposed budget for FY 1984 and accompanying materials.

9   The "truly needy" were asked to sacrifice . . . : According to an analysis of the administration's *Money Income and Poverty Status of Families and Persons in the United States: 1982*, conducted by the staff of the Select Committee on Children, Youth, and Families and released by Congressman George Miller, "Between 1980–1982, over two million children have become poor. . . . [This is] the greatest rate of increase over any 2-year period (19%). . . . more than one half of the over two million children cast into poverty live in two-parent families."

9   expectations of renewed inflation . . . : See, for instance, James E. McNulty, "Inflation and Monetary Growth: Will the Roller Coaster Continue?," *ABA Banking Journal* (September 1983), pp. 106–08, this article

charts the predicted time lag between monetary expansion and inflation at about eighteen months. See also Philip Dion, "Worries About Higher Interest Rates Linger Despite the Economic Recovery," *National Journal* (September 10, 1983), pp. 1841–844.

9 David Stockman . . . : William Greider, "The Education of David Stockman," *Atlantic* (December 1981), p. 27ff.

11 helping the well-to-do while hurting the poor . . . : Joel Havemann, "Sharing the Wealth: The Gap Between Rich and Poor Grows Wider," *National Journal* (October 23, 1982), pp. 1788–95; and Linda E. Demkovich and Joel Havemann, "The Poor and the Near Poor May Be Bearing the Brunt," *ibid.* pp. 1796–1800.

12 The true believers in . . . supply-side . . . : See George Gilder's *Wealth and Poverty* (New York: 1981); Jack Kemp, *An American Renaissance* (New York: 1981); and Bruce Bartlett, *Reaganomics* (New York: 1981), for example.

12 supply creates its own demand: Say's law. It can't be valid if prices are not permitted to fall. It may not be valid even if they are.

12 Our decline in productivity . . . : Joint Economic Committee, *Special Study on Economic Change*, Vol. 10, *Productivity: The Foundation of Growth* (Washington, D.C.: December 29, 1980); the growth rate in output per person hour in the American private sector has fallen from 3.44 percent in the period from 1947 to 1966, to 1.15 percent in the period from 1973 to 1978 (p. 3).

12 Supply . . . covers many factors: These are found throughout the economic literature from texts like Paul Samuelson's to analyses such as those of Edward Denison. See Denison, "The Contribution of Capital to Economic Growth," *American Economic Association Papers and Proceedings* (May 1980), pp. 2201–24; see also Denison, *Accounting for Slower Economic Growth: The United States in the 1970's* (Washington, D.C.: 1979), *passim*.

13 look in the want ads: Cited by Nick Kotz, "The War on the Poor," *New Republic* (March 24, 1982), p. 23.

14 demand stimulus . . . has not called forth supply . . . : Peniti J. K. Kouri, "Macroeconomics of Stagflation Under Flexible Exchange Rates," *American Economic Association Papers and Proceedings* (May 1982), pp. 390–94.

14 the reciprocal relationship . . . : This is the famous migration of the Phillips Curve. The relationship between inflation and unemployment is still debated. See Lester Thurow, *Dangerous Currents* (New York: 1983), especially diagram, p. 74.

15 With ever-larger deficits . . . : The deficit designed to end the recession of 1958 was $12 billion; the recession of 1970–71, $23 billion; the recession of 1974–76, $66 billion; the Great Recession, $200 billion this year (1983). See *Statistical Abstract of the United States 1982–83* (Washington, D.C.), p. 246.

15 heady times . . . : In the memory of an admiring student of Otto Eckstein's, this noted economist in his opening lecture in Economics 1 at Harvard in 1961 stated, "We think we've licked the business cycle. But in economics, you can never tell about these things. . . . " Bravo.

15 Richard Nixon shook . . . : David P. Calleo, *The Imperious Economy* (Cambridge, Mass.: 1982), especially pp. 62–102.

16 Jimmy Carter pursued . . . stop-and-go . . . : *Ibid.*, pp. 141–153.

16 more than $65 billion . . . : *Statistical Abstract of the United States 1982–83, loc. cit.,* p. 842.

16 "Industrial Policy" . . . : I do not know the origin of this term. I first proposed one (quite different from the Democrats' version) in October 1979.

16 The Republican party . . . nominating process . . . : See Epilogue.

Chapter 2: Stagnation and Stagflation

19 Auto salespeople looking for tire kickers . . . : Generally true. But in the summer of 1983 there was a supply shortage in cars.

20 trade deficit burgeoned to more than $18 billion with Japan . . . : Federal Reserve Bank of San Francisco, "U.S.-Japan Trade," April 8, 1983, p. 2.

20 Our total imbalance was over $35 billion: Council of Economic Advisers, *Economic Indicators* (Washington, D.C.: June 1983), p. 36.

20 neither our vices nor their remedies: Livy, *History*, Prologue.

21 the Eurocurrency market . . . : Congressional Research Service, Arlene Wilson, *The Stability of the International Banking System*, Issue Brief No. IB 82107, updated (Washington, D.C.: July 19, 1983). See also series of articles *Columbia Journal of World Business* (Fall 1979).

21 American loans to foreign governments . . . : See, for example, *Time* (January 10, 1983), chart, p. 430. See also Robert Solomon, *The International Debt Problem*, Center for National Policy (Washington, D.C., October 1982).

22 Following a period of growth . . . : Raymond Vernon, "International Investment and International Trade in the Product Cycle," *Quarterly Journal of Economics* (May 1966), pp. 190–207.

22 They are reluctant to make major innovative changes . . . : William Abernathy and James Utterback, "Patterns of Industrial Innovation," *Technology Review* (June-July 1978), pp. 40–47. This important article traces the three-stage development that I have used here.

23 minor . . . improvements in the production process: Burton H. Klein, "Hidden-Foot Feedback: Wellspring of Economic Vitality," *Technology Review* (October 1980), p. 46ff.

23 Bureaucracy sets in: William Dugger, "Corporate Bureaucratic Process," *Journal of Economic Issues* (June 1980), pp. 399–409. See also Joseph Stanislao and Bettie Stanislao, "Dealing with Resistance to Change," *Business Horizons* (July-August 1983), pp. 74–78.

23 Blame becomes easy to shift . . . : Klein, *op. cit.*, p. 52.

23 Work rules are established: For a critical view of this process, see Robert M. Kaus, "The Trouble with Unions," *Harper's* (June 1983), p. 23.

24 attorneys in the 1970s . . . : See Robert Reich, *The Next American Frontier* (New York: 1983), pp. 229–82, for a discussion of social stagnation. He states (p. 281) that Naples during its period of stagnation (my term) had 30,000 attorneys out of a population of 500,000.

24 Managers . . . are . . . sensitive to the short-term performance . . . : See, for example, the now classic article, by Robert H. Hayes and William Abernathy, "Managing Our Way to Decline," *Harvard Business Review* (July-August 1980), pp. 67–77.

25 Raising prices is more promising: There is a vast literature on

this. See Arthur Okun's brilliant *Prices and Quantities* (Washington, D.C.: 1981). For a provocative view of pricing policies, see Floyd B. McFarland, "Markup Pricing in the Auto Industry," *American Journal of Economics and Sociology* (January 1982), pp. 1–15. "Administered prices," of course, is John Kenneth Galbraith's old trumpet call.

26 a flair for creative financing . . . : See Reich's discussion of paper entrepreneurship, *op. cit.*, pp. 100–72.

27 technology . . . will bounce right off them: Shelby H. McIntyre, "Obstacles to Corporate Innovation," *Business Horizons* (January-February 1982), pp. 23–28.

28 Competitive conditions . . . : Klein, *op. cit.*

28 Corning Glass . . . : *Ibid.*, p. 48.

28 "bet the company" . . . : John Newhouse, *The Sporty Game* (New York: 1982).

28 Computer technology advances so rapidly . . . : The industry has lively giants, including IBM. See "Personal Computers: And the Winner Is IBM," *Business Week* (October 3, 1983), p. 76ff. The IBM personal computer story is a classic case of how a company can keep alive with new products.

28 the central role seems to be played by management: Arnold S. Judson, "The Awkward Truth About Productivity," *Harvard Business Review* (September-October 1982), p. 93. See also Carlton P. McNamara, "Productivity Is Management's Problem," *Business Horizons* (March-April 1983), pp. 55–61.

28 It expands: Sumer C. Aggarwal, "Manager, Manage Thyself," *Business Horizons* (January-February 1983), pp. 25–30.

28 It seems progressively more inflexible: Reich, *op. cit.*, especially pp. 83–114.

29 measures designed only to encourage the manager . . . : We might note that the salaries of contemporary American managers are considerably higher than those of their overseas counterparts. See Mark Green, "Richer Than All Their Tribe," *New Republic* (January 6 and 13, 1982), p. 21.

29 We need more entrepreneurs: Subrata N. Chakravarty, "Let Them Become Entrepreneurs [an interview with Robert E. Levinson]," *Forbes* (August 15, 1983), p. 82.

29 As a result, a fall in demand . . . : The relationship between stagflation and industrial stagnation is very complex. See Mancur Olsen, *The Rise and Decline of Nations* (New Haven: 1982); Okun, *op. cit.*; and Klein, *op. cit.*, for three very different approaches.

30 Stagnant industries can influence . . . : Much has been written on the problems of inflexible prices. See Thurow, *op. cit.*, pp. 3–28; also Okun, *op. cit.*

31 businesses in the flexible sectors . . . : Olsen, *op. cit.* There seems to be a Gresham's law at work, with economic and social rigidities driving out flexibility.

32 Macroeconomic policies operating on an economy . . . : Richard Lipsey, "The Understanding and Control of Inflation: Is There a Crisis in Macroeconomics?," *Canadian Journal of Economics* (November 1981), pp. 545–73.

32 economic structure that tends to discourage . . . : American investment rates seem to be significantly lower than those of other developed

countries. See, for example, Michael J. Boskin, "Economic Growth and Productivity," in his *The Economy in the 1980's: A Program for Growth and Stability* (New Brunswick, N.J.: 1980), pp. 23–50, especially Table 2, p. 31.

32 Inflation has been a major villain: Peter K. Clark, "Inflation and the Productivity Decline," *American Economic Association Papers and Proceedings* (May 1982), pp. 149–54.

33 a nation of loan sharks . . . : "Observer," *New York Times*, March 31, 1982, p. 31.

33 savings fell instead: Council of Economic Advisers, *Economic Indicators* (Washington, D.C.: September 1983), p. 6. Savings as a percentage of disposable personal income fell from 6 percent in 1980 to a projected 4 percent in the second quarter of 1983.

33 Many stagnant industries, resisting the introduction . . . : The dangers of incremental investments are set forth in Robert H. Hayes and David A. Garvin, "Managing As If Tomorrow Mattered," *Harvard Business Review* (May-June 1982), p. 71.

35 As the quality of our investments has declined . . . : David Fusfeld, "The Next Great Depression II: The Impending Financial Collapse," *Journal of Economic Issues* (June 1980), pp. 493–503. The author emphasizes the alarming disparity between interest rates and returns to real capital as a source of instability.

35 Ponzi finance . . . : Hyman Minsky, "Finance and Profits: The Changing Nature of American Business Cycles," in Joint Economic Committee, *Business Cycles and Public Policy 1929–1980* (Washington, D.C.: November 1980), p. 209.

Chapter 3: The New Technology

40 It stands to reason, therefore . . . : Edwin Mansfield, "How Economists See R & D," *Harvard Business Review* (November–December 1981), p. 98.

40 new methods of production . . . and help reestablish . . . : I don't want to take sides in the Keynes-Schumpeter debate, but see Peter F. Drucker, "Schumpeter and Keynes," *Forbes* (May 23, 1983), pp. 124–28.

40 Technological changes have played a central role . . . : David Dickson, "Technology and Cycles of Boom and Bust," *Science* (February 25, 1983), pp. 933–36.

41 Genetic engineering . . . : See, for example, Gary A. Sojka. "Where Biology Could Take Us," *Business Horizons* (January–February 1981), pp. 60–69; and the entire September 1981 issue of *Scientific American*.

41 computer chip . . . a tiny flake: See, for example, the imaginative essay, Blake M. Cornish, "The Smart Machines . . . ," *Futurist* (August 1981), p. 5; or Jon Roland, "The Microelectronic Revolution," *Futurist* (April 1979), pp. 81–90.

43 Many opportunities will present . . . : Martin L. Ernst, "The Mechanization of Commerce," *Scientific American* (September 1982), pp. 132–47.

43 Electronic shopping . . . : Larry J. Rosenberg and Elizabeth C. Hirschman, "Retailing Without Stores," *Harvard Business Review* (July-August 1980), pp. 103–12.

43 *Capital* will be affected . . . : See, for example, the series "Banking

and the New Technology" in *Bankers Magazine* (March–April 1983), pp. 24–52.

44 The age of robotics is upon us: Excellent materials on robotics have been collected by the Subcommittee on Investigations and Oversight of the Committee on Science and Technology of the U.S. House of Representatives in hearings conducted in the summer of 1982. See also *Omni's* April 1983 issue.

44 negative relationship between efficiency and flexibility: Reich, *op. cit.*, pp. 133–39.

45 Computer-aided design and computer-aided manufacture . . . : Thomas G. Gunn, "The Mechanization of Design and Manufacture," *Scientific American* (September 1982), pp. 114–31.

45 Economies of scope will replace economies of scale: Mariann Jelinek and Joel D. Golhar, "The Interface Between Strategy and Manufacturing Technology," *Columbia Journal of World Business* (Spring 1983), p. 26.

47 In the air controllers' strike . . . : Harley Shaikan, "Computers and Strikebreakers," *Technology Review* (April 1982), pp. 50–51; and Hoo-min D. Toong and Amar Gupta, "Automating Air-Traffic Control," *Technology Review* (April 1982), p. 41.

47 To the degree that unions . . . : Marvin Cetron and Thomas O'Toole, "Careers with a Future," *Futurist* (June 1982), especially pp. 16–17.

47 Many young people are now training . . . : Roland, *op. cit.*, p. 90.

48 4 million out of 8 million . . . : Robert Ayers and Steve Miller, "Industrial Robots on the Line," *Technology Review*, (May/June 1982), p. 42.

48 no guarantee that the new jobs . . . : Barry Bluestone, *The Deindustrialization of America* (New York: 1982), pp. 92–98.

49 a serious approach to this problem goes far beyond retraining . . . : *Ibid.*, pp. 49–81.

49 It is a problem of pride and initiative . . . : Bruce Gilchrist and Ariaana Shenkin, "Disappearing Jobs: The Impact of Computers on Employment," *Futurist* (February 1981), pp. 44–49.

49 dual economy: Bluestone, *op. cit.*; and Harrington and Adelman, *op. cit.*, pp. 48–53.

50 The office itself will be revolutionized . . . : See Marvin Kornbluh, "The Electronic Office," *Futurist* (June 1982), p. 37; see Vincent Biuliano, "The Mechanization of Office Work," *Scientific American* (September 1982), pp. 148–65; and just scan the advertisements in *Fortune*.

50 Lower-level management will be decimated . . . : Robert Schrank, "Horse Collar Blue Collar Blues," *Harvard Business Review* (May-June, 1981), especially pp. 137–38.

50 inspiring and directing its valuable human capital . . . : The clash between "professionalism" and "bureaucracy" is well discussed by Kenneth O. Alexander, "Scientists, Engineers, and the Organization of Work," *American Journal of Economics and Sociology* (January 1981), p. 51. See also Tracy Kidder, *The Soul of a New Machine* (New York: 1981).

51 superclass of cognoscenti . . . : David Burnham, *The Rise of the Computer State* (New York: 1980), p. 226ff.

51 centralize information . . . : *Ibid.*, pp. 49–87.

52 spy on people . . . : *Ibid.*, pp. 20–48.

52 large industrial constituents . . . : Michael Wines, "The Admini-

stration, in High-Tech's Name, Takes Aim at Antitrust Laws," *National Journal* (May 4, 1983), pp. 1000–04.

52 a model for the future control of knowledge: See, for example, Floyd Abrams, "The New Effort to Control Information," *New York Times Magazine* (September 25, 1983), p. 22.

Chapter 4: Japan—the Strategic Challenge

55 The real Japanese challenge, however, is not . . . : The literature on the Japanese challenge is staggering. I can only begin to do justice to all the articles and books I have perused. It is a growth industry all by itself. The best known are Ezra Vogel, *Japan as Number One* (Cambridge, Mass.: 1979), and William Ouchi, *Theory Z* (Reading, Mass.: 1981).

56 the war destroyed the old social and economic structure . . . : Olsen, *op. cit.*

56 The West German miracle is disintegrating: This sovereign occurrence first came to my attention in the summer of 1982 when I visited Europe. See Bruce Scott, "Can Industry Survive the Welfare State?" *Harvard Business Review* (September–October 1982), p. 77. See also Bruce Nussbaum, *The World After Oil* (New York: 1983), pp. 76–103; he makes a convincing argument that Germany, with an obsolete capital plant, will be forced to turn east for markets.

56 Entrepreneurship and innovation are rewarded: See, for example, *Newsweek* (August 9, 1982), p. 56.

56 Capital is formed . . . : See Chapter 5.

56 . . . technical knowledge . . . : See, for example, *Newsweek* (August 9, 1982), pp. 48–54.

56 Resources are carefully managed . . . : Daniel Yergin and Martin Hillenbrand, *Global Insecurity* (Boston: 1982), pp. 138–67.

56 People are well trained and educated . . . : Vogel, *op. cit.*, pp. 158–83.

56 special encouragement by management: Haruo Shimada, "Japan's Success Story: Looking Behind the Legend," *Technology Review* (May–June 1983), p. 47; and Rodney Clark, *The Japanese Company* (New Haven: 1979).

56 Management itself . . . : Sang M. Lee and Gary Schwendiman, eds., *Japanese Management: Culture and Environmental Considerations* (New York: 1982), especially Part II, in which cultural factors are emphasized.

57 West Germany . . . has neglected a key factor: knowledge: Characteristically, Germany is given but one short paragraph in Edward A. Feigenbaum and Pamela McCorduck, *The Fifth Generation* (Reading, Mass.: 1983), a discussion of national artificial intelligence programs; see p. 172.

57 market penetration strategy . . . : For an example of this strategy at work in a single industry, see Liam Fahey and Michael Radnor, "The Product-Market Strategies of U.S. and Japanese Firms in the U.S. Consumer Electronics Marketplace," in Lee and Schwendiman, *op. cit.*, pp. 334–46.

58 quality-oriented production process: Robert E. Cole, "The Japanese Lesson in Quality," *Technology Review* (May 1981), pp. 29–40.

59 debt burdens . . . : "Debtor's Merry-Go-Round," *Business Week* (September 12, 1983), pp. 73–74.

61 757s and 767s . . . : Howard Banks, "Holding for Takeoff," *Forbes* (June 20, 1983), p. 50.

62   cutting heavily into the machinery and machine tool . . . : In 1980, 25 percent of machine tools purchased by U.S. industry were imports; in 1982 the figure was 42 percent. See Seymour Melman, "How the Yankees Lost Their Knowhow," *Technology Review* (October 1983), p. 56ff.

62   The American microelectronic industry . . . : *Business Week* (May 23, 1983), pp. 80–105. An editorial in *Science* (March 4, 1983, p. 1025) flatly concluded, "The Japanese are moving vigorously toward a national goal of world domination in semi-conductors."

64   technologies needed for . . . computers . . . : Richard Corrigan, "The Latest Target of the Japanese—U.S. Preeminence in Supercomputers," *National Journal* (April 2, 1983), pp. 688–92.

64   The American civilian aircraft industry . . . : See, for example, Gene Gregory, "Japan's Industrial Revolution," *Futurist* (August 1982), pp. 30–32.

64   Pratt & Whitney . . . : "Seven U.S., European, Japanese Firms Set to Sign Accord This Week for Jet Engines," *Wall Street Journal*, March 9, 1983, p. 6.

65   making F-15 fighter planes . . . : *Business Week* (March 14, 1983), p. 106.

66   competition of the newly industrialized countries of Asia: Gene Gregory, "Japan's Asian Challenge," *Columbia Journal of World Business* (Summer 1979), pp. 65–73.

67   disassociate the interests of the banking community . . . : Calleo, *op. cit.*, pp. 184–86.

Chapter 5: Rebuilding the Economy

70   domestic-content legislation . . . : For a description of domestic-content legislation, see Douglas A. Fraser, "Domestic Content of U.S. Automobile Imports: A UAW Proposal," *Columbia Journal of World Business* (Winter 1981), pp. 57–61.

70    $160,000 per job created: Dick Nanto, *Automobile Domestic Content Requirements, Congressional Research Service,* Issue Brief IB No. 82056, updated (Washington, D.C.: June 29, 1983), p. 5. This is an excellent analysis of domestic-content legislation and its cost to America.

71   Let's compete: Let's also go on the offensive. See Craig M. Watson, "Counter-Competition Abroad to Protect Home Markets," *Harvard Business Review* (January–February 1982), p. 40.

71   postindustrialism?: The term *postindustrial* was popularized by Daniel Bell's seminal *The Coming of Post-Industrial Society*, which appeared in 1973. Bell raises all the questions: the relationship between manufacturing and services, the impact of technology, the rise of meritocracies, the emerging role of knowledge, and the impact of postindustrialism on democracy. Bell rightly focuses on the need for a new infrastructure. The term *postindustrial* has come to mean an end to manufacturing, instead of its transformation into a knowledge-based enterprise. This is not really Bell's doing, and it is here that I part company with the concept as currently used.

74   comparative advantage in services?: Ronald K. Shelp, *Beyond Industrialization: Ascendancy of the Global Economy* (New York: 1981), especially pp. 85–88.

74 neoliberalism: Randall Rothenberg, "The Neoliberal Club," *Esquire* (February 1982), pp. 37–46.

74 Ax the losers: Lester Thurow, *The Zero-Sum Society* (Harmondsworth, England: 1981), especially pp. 80–82.

75 rid itself of the old and support the new: The difference between a "dying" industry and a "growing" industry is well shown in *ibid.*, p. 81.

76 The Democrats envision . . . : Sidney Blumenthal, "Drafting a Democratic Industrial Plan," *New York Times Magazine* (August 28, 1983), p. 30ff.

79 Ministry of International Trade and Industry . . . : For a truly superb analysis of the investment approach of Japanese industrial policies and their institutional support, see the Comptroller General, *Report to the Chairman, Joint Economic Committee. . . . Industrial Policy: Japan's Flexible Approach*, (GAO ID–82–32) (Washington, D.C.: June 23, 1982).

79 American agricultural sector: Gary Hart, *A New Democracy* (New York: 1983), p. 53.

Chapter 6: Entrepreneurship

95 Two hundred companies control . . . : TRB, *New Republic* (July 25, 1981).

97 leaves an established company to start his or her own firm: Robert N. Noyce, "Innovation: The Fruit of Success," *Technology Review* (February 1978), pp. 24–27.

99 This is a complex area [patents]: For just a sample of the complexity, see Ben T. Yu, "Potential Competition and Contracting an Innovation," *Journal of Law and Economics* (October 1981), p. 215.

102 salaries of many research and development workers . . . : Joel Kotkin and Don Gevirtz, "Why Entrepreneurs Trust No Politician," *Washington Post*, January 16, 1983.

102 a more predictable regulatory environment: Only a suggestion of the materials I have encountered on regulation is James Q. Wilson, *The Politics of Regulation* (New York: 1980), and Barry M. Mitnick, *The Political Economy of Regulation* (New York: 1980).

103 A whole industry has been created . . . : Robert Reich, "Regulation by Confrontation or Negotiation," *Harvard Business Review* (May–June 1981), especially pp. 84–91.

104 J. R. Fox . . . : "Breaking the Regulatory Deadlock," *Harvard Business Review* (September–October 1981), pp. 97–105.

104 I would recommend . . . : Reich, "Regulation by Confrontation . . . ," *loc. cit.*, p. 92.

105 $82.6 billion . . . : *National Journal* (July 10, 1982), p. 1204.

105 The Great Recession dampened the game somewhat . . . : "Merger Drive Goes into Reverse," *U.S. News & World Report* (May 2, 1983), p. 55.

105 Mergers absorb corporate talent . . . better used elsewhere: Peter Drucker, "Why Some Mergers Work and Many More Don't," *Forbes* (January 19, 1982), pp. 34–36.

105 There are several ways of addressing [mergers]: See Bruce Scott's suggestions for a special form of corporate charter to enable companies to in-

corporate in such a way that takeovers would have to receive an affirmative vote of employees to proceed, *loc. cit.*, p. 83.

106 limit . . . the extension of . . . credit . . . : For credit control proposals, see Ronald Bronstein, "Merger Wars—Congress, SEC Take Aim at Hostile Corporate Take-over Moves," *National Journal* (July 23, 1983), p. 1540.

106 Small businesses . . . labor under disadvantages . . . : *Small Business Innovation Research Act*, House Report 97–349, Part I, issued November 20, 1981; and *Small Business and Small Business Investment Act of 1958 Amendments, Bill # HR 6086*, House Report 97–564, reported May 17, 1982.

107 most of the new jobs in America . . . : Kevin Farrell, "The New Face of Manufacturing," *Venture* (October 1982), p. 80.

107 disproportionate share of America's new inventions: Kotkin and Gevirtz, *op. cit.*, ". . . small and medium-sized firms produce from four to 24 times more innovations per research dollar than *Fortune* 500 corporations," according to the National Science Foundation.

107 Its tax cuts for business aided large companies more than small: "No Big Breaks for Small Business in the Tax Cuts," *Business Week* (August 24, 1981), p. 100.

107 land office business . . . : Lawrence Mosher, "Despite Setbacks, Watt Is Succeeding in Opening Up Public Lands for Energy," *National Journal* (June 11, 1983), pp. 1230–34.

108 Ted Kennedy's industrial planning . . . : Sidney Blumenthal, "Drafting a Democratic Industrial Plan," *New York Times Magazine* (August 28, 1983), p. 30ff. This presents Kennedy's aspiration to be the tribune of industrial policy.

108 Even the neoliberal Atari Democrats have the wrong approach: Kotkin and Gevirtz, *op. cit.*

Chapter 7: Capital

110 60 percent of all new savings . . . : Congressional Budget Office, *The Economic and Budget Outlook: An Update* (Washington, D.C., August 1983), Figure, p. 9.

111 Henry Kaufman . . . "one in six" . . . : See Hobart Rowan, "Dr. Doom Quotes Worldwide Economic Collapse Odds at 6 to 1," *Washington Post* (January 2, 1983), p. B3.

112 reasons for the financial system's instability: Congressional Research Service, "The stability of the International Banking System," *loc. cit.*

112 The *Wall Street Journal* . . . : See "Script for Collapse . . . ," *Wall Street Journal* (November 10, 1983), p. 1.

112 The oil contretemps . . . : See, for example, Bruce R. Scott, "OPEC, the American Scapegoat," *Harvard Business Review* (January–February 1981), p. 6.; see also *Time* cover story, "The Repairing of America," (January 10, 1983); for an excellent overview see Richard Weinert, "International Finance: Banks and Bankruptcy," *Foreign Policy* (Spring 1983), pp. 138–49.

113 A London lender . . . : David Ashby, quoted by *Time* (January 10, 1983), p. 45.

113 tender mercies of the commodity markets: *Time* (January 10, 1982), p. 46: in addition to oil, sugar, copper, and cotton have fallen. Com-

modities, excluding oil, "have fallen 35% to the lowest real level in three decades."

116 Banks are rapidly entering new financial areas . . . : Dwight B. Crane and Samuel L. Hayes III, "The New Competition in World Banking," *Harvard Business Review* (July–August 1982), pp. 88–93; and George G. C. Parker, "Now Management Will Make or Break the Bank," *Harvard Business Review* (November–December 1981), pp. 140–148.

116 Interstate ownership is now growing rapidly: "States Rights," *Forbes* (May 23, 1983), p. 36.

117 Walter Wriston expects only a half dozen . . . : Robert A. Bennett, "Inside Citicorp," *New York Times Magazine* (May 29, 1983), p. 15.

118 local development banks: The germ of this idea is to be found in Ronald E. Müller, *Revitalizing America* (New York: 1980), pp. 269–71. Müller restricts his banks to energy-related projects.

120 capital investment banks: See, for example, Lester Thurow, "The Economy," *New Republic* (March 31, 1982), pp. 24–25.

Chapter 8: Knowledge

125 spirit of enterprise: George Gilder, *The Spirit of Enterprise*, forthcoming.

126 to $14.8 billion: American Association for the Advancement of Science, *AAAS Report VIII: Research and Development FY 1984* (Washington: 1983), p. 30.

126 The federal government today is spending about three-quarters . . . : *Ibid.*, pp. 24, 26.

126 "seed corn" . . . : The phrase is that of president Paul E. Gray of MIT, cited in Robert Cowen, "Federal R & D: Let Them Eat Seed Corn," *Technology Review* (August–September 1981), pp. 8–9.

126 campus laboratories . . . : George E. Parks, "Universities' Obsolete Instrumentation," *Physics Today* (August 1982), p. 88.

127 Industrial Science Foundation (ISF) . . . : This idea was suggested to me by Dr. Peter Zimmerman of Louisiana State University.

128 Multiple funding sources . . . : See Magoroh Moruyama's plea for diversity in research "Wanted: New Ideas . . . ," *Futurist* (August 1980), p. 35.

128 We need to rebuild . . . our engineering schools . . . : James Botkin, Dan Dimancescu, and Ray Stata, "High Technology, Higher Education, and High Anxiety," *Technology Review* (October 1982), p. 49; and Robert C. Seamans and K. F. Hansen, "Engineering Education for the Future," *Technology Review* (February–March 1981), p. 4ff.

129 design methods, production methods, and systems research: For an analysis of these, see Sydney B. Newell, Sart J. de Geus, and Ronald A. Rohner, "Design Automation for Integrated Circuits," *Science* (April 29, 1983), pp. 465–71.

129 the Japanese, who use robotics at home . . . : Charles Ferguson, "The Microelectronics Industry in Distress," *Technology Review* (August–September 1983), p. 24.

130 In 1980 only sixty-nine commercial ships . . . : *Statistical Abstract of the United States 1981* (Washington, D.C.), p. 651.

131 there are no guarantees that this will happen: Joseph Morone

and Richard Ivins, "Problems and Opportunities in Technology Transfer from the National Laboratories to Industry," *Research Management* (May 1982), p. 35.

131 Technology transfer . . . : For a discussion, see Richard Nelson and Richard Langlois, "Industrial Innovation Policy: Lessons from American History," *Science* (February 18, 1983), pp. 814–18; Richard Nelson, ed., *Government and Technical Progress* (New York: 1982); and Ubiratan D' Ambrosio, "Knowledge Transfer and the Universities: A Policy Dilemma," *Impact of Science on Society*, 1979, p. 223.

131 technology would be effectively transferred . . . : *Technology Review*'s series on innovation presents many provocative ideas. For example, see George R. White, "Management Criteria for Effective Innovation" (February 1978); Edward B. Roberts and Alan L. Frohman, "Strategies for Improving Research Utilization" (March–April 1978); Sumner Myers and Eldon Sweezy, "Why Innovations Fail" (March–April 1978); and Alan Fusfeld, "How to Put Technology into Corporate Planning" (May 1978). The emphasis in most cases is upon people.

132 The states would be given the final say . . . : The relationship between universities and industry, like the relationship between universities and government, is an area of great controversy. One reason I recommend that the Regional Technology Institutes be created separately in most cases is to enable existing institutions to preserve their distance from both. See, for example, Katherine Bouton, "Academic Research and Big Business: A Delicate Balance," *New York Times Magazine* (September 11, 1983).

133 encourage private-sector research and development . . . : Private-sector research and development increased about 15 percent between 1980 and 1981 despite the recession. *Business Week* (July 5, 1982), p. 54.

133 cut the space budget by more than half . . . : The space research budget was cut from $4.9 billion to an estimated $2.3 billion between FY 1981 and FY 1983. See American Association for the Advancement of Science, *op. cit.*, p. 26.

134 A full program of planetary and solar probes . . . : E. Margaret Burbidge, "Adventure into Space," *Science* (July 29, 1983), pp. 421–27.

134 The commercialization of space . . . : Jerry Grey, "Implications of the Shuttle: Our Business in Space," and Giuseppe Colombo, "Space Technology: Where Will Fiction Meet Reality?" both *Technology Review* (October 1981); John Noble Wilford, "Big Business in Space," *New York Times Magazine* (September 18, 1983), p. 47ff.

135 We must build a fifth-generation computer: Feigenbaum and McCorduck, *op. cit.* The authors emphasize the commercial possibilities of the computer's "human" qualities; I believe, however, its complex modeling capacity will be its most profitable initial commercial use.

135 The Japanese are making a major effort to be the first . . . : The computer competition between us and the Japanese is intense. See Stephen Solomon, "Superbrain," *Science Digest* (September 1983), p. 42ff.; and *Newsweek* (August 9, 1982), p. 55.

135 A few large companies have created a consortium . . . : There are two combines: Semiconductor Research Corporation (SRC) and Microelectronics and Computer Technology Corporation (MCC). SRC is headed by Larry W. Sumney, who ran the Pentagon's Very High Speed Integrated Circuit (VHSIC) project; MCC is headed by Bobby Inman, former head of the

National Security Agency. See "Chipmakers Pool Their Research to Stay Competitive," *Business Week* (May 23, 1983), pp. 84–85.

136   new national research and teaching facility . . . : Feigenbaum and McCorduck, *op. cit.* Their "National Center for Knowledge Technology" is not a bad idea, as long as it is part of a larger decentralized system of artificial intelligence research.

136   significance of being human: Kenneth R. R. Gros Louis, "Why the Humanities Are More Important Than Ever," *Business Horizons* (January–February 1981), pp. 19–24.

137   Frankenstein myth: For a fascinating discussion of the ancient question of the utility of knowledge and the virtues (and vices) of its possession, see Jonathan Schell, *The Fate of the Earth* (New York: 1982).

137   a legislative Bill of Rights . . . : A thoughtful discussion of the impact of technology on our rights as citizens is Burnham's *The Rise of the Computer State, loc. cit.* Many of the caveats I set forth here are to be found in Burnham. The need for legal controls is eloquently set forth, pp. 165–225. I formulate rights somewhat differently from Burnham, but the general principles are the same.

138   scientific and technical literacy . . . : The need for broad-based scientific awareness in a democracy is discussed in Kenneth Prewitt, "Scientific Illiteracy and Democratic Theory," *Daedalus* (Spring 1983), pp. 49–64. For an interesting minisymposium on the "new literacy," see *Science Digest* (March 1983), pp. 16–19. My own belief is that the country that introduced universal literacy to the world should take the lead in bringing this new literacy to all our citizens. The task should be no more formidable.

138   Recent government attempts to limit the private dissemination of knowledge . . . : There is a broad consensus outside the government that this should not be done. It embraces the academic, and business, and scientific communities. See, for example, Robert A. Rosenbaum, Morton J. Tenzer, Stephen H. Unger, William Van Alstyne, and Jonathan Knight, "Academic Freedom and the Classified Information System," *Science* (January 21, 1983) pp. 257–259; and Roland Schmitt, vice-president of General Electric, who stated that Soviet engineering research is seriously retarded by "the oppressive bureaucratic ambiance that constantly surrounds the Soviet technologist. . . . Do we want to encumber our system in the same way?," "Fresh Funds for Scientific R & D, but with Strings," *Christian Science Monitor*, August 17, 1983, p. 6; and the National Academy of Sciences' opposition, as reported in "Science Panel Says U.S. Shouldn't Classify Research. . . ," *Wall Street Journal*, October 1, 1982, p. 37.

139   patent infringements . . . : Congress has begun to make changes in the patent laws, but it has not yet grappled with the truly fundamental issues at stake in a knowledge-based economy. See, for example, *Wall Street Journal*, July 16, 1982, p. 19.

Chapter 9: Resources

141   Oil does not mix easily with fish in Massachusetts: William MacLeish, "Resources: Oil, Fish, and Georges Bank," *Atlantic* (September 1981), p. 18ff.

143   The oil industry . . . seismic boom-and-bust cycle: "The Morning After the Oil Binge," *U.S. News & World Report* (September 20, 1982)

p. 47, for drops in oil profits; see also "When an Oil Boom Fades," *New York Times,* June 11, 1982, p. D1.

143 The oil hostage crisis is not over: See, for example, Daniel Yergin, "Awaiting the Next Oil Crisis," *New York Times Magazine* (July 11, 1982), p. 19; or Nazli Choucri, "Power and Politics in World Oil," *Technology Review* (October 1982), p. 24.

144 put the synfuels program on stall: "Synfuels Subsidies—What Some Call 'Insurance,' Others Call a Giveaway," *National Journal* (May 5, 1983), pp. 965–68.

146 an energy tax still makes very good sense: For example, see "Gasoline Tactics," *New Republic* (October 25, 1982), p. 7. My suggestions here are the result of conversations with Robert Pindyk, among others.

147 strategic petroleum reserve: Franklin A. Lindsay, "Plan for the Next Emergency," *Harvard Business Review* (September–October 1981), p. 152. Lindsay lists other steps that could be taken.

148 abandon the oil game . . . : But see "Twilight Nears for the Age of Oil," *New York Times,* August 29, 1982.

148 invest heavily in alternative energy sources . . . : This is precisely what we are *not* doing. See Stuart Eizenstat's Op-Ed piece in the *New York Times,* June 1, 1982, p. A23.

148 gas market is in even more of a mess . . . : See, for example, Richard Corrigan, "Soaring Prices for Gas from Deep Wells May Force Early Rewriting of 1978 Law," *National Journal* (November 21, 1981), pp. 2063–67.

149 We must also expand the use of coal . . . : Robert Stobaugh predicts a major expansion of coal usage and American production by the year 2000. See "World Energy to the Year 2000," in Yergin and Hillenbrand, *op. cit.,* pp. 44–47.

149 intense attack upon the environmental problems of coal: For example, see the classic Francis X. Murry, ed. *Where We Agree . . . The Report of the National Coal Policy Project* (Boulder, Colo., 1978).

149 transportation of coal . . . stringent environmental controls: For some of the environmental problems of slurry pipelines, see Peter Gwynne, "Piping Coal to the Southeast," *Technology Review* (October 1982), p. 14.

149 magnetohydrodynamic processes . . . : Ernest Volkman, "Firepower Plant," *Omni* (February 1983), p. 44ff.

150 [nuclear] waste problems . . . : Alan Jakimo and Irvin C. Bupp, "Nuclear Waste Disposal: Not in My Backyard," *Technology Review* (March–April 1978), pp. 64–72.

150 I would not . . . halt . . . fusion power: International Fusion Research Council, "Controlled Thermonuclear Fusion: Status Report," *Impact of Science on Society* Vol. 29, No. 4 (1979), p. 327.

150 cut back federal support . . . 90 percent by 1986 . . . : Congressional Research Service, Gary Paolino, *Conserving Energy: The Reagan Budget and the Federal Role,* Issue Brief No. IB 83003, updated (Washington, D.C.: July 25, 1983), pp. 1–2.

150 The GNP is now growing faster than energy consumption . . . : Yergin and Hillenbrand, *op. cit.,* p. 9.

151 encourage . . . individuals to become producers of electricity: Robert W. Gilmer, "Power to the People: The Promise of Decentralized Solar," *Technology Review* (August–September 1981), p. 37.

151 Wind and low head hydro . . . : V. Torrey, "Blowing Up More

Kilowatts from Wind," *Technology Review* (February 1980), p. 12; William A. Loeb, "How Small Hydro Is Growing Big," *Technology Review* (August–September 1983), p. 51; and Richard Corrigan, "With an Off-handed Push from Congress, Speculators Plunge into Small Hydro," *National Journal* (May 30, 1981), pp. 974–77.

151   geothermal . . . : Cummings, Morris, Tester, and Bivins, "Mining Earth's Heat . . . ," *Technology Review* (February 1979), p. 58.

151   ocean thermal energy conversion . . . : William Whitmore, "OTEC: Electricity from the Ocean," *Technology Review* (October 1978), p. 58.

151   tidal energy: Roy Bongartz, "A New Tidal Wave," *Science Digest* (September 1983), p. 12.

152   shortage of materials as well: Lee R. Murphy, "A Report on the Potential for Supply Dislocation of Selected Nonenergy Materials," in Joint Economic Committee, *Special Study on Economic Change*, Vol. 2, *Energy and Materials: A Shortage of Resources or Commitment?* (Washington, D.C.: 1980), pp. 185–253; and Julian L. Simon, "The Scarcity of Raw Materials," *Atlantic* (June 1981), p. 33.

152   Dumping the [waste] problem . . . : I am not persuaded, for example, by William Lahey and Michael Connor, "The Case for Ocean Waste Disposal," *Technology Review* (August–September 1983), p. 60.

152   a large cutback in funding for research on hazardous waste: American Association for the Advancement of Science, *op. cit.*, p. 80.

153   great interests are at stake: The peculiar susceptibility of resources to special-interest consideration is well illustrated by Julian L. Simon, "The Scarcity of Raw Materials," *Atlantic* (June 1981), especially pp. 39–41.

Chapter 10: People

157   The age of perpetual education and training is at hand: See the May 1982 issue of *Education and Urban Society*, devoted to lifelong learning.

158   an underclass of millions . . . : George C. Lodge and William R. Glass, "The Desperate Plight of the Underclass," *Harvard Business Review* (July–August 1982), p. 60.

160   the Reagan administration decided not to invest in people . . . : Kotz, *op. cit.*, p. 18.

160   number of students in college rise from 3.5 million . . . : *Statistical Abstract of the United States 1982–83, loc. cit.*, p. 166.

160   We ought to aim . . . in many respects professionalized: One out of four Americans today can be called a professional. In 1940 it was one out of twenty. See Eli Ginzberg, "The Professionalization of the U.S. Labor Force," *Scientific American* (March 1979), pp. 48–53.

160   the [school] problem is staggering: See National Commission on Excellence in Education, *A Nation at Risk*, A Report to Secretary of Education, Department of Education, April 26, 1983, or just ask a parent.

161   far from what it should be: For a discussion of the problems and approaches to solutions, see the *National Journal*'s series on education, July 9, 1983.

161   As Seymour Papert . . . : Seymour Papert, *Mindstorms: Children, Computers, and Powerful Ideas* (New York, 1980).

161   The electronic classroom of the future . . . : Even today just scan

an issue of *Electronic Learning.* See also *Time* (October 11, 1982), p. 66, or *Newsweek* (November 1, 1982), p. 91.

163 advanced computer literacy: The importance of scientific literacy to economic productivity is well argued in Herbert J. Walberg, "Scientific Literacy and Economic Productivity in International Perspective," *Daedalus* (Spring 1983), pp. 1–28. See the rest of this excellent issue, which is devoted to the topic of scientific literacy.

163 mathematics and science . . . : John Walsh, "Science Education Redivivus?," *Science* (March 11, 1983), pp. 1198–99.

164 released time . . . : An intriguing suggestion is that entrepreneurial youth projects be set up with young people in management roles. This practice, although designed as a training program to confront unemployment, could also be part of a standard released time program. See Stephen F. Hamilton and John F. Claus, "Inequality and Youth Unemployment: Can Work Programs Work?," *Education and Urban Society* (November 1981), pp. 103–126.

164 now called guidance: For a range of issues in the area, see Joan P. Avis, "Counseling: Issues and Challenges," *Education and Urban Society* (November 1982), pp. 70–87.

164 encourage students . . . not to drop out early from the system: Fred M. Newmann, "Reducing Student Alienation in High Schools . . . ," *Harvard Educational Review* (November 1981), pp. 546–64; and Trevor E. Sewell, Artis Palmo, and John L. Manni, "High School Dropout . . . ," *Urban Education* (April 1981), pp. 65–76.

164 Outreach programs . . . : For some difficulties in extending the community role of the school, see Clement B. G. London and Albert Griffith, "Inner City Teachers and School-Community Relations," *Urban Education* (January 1981), pp. 435–49; and Stephen H. Wilson, "Strengthening Connections Between Schools and Communities," *Urban Education* (July 1983), pp. 153–76. The advantages of involving students in community activities are shown in W. Marvin Will, "Socializing to Participate . . . ," *Urban Education* (January 1980), pp. 415–36.

165 special classes for the parents . . . : The experience of the Houston Independent School District's Operation Failsafe, designed to involve parents more directly in the educational process, demonstrates the importance of parental involvement.

165 adult and continuing education . . . : For a discussion of the range of issues here, see Carol H. Hoare, "Future Issues in Adult Education . . . ," *Adult Education* (Fall 1982), pp. 56–69.

165 adult illiteracy: By one estimate, 23 million Americans are functionally illiterate. See *Washington Post* series on adult illiteracy, November 25–27, 1982, by Joanne Omang. For a view of the complexities of the issue, see Larry Mikulecky and Dorothy Winchester, "Job Literacy and Job Performance Among Nurses at Various Employment Levels," *Adult Education Quarterly* (Fall 1983), pp. 1–15; and Kenneth Levine, "Functional Literacy: Fond Illusions and False Economies," *Harvard Educational Review* (August 1982), pp. 249–66.

165 Quality public education must become a major national priority . . . : See the excellent issue of *Daedalus* (Summer 1983), "The Arts and Humanities in America's Schools."

166 Our system of vocational schools . . . expanded . . . : There is

much politics involved with vocational education. I believe that the system should be strengthened and expanded. For a sample of the problems and solutions, see Charles Benson and Annette P. Lareau, "The Uneasy Place of Vocational Education," *Education and Urban Society* (November 1982), pp. 104–24; and Paul E. Barton, "Vocational Education: Federal Policies for the 1980's," both in *Education and Urban Society* (November 1981), pp. 83–102.

167 help for the handicapped . . . : For a discussion of the potential impact of the Reagan philosophy on programs for the handicapped, see Bette Everett Hamilton and Daniel Yoholem, "The Effects of Federal Deregulation: The Case of Handicapped Children," *Education and Urban Society* (August 1982), pp. 399–423.

167 Reagan administration . . . object[s] to . . . : inoculation . . . : Jane Stein, "Budget Cuts Hit Chief Weapon in War on Childhood Diseases, Say Critics," *National Journal* (March 13, 1982), pp. 462–64.

167 starvation and disease . . . : Elin Schoen, "Once Again, Hunger Troubles America," *New York Times Magazine* (January 2, 1983), p. 21.

167 money invested in these areas . . . fully paid back . . . : For example, the WIC program, which provides nutritional supplements for women, infants, and children, was investigated by a Harvard group. It concluded that for every $1 spent on WIC, $3 was saved in future hospital costs. See Linda E. Demokovich, "Feeding the Young . . . ," *National Journal* (April 10, 1982), p. 625.

168 It is not simply a case of people "between jobs" . . . : There is a great debate between economists about the nature of unemployment. Martin Feldstein, head of President Reagan's Council of Economic Advisers, has held that unemployment is mainly a case of people's voluntarily being between jobs while looking for better ones: "The Economics of the New Unemployment," *Public Interest* (Fall 1973), p. 1; and "Unemployment Insurance: Time for Reform," *Harvard Business Review* (March–April 1975), pp. 51–61. The opposite view is convincingly presented by Kim B. Clark and Lawrence H. Summers in "Unemployment Reconsidered," *Harvard Business Review* (November–December 1980), p. 171. See also Sar A. Levitan and Clifford M. Johnson, "The Politics of Unemployment," *New Republic* (September 20 and 27, 1982), p. 22; and George A. Akerlof and Brian G. M. Main, "Unemployment Spells and Unemployment Experience," *American Economic Review* (December 1980), p. 885.

169 (CETA) programs . . . have provided limited . . . opportunities . . . : The disappointing results of CETA for adults are documented in Congressional Budget Office et al., *CETA Training Programs—Do They Work for Adults?*, (Washington, D.C.: July 1982). The study showed a small positive effect on female trainees and hardly any effect at all on males.

169 Republicans do not want to give stipends . . . : Richard Corrigan, "Private Sector on the Spot . . . ," *National Journal* (April 30, 1983), pp. 894–97, especially p. 896.

170 exempt from Davis-Bacon . . . : Davis-Bacon requires that all work done on federal construction contracts be done at the "prevailing wage" in an area. This means, effectively, the highest wage. This is an area of hot controversy. Reform is needed. See Kenneth Kovach, "Should Davis-Bacon Be Repealed?," *Business Horizons* (September–October 1983), pp. 33–37. I favor modification.

170 deduct as a taxable expense 200 percent . . . : See the arguments

for wage subsidies in Clark and Summers, *op. cit.*, especially pp. 178–79.

171 We need to make it possible . . . to hire . . . : The PECs fulfill Lester Thurow's criteria for a jobs program: They would not operate at minimum wages, promotions would be possible, the program would be open to people in all social categories, ability and talent would count, and the programs would not be temporary. See Thurow, *The Zero-Sum Society*, *loc. cit.*, pp. 204–05.

171 two-tiered employment: Work sharing and reducing the length of the workweek are other suggestions. There are many problems associated with these. See, for example, John D. Owen, "Hours of Work . . . ," Joint Economic Committee, *Special Study on Economic Change*, Vol. 1, *Human Resources and Demographics: Characteristics of People and Policy* (Washington, D.C.: 1980), pp. 186–251.

172 (WPA)?: Robert M. Kaus, "Jobs for Everyone," *Harper's* (October 1982), p. 11.

174 Business needs literate . . . people . . . : Charles Ping, "Bigger Stakes for Business in Higher Education," *Harvard Business Review* (September–October 1981), p. 122, and Robert J. Wise, "Schools, Businesses, and Educational Needs . . . ," *Education and Urban Society* (November 1981), pp. 67–82.

174 possible to assemble a powerful coalition . . . : Stephen K. Bailey, "Political Coalitions for Public Education," *Daedalus* (Summer 1981), pp. 27–43.

Chapter 11: Management, Labor, and the Building of a New
Industrial Relationship

177 Tax-based Incomes Policy (TIP): For an extended discussion of TIP, see Sidney Weintraub, *Capitalism's Inflation and Unemployment Crisis: Beyond Monetarism and Keynesianism* (Newton, Mass.: 1978); see also Arthur Okun and George L. Perry, eds., *Curing Chronic Inflation* (Washington, D.C., 1978).

178 an option for employees to take payment in . . . stock. . . . : Employee Stock Ownership Plans (ESOPs) have become a new source of corporate finance. See Jeffry R. Gates and John E. Curtis, Jr., "ESOPs—an Emerging Technique for Development Financing," in Peter J. Bearse, ed., *Mobilizing Capital* (New York: 1982), pp. 161–85.

179 bring the two more closely together: See, for example, Y. K. Shetty, "Key Elements of Productivity Improvement Programs," *Business Horizons* (March–April 1982), pp. 15–22.

179 can be improved . . . more efficient use of existing plant and equipment: See, for example, William Abernathy, Kim Clark, and Alan Kantrow, *Industrial Renaissance* (New York: 1983).

179 close cooperation . . . on the factory floor: Robert R. Rehder, "What American and Japanese Managers Are Learning from Each Other," *Business Horizons* (March–April 1981), pp. 63–70.

179 "quality circles" . . . : Lee and Schwendiman, especially pp. 450–94.

179 If plants must be closed . . . : Bluestone, *op. cit.* Although I do not agree with all of Bluestone's proposals, he is on the right track.

180 a series of Industrial Development Councils . . . : This suggestion

appeared in my 1980 platform. For some similar suggestions, see Robert A. Leone and Stephen P. Bradley, "Toward an Effective Industrial Policy," *Harvard Business Review* (November–December, 1981), p. 91.

180   The agenda of these councils . . . : For an example of how management/labor/government cooperation can help revitalize an industry (in this case the shoe industry), see Müller, *op. cit.*, pp. 224–26.

182   Another approach is . . . industrial policy . . . : Blumenthal, *op. cit.*; and Felix Rohatyn, "Alternatives to Reaganomics," *New York Times Magazine* (December 5, 1982), p. 72ff.

183   market allocation schemes . . . : Ironically, the best analysis of why industrial planning of the variety advocated by the Democrats will lead to market allocation schemes is set forth in Reich, *The Next American Frontier, loc. cit.*, pp. 83–105.

183   industrial planning . . . concentration of . . . power: Robert Kaus, "Can Creeping Socialism Cure Creaking Capitalism?" *Harper's* (February 1983), pp. 17–22.

191   This . . . not utopian. . . . Many companies today . . . : Thomas J. Peters, *In Search of Excellence* (New York: 1983); and Edward B. Roberts, "New Ventures for Corporate Growth," *Harvard Business Review* (July–August 1980), pp. 134–42.

Chapter 12

201   no single instrument . . . adequate: Arthur Okun, *Prices and Quantities* (Washington, D.C., 1981); and also the interesting collection of essays in Michael Piore, ed., *Unemployment and Inflation* (White Plains, New York, 1979); and Wolfgang Blaas, "Institutional Analysis of Stagflation," *Journal of Economic Issues* (December 1982), pp. 955–75.

205   big budget deficits pose an enormous . . . threat: Herbert Stein, "Why Deficits Matter," *AEI Economist* (January, 1982), p. 1.

207   David Stockman's imagination . . . : The highest figure I have seen for federal capital spending is $155.3 billion for FY 1983. This, however, I believe to be exceedingly high when it comes to estimating expenditures on which actual returns will be realized. See David Mahoney, "Financing Federal Capital Investments: A Project-Specific Approach," prepared for the Conference Board, December 2, 1982.

212   There are no easy ways to reduce the deficit . . . : The figures I use in this and subsequent paragraphs are based on Congressional Budget Office (CBO) *Reducing the Deficit: Spending and Revenue Options* (Washington, D.C.: 1983). See also, CBO, *Tax Expenditures: Budget Control Options and Five-Year Budget Projections for Fiscal Years 1983 through 1987* (Washington, D.C., 1982).

213   "entitlement" programs . . . : James Fallows, "Entitlements," *Atlantic* (November, 1982), pp. 51–59.

213   escalating costs of medical care . . . : Richard Price and Janet Lundy, *Health Care Expenditures and Prices*, Issues Brief IB 77066 (Washington, D.C.: August 23, 1983 Congressional Research Service), *passim*; and Linda E. Demkovich, "Medicare on the Critical List . . . ?," *National Journal* (July 30, 1983), pp. 1580–85.

214   indifferent to the health needs . . . elderly . . . : Marylin Moon, "The Incidence of Poverty Among the Aged," *Journal of Human Resources*,

(Spring 1979), pp. 211–21.; and Didi Moore, "America's Neglected Elderly," *New York Times Magazine* (January 30, 1983), p. 30.

216 Al Sommers . . . : Albert Sommers, "The Federal Budget Should Be Built from the Bottom Up," *Across the Board* (May, 1982), pp. 18–23; and the paper "An Historical and Institutional View of Policy Needs for the Coming Decade."

219 stockpiling . . . : Prudent stockpiling could also prevent some of the catastrophic swings in primary materials production. The Great Recession was peculiarly devastating to many industries. See *Wall Street Journal* (September 16, 1982), p. 56.

Chapter 13: The Contribution of Creative Federalism

224 By 1980 investment . . . forty percent less of the gross national product: According to Congressional Budget Office, *Public Works Infrastructure: Policy Considerations for the 1980's*, April 1983, p. 6, estimated capital outlays in seven major categories of infrastructure represented 2.2 percent of the GNP in 1960. By 1980 this had fallen to 1.3 percent of the GNP.

224 Many cities still suffer . . . social service burdens . . . : Paula Span, "Newark's Failing Dream," *New York Times Magazine* (October 2, 1983), p. 55ff.

224 poor competitive situation . . . : For an extended analysis, see Robert W. Burchell and David Listokin, eds., *Cities Under Stress: The Fiscal Crises of Urban America* (New Brunswick, N.J.: 1981).

225 Ronald Reagan's New Federalism . . . : *National Journal* (February 27, 1982), especially pp. 356–79.

227 the Department of Transportation (DOT) estimates that $33 billion . . . : The statistics in this paragraph and the next two paragraphs are taken from "The Decaying of America," *Newsweek* (August 2, 1982), pp. 12–15. There are many other sources which could be cited. See, for example, Pat Choate and Susan Walter, *America in Ruins: Beyond the Public Works Pork Barrel* (Washington, D.C.: 1981).

229 matching grant formula . . . maintenance . . . supported . . . : Blair Birdsall, "The Brooklyn Bridge at 100," *Technology Review* (April 1983), p. 61ff; and Rochelle L. Stansfield, "Building Streets and Sewers Is Easy—It's Keeping Them Up That's the Trick," *National Journal* (May 24, 1980), pp. 844–47.

231 the enterprise zone: For a critical evaluation, see the symposium on enterprise zones in *Urban Affairs Quarterly* (September 1982).

232 banks . . . can also become active in the energy resource area: There are still dozens of ways for consumers to save energy. Local financing can help. See Bruce Stokes, *Helping Ourselves* (New York: 1981), pp. 41–60.

233 neighborhood improvement tax credit . . . : *Ibid.*: p. 127: "The Office of Neighborhood Self-Help Development in the Department of Housing and Urban Development estimates that for every million dollars it invests in self-help projects, $16 million is contributed from local resources. Few government programs can boast of such a return on the public's money."

234 1.1 million housing starts . . . fewest . . . : *Statistical Abstract of the United States 1982–83, loc. cit.*, and previous issues. See also Council of Economic Advisers, *Economic Indicators* (Washington, D.C.: 1983), p. 19.

234 In the household-forming age-group . . . unemployment rose . . . : Congressional Research Service Review, Morton J. Schussheim, *Looking Ahead in Housing*, CRS document IP 0207 H (Washington, D.C.: February 1983).

235 fewer than three out of ten families . . . : *Ibid.*

235 A countercyclical mortgage subsidy program . . . : See, for example, *CQ Almanac, 1975* (Washington, D.C.), p. 429, and related articles.

235 The problems of . . . high-rise slums . . . : Robert Reich makes the interesting point that public housing decreases mobility: *The Next American Frontier, loc. cit.*, pp. 216–18. This must be studied further.

236 Urban homesteading programs . . . : See, for instance, Stokes, *Helping Ourselves, loc. cit.*, pp. 70–75.

Chapter 14: Exporting to the Global Economy

239 the dollar, the high value . . . : According to "World Financial Markets," May 1983, published by the Morgan Guaranty Trust Company, the dollar by the end of 1982 had risen to 120 percent of its 1975–79 average.

239 record trade deficits: See, for example, "Dangers of the Burgeoning Trade Deficit," *Dun's Business Month* (September 1983), pp. 36–40.

239 In former years the value of the dollar . . . : One of the best accounts of America's postwar world economic role is Calleo's *The Imperious Economy, loc. cit.*

239 decentralized structure . . . : Luther Tweeter, "The Economics of Small Farms," *Science* (March 4, 1984), pp. 1037–41, and Congressman Byron L. Dorgan's article "America's Real Farm Problem: It Can be Solved," in the *Washington Monthly* (April 1983), p. 12.

239 conserve our topsoil . . . : W. E. Larson, J. F. Pierce, and R. H. Dowdy, "The Threat of Soil Erosion to Long-term Crop Production," *Science* (February 4, 1983), pp. 458–65; and Michael Lenehan, "Will the Corn Belt End Up in the Rivers?," *Atlantic* (December 1981), pp. 22–25.

239 Genetic engineering . . . : See, for example, "Creating Plants That Feed Themselves," *Technology Review* (July 1982), p. 65.

240 Timber exports can also be expanded: The U.S. share of the world forest product market has risen from 13 to 17 percent during the last decade: *Industry Week* (June 14, 1982), p. 66.

240 Coal exports . . . : America has doubled its coal exports since 1979—to 90 million tons. See *Industry Week* (June 14, 1982), p. 66.

241 do manufactured goods?: The magnitude of the task must be considered against the recent history of serious declines in the American share of world exports in transportation equipment, steel, textiles and apparel, machine tools, consumer electronics, industrial fasteners, aircraft, chemicals, and microelectronics. *Ibid.*, pp. 61–65.

241 Digital televisions . . . : *Business Week* (September 16, 1983), pp. 160–63. The Japanese, of course, are well aware of this possibility and today appear to be ahead of us in the technology.

242 Let us not concede . . . : Marilyn Wilson, "Smokestack America: The Future Is Better Than You Think," *Dun's Business Month* (July 1983), pp. 30–35.

242 The computer and communications revolutions . . . : Bernard J. Wunder, Jr., "International Commerce in Telecommunications and Infor-

mation Products," *Columbia Journal of World Business* (Spring 1983), pp. 62–67; and Herbert S. Dordick, "The Emerging World Information Business," *ibid.*, pp. 69–76.

242 educational services . . . : Joseph N. Pelton, "The Communication Satellite: Revolutionary Change Agent?," *ibid.*, pp. 77–84.

246 avoid the trade war . . . : Thomas R. Graham, "War and Peace," *Foreign Policy* (Spring 1983), pp. 124–37.

246 liberalize world trade in services: Shelp, *op. cit.*, pp. 165–213.

Chapter 15: Access to Employment and Income

250 keep ahead of the demographics . . . : See, for example, Eli Ginzberg, "The Social Security System," *Scientific American* (January 1982), pp. 51–57.

252 a strategy of growth: See Patrick G. Grasso and Ira Sharkansky, "Economic Development and the Distribution of Income in the American States," *Social Science Quarterly* (December 1980), pp. 446–57. The authors argue that in times of zero growth the tendencies are not to redistribute.

253 "Latin Americanization" . . . : The term is from Carlos Díaz Alejandro and is discussed in Müller, *op. cit.*, especially pp. 72–74.

253 Democrats have not only failed . . . policies . . . to create new wealth . . . : See Michael Barone's pessimistic prognostication concerning the probability that the Democrats will abandon redistributionist policies, "The Battle for the Democratic Party," *Washington Post*, Op. Ed, November 29, 1982.

254 Redistributionism is not a viable policy . . . : Arthur Okun, *Equality and Efficiency: The Big Tradeoff* (Washington, D.C.: 1975).

255 double-digit unemployment persisted in the megastates . . . : Democratic Study Group, *Special Report: Unemployment and the Recovery* (Washington, D.C., September 16, 1983), p. 20.

255 In the construction industry . . . : *Ibid.*, p. 17.

255 Black unemployment . . . : *Ibid.*, p. 16; for an in-depth analysis of unemployment statistics, see Eli Ginzberg, "Youth Unemployment," *Scientific American* (May 1980), pp. 43–49.

255 Black median family income . . . : Ransford W. Palmer, "Equality, Incentives, and Economic Policy," *American Economic Association Papers and Proceedings* (May 1980), pp. 123–24.

255 On the average [women] receive about fifty-nine cents . . . : Women's Equity Action League, *The WEAL Washington Report* (June–July 1983), p. 2.

255 Only 2 percent of higher-level business managers are women: J. Benjamin Forbes and James E. Piercy, "Rising to the Top: Executive Women in 1983 and Beyond," *Business Horizons* (September–October 1983), pp. 38–47. (The percentage of new appointees has doubled—to 4 percent recently.)

255 Women's median earnings . . . : For the statistics in this paragraph, see WEAL, *op. cit.*

255 To give all Americans access to . . . wealth . . . : Palmer, *op. cit.*, p. 123, put it thus: " . . . from the point of view of blacks, the scenario for the best of all possible worlds is one in which economic policy strives actively to

achieve full employment while educational policy stimulates the growth of human capital investment to upgrade the occupational distribution of the black labor force. No one policy without the other can be fully successful in reducing persistent income disparity."

255   the job profile . . . will be quite different . . . : It is impossible to predict with certainty, but see Cetron and O'Toole, *op. cit.*

256   the chance to build video games will not solve . . . : Steve Huntley, "High Tech: No Panacea for the Jobless," *U.S. News & World Report* (March 7, 1983), p. 74.

257   capital equipment . . . sufficiently sophisticated to build itself. For a futuristic view of automatons building themselves, see Robert Freitas, Jr., "Roboclone," *Omni* (July 1983), p. 44.

257   marketing . . . emphasis on quality and variety . . . : See Leslie M. Dawson, "Marketing for Human Needs in a Human Future," *Business Horizons* (June 1980), pp. 72–82, for a discussion of the "professionalization" of marketing.

258   the service sector . . . rapidly growing employer: Services are now the largest sector by far. See Eli Ginzberg and George J. Volta, "The Service Sector of the U.S. Economy," *Scientific American* (March 1981), pp. 48–55.

258   Even in construction . . . automation . . . : Francis T. Ventre, "Innovation in Residential Construction," *Technology Review* (November 1979), pp. 51–59.

259   We simply must increase the level of professional training . . . : There is evidence that the gains already made by blacks are not a result of relative improvements with respect to whites within given job categories but are a result of a changing profile of black-held jobs. See the striking statistics in Michael Reich, "The Persistence of Racial Inequality in Urban Areas and Industries, 1950–1970," *American Economic Association Papers and Proceedings* (May 1980), p. 128.

260   job segregation [for women] . . . : Barbara Bergman, "The Shibboleth of the Shrinking Pie," *Perspectives* (Summer–Fall 1981), pp. 30–33.

260   create . . . special training programs for young women who . . . : WEAL, *op. cit.*, p. 7.

260   Department of Education's . . . adequate staff support . . . : *Ibid.*, p. 5.

261   Still, access to jobs . . . outright discrimination . . . : Discrimination exists in many forms. See Barbara Bergman, Testimony Before the U.S. Department of Labor, Hearings on Affirmative Action in Universities, October 10, 1975.

262   Equal Rights Amendment (ERA): Now, *The ERA Countdown Campaign, 1982*, revised edition (Washington, D.C., 1982), p. 2.

262   litigation to enforce . . . curtailed: Coalition on Women and the Budget, *Inequality of Sacrifice: The Impact of the Reagan Budget on Women* (Washington, D.C.: March 1983), p. 48.

262   Back pay claims . . . decreased . . . : *Ibid.*

263   We should have a national policy on child care . . . : WEAL, *op. cit.*, p. 8.

263   mechanism for collecting . . . child support . . . : Barbara Bergman, "The Share of Women and Men in the Economic Support of Children," *Human Rights Quarterly* (August 1980), pp. 103–12.

Chapter 16: Arms and the American Economy

269 *increase* military spending . . . $1 trillion . . . : Based on *Budget of the United States Government FY 1984*, issued by the Executive Office of the President, Office of Management and Budget.

270 8.4 percent more jobs are lost . . . : Congressional Research Service, Carolyn Brancato and Linda Le Grande, *The Impact on Employment of Defense Versus Non-Defense Government Spending*, Mini Brief No. MB 82246, updated (Washington, D.C.: August 10, 1983).

271 Goldman, Sachs estimates . . . defense spending as a percentage . . . : Congressional Research Service, Barry Molefsky, *Inflationary Consequences of the Defense Buildup*," Mini Brief No. MB 81256 (Washington, D.C.: July 6, 1983).

271 High-technology research . . . under defense . . . control: David Burnham, "The Silent Power of the NSA," *New York Times*, March 27, 1983, p. 60.

272 Russia has sacrificed all else to arms: Nussbaum, *op. cit.*, pp. 104–33.

274 verifiable nuclear freeze: McGeorge Bundy, George F. Kennan, Robert S. McNamara, and Gerard Smith, "Nuclear Weapons and the Atlantic Alliance," *Foreign Affairs* (Spring 1982), pp. 753–68; and Randall Forsberg, "A Bilateral Nuclear Weapon Freeze," *Scientific American* (November 1982), pp. 52–61.

274 freeze on the deployment of the MX and Pershing . . . : Richard Ullman, "Out of the Euromissile Mire," *Foreign Policy* (Spring 1983), pp. 39–52.

276 a comprehensive test ban treaty: Lynn R. Sykes and Jack F. Evernden, "The Verification of a Comprehensive Nuclear Test Ban," *Scientific American* (October 1982), pp. 47–55.

276 chemical and biological weapons: See, for example, Matthew Meselson, "Chemical Warfare and Chemical Disarmament," *Scientific American* (April 1980), pp. 38–47.

276 conventional war . . . in Europe . . . deadly war of attrition . . . : See the extraordinary projections of Seymour J. Deitchman, *New Technology and Military Power: General Purpose Military Forces for the 1980's and Beyond* (Boulder, Colo. 1979).

276 limit the flow of arms to the developing world: Andrew Pierre's excellent anthology *Arms Transfers and American Foreign Policy* (New York: 1979) shows the difficulties of negotiating a conventional arms transfer agreement, but he also advocates that we try.

277 forty separate wars . . . : "Even in Peacetime, 40 Wars Are Going On," *U.S. News & World Report* (July 11, 1983), pp. 44–45.

278 the MX, the B-1 bomber . . . : The FY 1984 requests for the MX and the B-1 are about $7 billion apiece. Producing and testing nuclear warheads are budgeted at $6.4 billion. See "Reagan's Major Budget Proposals for Fiscal 1984," *Wall Street Journal* (January 31, 1983), pp. 3, 6.

278 The F-16 . . . cheaper . . . reliable . . . : James Fallows, *National Defense* (New York: 1982), pp. 95–106.

278 smaller ships at greatly reduced costs: There is a raging controversy over this issue. I side with the advocates of smaller. See Hart, *op. cit.*, pp. 136–38.

278 number of people who stand "behind" . . . is greater . . . : Steve Canby, "Strong Defense Does Not Need More Money," *Christian Science Monitor* (August 23, 1982), p. 23.

279 Managers and employees replace commanders and soldiers: Fallows, *op. cit., passim*, especially pp. 106–38.

279 armies ripe for defeat: Hart, *op. cit.*, pp. 125–26 and 138–40.

279 Several billion . . . could probably be saved . . . : See, for example, Laurence Grafstein, "Wallowing in Waste," *New Republic* (October 4, 1982), p. 17.

279 larger savings . . . possible . . . procurement of major weapons . . . : See Jacques Ganzler's classic *The Defense Industry* (Cambridge, Mass.: 1982).

280 major inefficiencies . . . in which one party is the sole purchaser . . . : *Ibid.*, pp. 29–70.

280 Reform is needed: *Ibid.*, pp. 99–108.

281 subcontractor level . . . : *Ibid.*, pp. 128–61.

282 Better training programs . . . : Fallows, *op, cit.*, pp. 105–38. I do not, however, favor a reintroduction of the draft.

284 We believe America . . . : From "Declaration of the National Unity Party," adopted December 3, 1983, Chevy Chase, Maryland.

Chapter 17: Building a More Prosperous and Secure World

286 Europe['s] . . . economic stagnation: Edward Jay Epstein and Jeffrey Steingarten, "Europe: The End of a Miracle," *Atlantic* (July 1981), pp. 11–18; and Lawrence Minard, "Can Europe Catch Up?," *Forbes* (July 4, 1983), p. 84.

286 We should applaud the efforts . . . community-wide basis: We should encourage European scientific cooperation. See David Dickson, "New Push for European Science Cooperation," *Science* (June 10, 1983), pp. 1134–36.

287 selling its inferior products only to the Soviet bloc . . . : Nussbaum, *op. cit.*, especially pp. 76–103.

287 time to rethink our policies toward Japan: Stephen J. Solarz, "America and Japan: A Search for Balance," *Foreign Policy* (Winter 1982–83), pp. 75–92.

287 It is . . . in neither Japan's diplomatic interests nor ours . . . : Neil Ulman and Urban C. Lehner, "Tokyo's Buildup," *Wall Street Journal*, November 22, 1982, p. 1; and Robert Keatley, "The Far East Worries as U.S. Presses Japan to Rearm," *Wall Street Journal*, November 29, 1982, p. 27.

290 Our trade with India . . . we showed a surplus: *Statistical Abstract of the United States 1981* (Washington, D.C.), p. 848.

291 it is in our own self-interest . . . : For example, "40% of U.S. exports (nearly 3% of GNP) and 28% of OECD exports" go to Third World countries. See "World Financial Markets," Morgan Guaranty Trust Company of New York, June 1983, p. 7.

291 Most of these countries face severe problems . . . : Carol Lancaster, "Africa's Economic Crisis," *Foreign Policy* (Fall 1983), pp. 149–66.

291 food . . . in short supply: Carl K. Eicher, "Facing Up to Africa's Food Crisis," *Foreign Affairs* (Fall 1982), pp. 151–74.

291 Some of these countries are dangerously dependent . . . : World

Bank, *World Development Report 1982* (Washington, D.C. 1982), pp. 114–115.

292 about 24 percent of export earnings . . . interest payments: Herbert Rowan, "IMF Forecasts World Industry Growth at 3%," *Washington Post* (June 22, 1983), p. D7–8.

292 our policy must reflect fundamental values . . . : Charles Maechling, Jr., "Human Rights Dehumanized," *Foreign Policy* (Fall 1983), pp. 118–35.

293 The 0.27 percent of the gross national product that we contribute . . . : World Bank, *op. cit.*, p. 14.

293 —A lack of adequate water facilities . . . : Robert Ambroggi, "Water," *Scientific American* (September 1980), pp. 100–16.

293 —Developing countries need energy: Wolfgang Sassin, "Energy," *Scientific American* (September 1980), pp. 119–32.

294 timely payment . . . the United States . . . remiss: International Development Agency, *IDA in Retrospect* (Washington, D.C.: 1982).

296 El Salvador . . . : Robert A. Pastor, "Our Real Interests in Central America," *Atlantic* (July 1982), pp. 27–39.

297 the truly impressive efforts . . . by the Mexican government . . . : "The Neighborhood Starts to Pick Up," *Economist* (August 20, 1983), pp. 19–22.

298 Mexico has tried to reduce its . . . deficit . . . : Norman Gall, "Can Mexico Pull Through?," *Forbes* (August 15, 1983), p. 74.

298 A socioeconomic and political disaster . . . : "Where Two Worlds Meet," *The Economist* (August 20, 1983), pp. 27–31; and Morris K. Udall, "Serious Trouble for U.S.—Close to Home," *Tucson Citizen*, August 12, 1983.

Chapter 18: An Economy of Values

303 An Economy of Values: For the importance of values and sense of purpose, see Amitai Etzioni's provocative *An Immodest Agenda: Rebuilding America before the 21st Century* (New York: 1982).

304 This approach of reducing everything to a single solution . . . : Warren Bennis, "A Bright Future for Complexity," *Technology Review* (February 1979), p. 16.

304 Greed is not enough . . . : Robert Lekachman, *Greed Is Not Enough: Reaganomics* (New York: 1982).

305 . . . "soul" . . . : Kidder, *op. cit.*

305 Markets . . . on the basis of a person's word . . . : Compare our penchant for litigation with Japan's preference for cooperation. See Frank Gibney, *Miracle by Design* (New York: 1982), pp. 118–31.

305 America will not work . . . without a measure of trust: Consider, for example, the recent rise of the underground economy. See Edward Tivnan, "Cashing In," *New York* (March 21, 1983), p. 26–31.

Epilogue

314 "The party is over": David Broder, *The Party's Over* (New York, 1972).

INDEX

Index

Kennedy, John F., 109, 270
Keynes, John Maynard, 12, 98
Keynesians, Keynesianism, 6, 14, 18, 108, 207–208, 209; as critics of tight money, 4
Knockoffs (unlicensed copies), 71, 100
Knowledge, 125–140; access to, vs. government control, 52–53, 137–140, 271; government support needed for generation of, 80, 82–83, 126, 132–133, measures for furthering of, 126–136, 195; national endowment funds advocated, 126–127, 132; as part of supply base, 12, 80; as part of supply base in Japan, 56, 58, 63, 64–65; as part of supply base, neglect in Germany, 57; private sector role, 127, 131, 132, 133, 134; role in computer-based work place, 46–47
Korea. *See* South Korea
Kuwait, 148, 253

Labor, 12, 13, 28, 321; in Asia, cheap, 44, 56, 241; dislocation of, 179, 180–181; effect of microchip revolution on, 47–48; Japanese, 56; job market of future, 47–50 (*see also* Job market; Job training); new party policies summarized for, 324–325; as part of supply base, 12, 41, 80, 83; profit sharing, 84, 178, 180, 188, 190, 193; in stagnant industries, 23, 176–179; training in robotics use, 46; under-class of jobless, 158–159. *See also* Government-labor-management cooperation schemes
Labor, organized, 11, 16, 36, 53; as Democratic power base, 16, 36, 38, 53, 91, 109, 326; future of, 191–194; and industrial policy proposals, 182; lobbying by, 90; microchip revolution and, 47, 51, 53; new party policies summarized for, 326; and PEC/PLC proposal, 171; relationship with management, 77, 85, 109, 178–180, 190, 192–194; wages and contracts, 176–178
Laboratories, national, 128
Laffer, Arthur, 6
Laffer curve, 6, 9
Laissez faire, 37, 41, 70
Land, as part of supply base, 12
Land-grant colleges, 80, 82, 129
Land speculation, 32, 39, 210
Laser technology, 41, 64, 130
Latin America, 273, 291, 296–299
"Latin Americanization," 253
Lay-offs, 7, 8, 29, 321. *See also* Unemployment
LDCs (less developed countries), 248, 289, 291–294. *See also* Developing nations
Liberal arts curriculum, 163–164
Liberals, 11, 14–15; acceptance of 1980s tax increases, spending cuts, 4. *See also* Neoliberals
Libraries, 226, 229, 232
Libya, 273
Lincoln, Abraham, 307
Literacy, scientific and technical, 138, 140. *See also* Computer literacy
Litigation, regulatory, 103, 104, 252
Loan business of future, 117–120
Lobbying, 31, 90–91, 103; defense industry, 37, 280, 284, 313–314; energy lobby, 37, 90, 91, 149, 154–155, 313–314

Local development banks, 118–120, 122, 151, 175, 226, 231–232; seed money cost, *table* 222
Local government(s), 132, 220, 223; and enterprise zones, 231; federal trust fund aid proposals, 228–230; and housing shortage, 235, 236; infrastructure problems, 171, 224, 225, 226–229; negative competition between, 224–225, 230, 236; positive competition, 230–233; public works spending figures, 224; role in creative federalism, 228–233, 235, 236–237; tax-based stagnation, 224–225, 226
London, as former world financial center, 68, 74
Low-tech industries, 256

M1 (basic money supply), 202–203
M-1 tank, 280
McDonnell Douglas, 65
McGovern, George, 33
Machinery, 129, 187, 241; unemployment in industry, 255
Machine tool industry, 21, 48, 129; Japanese competition, 62; recapitalization of, 67
Macroeconomics, xiv, 249, 251, 320
Mail order catalogues, 43
Malaysia, 289
Management, business, 12, 47, 96; accountant mentality in, 24, 50, 58, 61; of future, 50–51, 97, 190–191; and industrial policy proposals, 182; Japan juxtaposed to U.S., 56, 57; labor relations, 77, 85, 109, 178–180, 190, 192–194; lower-level, replaced by computer, 50; as main factor in stagnation, 28–29; middle-level, 50; as part of supply base, 80, 83–84; short-term result orientation of, 24–25, 26, 105; in stagnant industries, 23–26, 28–29, 83–84, 176, 178–179; style vs. substance, 24, 97; top-level, 50–51. *See also* Government-labor-management cooperation schemes
Management, government, 306–307; in the military, 279
Managerial training, 132, 188, 189
Manufacture, 72, 145; automation of, 44–46, 129–130, 252, 260; disassociation of banking from, 34, 67–68, 121, 122; exports, 74, 241–242; flexibility vs. efficiency in, 45, 64; flexibility and efficiency linked, 64, 86, 189; Japanese ascendancy in, 64, 65–67, 135; jobs of future in, 256, 260; standardized vs. "smart robot," 44–45; technology, 73, 129–131, 135. *See also* Production
Marathon Oil Company, 26, 71
Marketing, 60–61; electronic, of future, 43, 97, 100, 188; Japanese penetration strategy, in U.S., 43, 55, 57–60, 61, 62–63, 64; jobs in, 257; U.S. imitation of Japanese market penetration strategy, 130, 241
Marketing chains, 43
Marketplace, 77–78, 80, 194–195, 204; vs. government, 76, 77, 84–85, 187; present U.S., flaws in, 78; pricing rigidities, 29–32, 78, 176–177; short-term orientation of, 78. *See also* Private sector

363

Stockpiling, countercyclical, 219, 282
Strategic and Critical Materials Stockpiling Act, 219
Strategic arms reduction, 275
Strategic petroleum reserve, 147
Strikes, 176, 193; by public employees, 192
Strip mining, 149
Structural economic problems, 20, 182; in banking, 123; reasons for, 20–21; unemployment, 15, 168–169. *See also* Supply base; Supply-side crisis
Student loans and grants, 128–129
Suburbia, 224, 230, 236
Sun Belt, 227, 230, 316; economic growth in, 224; and Republican presidential politics, 315, 316
Sunrise industries, 75, 76
Sunset industries, 21, 75–76. *See also* Stagnant industries
Supplemental Security Income, 214
Supply base, 320; basic elements of, 12–13, 80, 99; basic factors present in 19th Century expansion, 40–41; decentralized approach to, 95–96, 118, 122, 184–191, 195; deterioration of, in U.S., 12, 15; government support needed, 78, 80–84, 85–87, 88, 196; healthy Japanese system, 56–57, 78–79; need for rebuilding in U.S., 16, 17, 78, 80–87, 99, 244, 246, 269; private sector role in rebuilding of, 85, 127, 132, 133, 134, 151, 168, 169–171, 173–174, 184–196; public strategy for rebuilding, 98–106, 109, 115–116, 118–123, 126–136, 151, 165–167, 169–172, 180–188, 210; strategy summarized, 194–197
Supply-side crisis, xiv, 12, 15, 16, 19–20; "industrial policy" no answer to, 16, 27; reasons for, 20–21, 80. *See also* Credit crisis; Investment, decline in quality long-term; Stagnation
Supply-side economics, xiii, 209, 210; failure of, 8, 12–13, 40; limited scope under Reagan, 12–13, 40, 194; no remedy for stagnation, 26–27
Supply-siders, 12–13, 16, 41, 91, 209; second thoughts on tight money, 4
Sweden, 279
Systems, combination of goods and services in, 72. *See also* Capital systems
Systems engineering, 125, 129–130

Taft, William Howard, 107
Taiwan, 19, 42, 60, 66, 288, 289, 290
Taxation, 210, 211, 251, 324; inflation as form of, 205–206, 207; interstate and local negative competition based on, 224, 225, 226; windfall profits, 212, 326
Tax-based Incomes Policy (TIP) proposal, 87, 177–178, 202, 204
Tax cuts, 4, 8, 12, 13, 33, 107; Congress and, 10; consumption-oriented, 205, 208, 210, 251; "monetizing" of, 6; a Reaganomics goal, 5; results of, 6–7; stimulus offset by cost of credit, 7, 33; stimulus offset by deficits, 8, 33
Tax "expenditures," 212
Tax incentives: for business, 12, 26–27, 81, 88, 100–102, 175, 176, 251; projected cost, *table* 222; dividend exclusion, 111; for merger, 105; for neighborhood improvement, 233, 236; for R & D, 27, 102, 133, 189; self-implementing subsidies, 235; for stockholders, 101–102, 111
Tax increases, 4, 9, 10, 207; contingent, for fiscal 1986, 8; need for, 109, 212, 322, 324; proposals for, 212–213, 214, 215, *table* 221
Tax indexing, 212, *table* 221
Tax laws, 99; of 1981, 101; of 1982, 101, 105; proposed liberalization, 100–102
Tax leasing provisions, 27, 102
Tax loopholes, 212, *table* 221
Tax penalties, for acquisitions, 101, 105, *table* 222
Tax revenues, 6, 7, 206, 207, 212–213, 215, 216–217, *table* 221
Teachers, 161, 162, 165–166, 257–258
Technology, 17, 28, 125–126, 252–253, 320; assessment (OTA), 139; development of new, 73, 82–83, 86, 97, 129–136, 246; dissemination, 16, 52–53, 81, 82–83, 97, 131–133; diversion to defense-related purposes, 271–272; exports, 244–245, 291, 293–294; facilitation of introduction of new, 180–181, 184–189; innovation resisted by stagnant industries, 22–23, 27, 33, 70; Japanese acquisition and use of, 56, 58, 63, 64–65, 135; job opportunities, 257; military sector ascendancy in, 138, 271–272; monopolistic tendencies of Reagan Right, 52–53, 138, 253; 19th Century revolution, 40–41; present revolution, 41–54 (*see also* Computer chip); of production, changes in, 44–45, 64, 129–131, 135; Reagan spending cuts, 13, 125–126; skills required for use, 156–158; support spending needed, 13, 16, 82, 88, 126–127, 132; use in avoidance of stagnation, 28
Telecommunications, international barriers in, 247
Television: advertising, 43; industry (TV sets), 22; Japanese competition, 62
Textile industry, 49, 63; recapitalization of, 67
Thailand, 289
Third World, 68; arms proliferation in, 271, 273, 276, 284, 296; loans to, 112–114, 146 (*see also* Overseas loans); trade with, 244, 248, 288–291. *See also* Developing nations; Newly industrializing nations
Three Mile Island, 149
Tight money policy, 4, 5, 6, 13, 27, 202, 204; coupled with fiscal expansion, 6, 204, 206
Timber exports, 240
Time magazine, 113
TIP. *See* Tax-based Incomes Policy
Tokyo, as future world financial center, 68
Toxic wastes, 141, 150, 152
Training. *See* Education; Job training
Training systems, 130, 161–162, 167, 168; exports of, 242–243, 244, 245
Transfer payments, federal responsibility for, 216, 217, 225, 226, 236
Transportation equipment, 129, 187, 241
Transportation systems, 78, 79, 85, 218, 225, 228–229, 242; job opportunities, 258; R & D, 130